Crystal Reports 10 For Dummies®

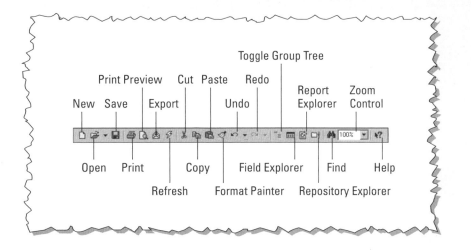

Toggle Group Tree

Print Preview — Cut — Paste — Redo

New — Save — Export — Undo — Report Explorer — Zoom Control

Open — Print — Copy — Field Explorer — Find — Help

Refresh — Format Painter — Repository Explorer

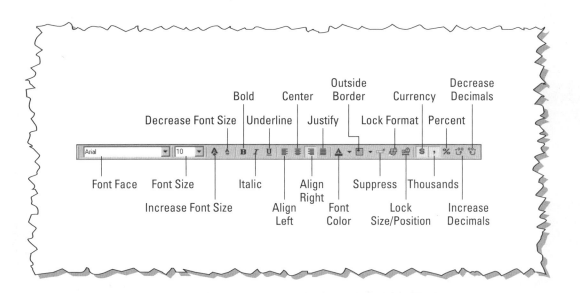

Outside Border — Decrease Decimals

Bold — Center — Currency

Decrease Font Size — Underline — Justify — Lock Format — Percent

Arial — 10

Font Face — Font Size — Italic — Align Right — Suppress — Thousands

Increase Font Size — Align Left — Font Color — Lock Size/Position — Increase Decimals

Crystal Reports 10 For Dummies®

Cheat Sheet

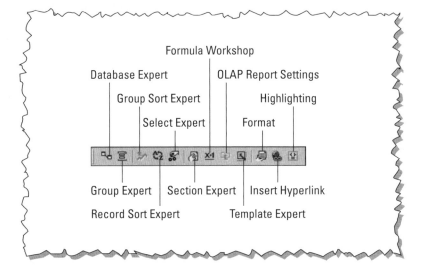

Formula Workshop

Database Expert

OLAP Report Settings

Group Sort Expert

Highlighting

Select Expert

Format

Group Expert

Section Expert

Insert Hyperlink

Record Sort Expert

Template Expert

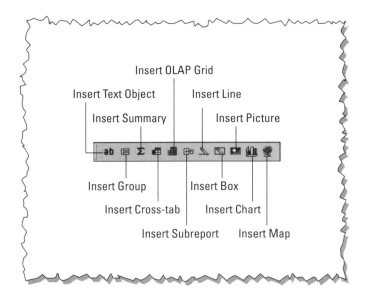

Insert OLAP Grid

Insert Text Object

Insert Line

Insert Summary

Insert Picture

Insert Group

Insert Box

Insert Cross-tab

Insert Chart

Insert Subreport

Insert Map

For Dummies: Bestselling Book Series for Beginners

Crystal Reports® 10

FOR

DUMMIES®

Crystal Reports® 10

FOR DUMMIES®

by Allen G. Taylor

Wiley Publishing, Inc.

Crystal Reports® 10 For Dummies®

Published by
Wiley Publishing, Inc.
111 River Street
Hoboken, NJ 07030-5774

WILEY

About the Author

Allen G. Taylor is a 30-year veteran of the computer industry and the author of over 20 books, including *SQL For Dummies, Access 2003 Power Programming with VBA, Database Development For Dummies,* and *SQL Weekend Crash Course.* He lectures nationally on databases, innovation, and entrepreneurship. He also teaches database development internationally through a leading online education provider and teaches digital circuit design locally at Portland State University. You can contact Allen at `allen.taylor@ieee.org`.

Dedication

This book is dedicated to my daughter, Valerie Joy Taylor, who is indeed a joy as well as being a psychologist and world traveler.

Author's Acknowledgments

Many people have contributed to the quality and content of this book. I would particularly like to recognize Jaylene Crick of Business Objects for her helpfulness, my acquisitions editor, Terri Varveris, for her overall management of the project, and my editor, Nicole Sholly, for keeping me honest.

I also appreciate the continued support of my family and the interest of my friends and colleagues. It would not have been possible to complete a project of this magnitude without the support of those close to me.

Publisher's Acknowledgments

We're proud of this book; please send us your comments through our online registration form located at www.dummies.com/register/.

Some of the people who helped bring this book to market include the following:

Acquisitions, Editorial, and Media Development

Associate Project Editor: Nicole Sholly

Acquisitions Editor: Terri Varveris

Senior Copy Editor: Barry Childs-Helton

Technical Editor: Wiley-Dreamtech India Pvt Ltd

Editorial Manager: Kevin Kirschner

Media Development Manager:
Laura VanWinkle

Media Development Supervisor:
Richard Graves

Editorial Assistant: Amanda Foxworth

Cartoons: Rich Tennant, www.the5thwave.com

Composition

Project Coordinator: Courtney MacIntyre

Layout and Graphics: Andrea Dahl,
Carrie Foster, Denny Hager,
Joyce Haughey, Kristin McMullan,
Lynsey Osborn, Heather Ryan

Proofreaders: Andy Hollandbeck,
Carl William Pierce;
TECHBOOKS Production Services

Indexer: TECHBOOKS Production Services

Publishing and Editorial for Technology Dummies

    Richard Swadley, Vice President and Executive Group Publisher

    Andy Cummings, Vice President and Publisher

    Mary C. Corder, Editorial Director

Publishing for Consumer Dummies

    Diane Graves Steele, Vice President and Publisher

    Joyce Pepple, Acquisitions Director

Composition Services

    Gerry Fahey, Vice President of Production Services

    Debbie Stailey, Director of Composition Services

Contents at a Glance

Table of Contents

Introduction

· ·

Crystal Reports 10 is the latest in a long and celebrated series of report writers for personal computers. Crystal Reports is by far the best-selling report writer package in the world, even though you may have never heard of it. In the past, it has been bundled with many of the most popular applications without being acknowledged by name. (A version of Crystal Reports is currently bundled into Microsoft's Visual Studio .NET, and Crystal Reports 10 is sold as a standalone product.) If you want to produce a high-quality report quickly, Crystal Reports is the top choice to do the job.

About This Book

Crystal Reports 10 For Dummies is an introductory level book that gets you using Crystal Reports quickly and effectively. It covers all the major capabilities of Crystal Reports but doesn't bog you down in intricate detail. The objective is to give you the information you need to produce the types of reports that most people need most of the time. I also get into some out-of-the-ordinary report types that you might be called upon to generate on occasion.

Use this book as a handy reference guide. Each chapter deals with an individual feature that you may need at one time or another. Pull out the book, read the chapter, and then do what you need to do. In many cases, step-by-step procedures walk you through commonly needed operations. You might find it worthwhile to put the book beside your computer and perform the operations as you read about them.

Anyone who may be called upon to produce a report based on database data can profit from the information contained in this book. It's also valuable to managers who may never personally produce a report, but have oversight of people who do. This book tells you what's possible, what you can do easily, and what takes a little more effort to accomplish. This knowledge can help you estimate how long it should take to produce reports of various types.

Conventions Used in This Book

When an instruction in the book says, for instance, File⇨Save, it means to click the left mouse button on File in the main menu, and then click Save on the submenu that drops down from it.

Anything you see that is printed in a monospaced font is code, or something you'll run across in the course of programming a database (field names, for example). `This is a monospaced font.` Crystal Reports executes code that you enter as formulas or SQL statements.

What You're Not to Read

You can read the book through from cover to cover, working through the examples, although you don't have to. Whether you read it all the way through or not, you can use it as a quick reference when you want to perform a particular operation that you have not used in a while.

There's another whole section of this introduction that explains the icons you'll normally run across, and there is a good reason for paying attention to each of them. There is, however, one icon that you get to skip: Consider yourself exempted from the requirement to read anything that appears by a Technical Stuff icon.

Material next to one of these icons may be interesting to techies like me (there must be some of you out there) but generally is not necessary for a full understanding of how to use Crystal Reports.

Foolish Assumptions

I've never met you, but because we're going to be together for a while, I'll make a few assumptions about you and what you know. I assume that you know how to use a personal computer and that you're somewhat familiar with Microsoft Word. If you know how to navigate around Microsoft Word, you already know almost all there is to know about navigating around Crystal Reports. The user interfaces of the two products are similar.

I assume that you've seen directory trees before, such as those extensively used in Microsoft Windows. You know that if you see a plus sign (+) to the left of a node that shows a folder (or other) icon, it means you can click the plus sign to expand that node, to see what the node contains. Crystal Reports treats directory trees in a similar way.

I assume you know how to perform a drag-and-drop operation with your mouse. In Crystal Reports, when you click an object and start dragging it, your progress is shown by a rectangular placement frame. When you release the mouse button to drop the item, the placement frame is replaced by a duplicate of the item that you dragged.

How This Book Is Organized

This book contains six major parts. Each part contains several chapters.

Part 1: Reporting Basics

Part I introduces you to Crystal Reports and the art of report creation. You find out what a report should accomplish and what it should look like. Then you fire up Crystal Reports and use it to create a simple report based on data held in a database.

Part II: Moving Up to Professional Quality Reports

You can do many things beyond the basics to make reports more focused, more readable, and easier on the eye. This part gives you the information you need to do all those things.

Part III: Advanced Report Types and Features

Part III gets into serious report creation. With the information in this part, you can zero in on exactly the data you want and display it in the most understandable way. You'll be able to nest one report within another, pull report elements from multiple non-database sources, present multidimensional data in OLAP cubes, and illustrate points with charts and maps. With these tools, you can produce reports fit for the eyes of the organization's CEO.

Part IV: Crystal Reports in the Enterprise

Crystal Enterprise is a companion product to Crystal Reports that controls and secures the distribution of reports. With it you can make your reports accessible to people on your local area network, or on the World Wide Web. Crystal Enterprise's new Business Views capability enables report developers to custom tailor a report based on the interests of the people who will be viewing it. There can be multiple different Business Views of a single report. Crystal Enterprise is also the home of the Crystal Repository, which is a great place to store formulas, custom functions, or Business Views, so they can be used again later.

Part V: Publishing Your Reports

After you create a report, you'll want to make it available to the people who need it. Crystal Reports makes it easy for you to distribute your report for viewing, whether to colleagues in your organization or to Internet users around the world. In addition, you can publish your reports using traditional methods. You can print it; export it to a file, or fax it to people far away. After you complete report development, distribution is easy.

Although Crystal Reports does a great job when used all by itself, you can also incorporate it into applications written in a computer language. Crystal Reports' SQL Commands facility gives you direct control over the data in a report's underlying database. Because a version of Crystal Reports is included as an integral part of Microsoft's .NET application development environment, you can incorporate the power of Crystal Reports into applications you write in Visual Basic, Visual C++, Visual C#, or any language compatible with the .NET framework. This gives the applications you write the sophistication of the world's leading report writer.

Part VI: The Part of Tens

It's always good to remember short lists of best practices. That's what the Part of Tens is all about. Listed here are pointers that help you produce outstanding reports with minimum effort, in the shortest possible time.

About the Web Site

This book has an accompanying Web site where you can find sample reports from the book, some exercises related to the sample reports, and links to sites for related information. To access the Web site, go to www.dummies.com/go/crystalfd.

Icons Used in This Book

Tips save you a lot of time and keep you out of trouble.

Pay attention to the information marked by this icon — you may need it later.

As mentioned earlier, Technical Stuff is detail that I find interesting and you may also. But if you don't, no big deal. It is not essential to gain an understanding of the topic being discussed. Skip it if you like.

Heeding the advice that this icon points to can save you from major grief. Ignore it at your peril.

Where to Go from Here

Now you're ready to start finding out about creating professional quality reports based on data stored in your databases, using Crystal Reports 10. Crystal Reports 10 is the latest version of the most popular report writer in the world. You can use it to quickly whip out simple reports, or you can take a little longer and generate a world-class executive report.

Part I
Reporting Basics

The 5th Wave   By Rich Tennant

"Let's check this report on your life.
'Courtesies', 'Kindnesses', not much
there. Helloooo, 'Transgressions'."

In this part . . .

There's data in the database, where it's not doing anyone any good. Your manager wants coherent information, based on that data, on her desk by the close of business today. What should you do? Panic? Consider joining the Foreign Legion?

There's no need to do anything drastic. The chapters in this part quickly tell you how to crank out the report your boss so desperately needs. It won't have all the bells and whistles that you find out about in other parts of this book, but it puts the needed information on the boss's desk before the lights go out tonight. And you'll start to build your reputation as a person who can deliver the goods when the pressure is on.

Chapter 1

Transforming Raw Data into Usable Information

Computers can store and process enormous amounts of data, and with the relentless advance of technology, those capabilities will soon become even more mind-boggling. Even now, the major challenge of getting value from computer systems is not to make them more powerful but to harness the power they already have — in a way that delivers useful information to people.

Megabytes or gigabytes of raw data are neither meaningful nor useful to people. Instead, we need organized information, distilled and focused on answering specific questions. In businesses and enterprises of all kinds, organizing and presenting information has traditionally been the job of documents called *reports*. These documents generally consist of multiple pages that can include text, numbers, charts, maps, and illustrations. The best reports convey the facts needed to make the best decisions, unobscured by a clutter of data irrelevant to the task at hand.

Crystal Reports has been a leading report-writing application package for more than a decade — and is by far the most commonly used report writer in the world. Many people have been using Crystal Reports unknowingly for years because it has been integrated with other applications and not specifically identified by name.

Major Features of Crystal Reports 10

Crystal Reports 10 includes all the features that made Crystal Reports 9 a worldwide best-seller, plus exciting new features that save you time and effort as you develop your reports. Crystal Reports 10 is tightly integrated, so all the individual components of the system work together seamlessly to support the creation, modification, distribution, and viewing of reports. The tight integration extends beyond Crystal Reports 10 to Crystal Enterprise 10, making the sharing of reports across large enterprises not just feasible, but downright convenient.

Data Explorer and Report Experts provide highly intuitive visual tools that step you through the process of creating a report. Features such as the Crystal Repository (which now can be shared across the enterprise) and report templates allow users throughout the organization to reuse components or entire reports. There is never any need to reinvent the wheel. If a component in the Repository or a report template comes close to meeting your requirements but doesn't meet them exactly, you can make minor modifications and have a usable report quickly — a vast improvement over creating an equivalent component or report from scratch.

Formatting a report

The primary job of a report writer such as Crystal Reports is to take data from a database and put it into a pleasing, logical, and understandable format for viewing by users. With Crystal Reports, you are well equipped to give your reports the appearance you want — without having to become a formatting guru.

Crystal Reports offers both absolute and conditional formatting:

- *Absolute formatting* enables you to put text, titles, charts, maps, columns of figures, cross-tabs, and graphics pretty much anywhere you want on the screen. You can handle preprinted forms. You can optimize for screen display or for printing on paper. This is close to the ultimate freedom in report creation — but not quite.

- *Conditional formatting* takes you one step further toward the ultimate: Using it, you can change the format of the data you're displaying in response to the content of the data itself. With conditional formatting, every time the data in a report changes, a formula that you include in the report can make the appearance of the report change accordingly.

One especially useful feature of Crystal Reports 10 — carried over from version 9 — is the report alert. Suppose that a value being displayed crosses a critical threshold that requires immediate action on the part of the report's target audience. When that threshold has been crossed, not only is its value displayed, but also a report alert dialog box pops up that can't be ignored.

Format Painter is a new feature of Crystal Reports 10. It saves you a lot of work if you have numerous objects in a report that all require the same formatting. You simply format the first of those objects and then — with one click — "clone" that formatting onto another object.

Another labor-saving feature is the Template Expert, which enables you to create and save a report template for later use. Imagine how much time you'll save if you have to quickly format multiple reports with a common look.

Enhancing a report with formulas and custom functions

Did I mention that conditional formatting makes use of formulas to change the format of a report? Well, you can use formulas for far more than that. A formula is like a little computer program that can do computations or other manipulations of data before displaying the result. This makes Crystal Reports more than merely a report writer that puts your data in a nice format. By using formulas, you can make it select specific records (or groups of records) and display them the way you want, controlling that process by declaring and using variables in your formulas. All the common flow-control structures (`If-Then-Else`, `Select Case`, `For`, `While Do`, and `Do While`) are available.

After you create a useful formula that you might want to use again later, you can save it as a custom function. Custom functions are added to the standard functions that come with Crystal Reports, keeping them available in one place.

Getting visual with charts and maps

Crystal Reports has excellent capabilities for the graphical display of data. All the most commonly used chart types are available, so you can display your data in the most meaningful way. If you have geographical data, Crystal Reports can display it in maps that show countries, regions, provinces, or cities. A variety of methods are available to associate values with specific regions, including colors, symbols of various sorts, and even charts.

Displaying a report

Crystal Reports is designed for distribution in today's highly connected business environment. You can build reports that are optimized for viewing by people at any computer attached to your organization's local area network. You can also put a report on the Web, for viewing by anyone who has a Web connection and a browser. Of course, you can also distribute your reports the old-fashioned way, printing them on paper and putting them on the target readers' desks.

Distributing a report

You can get your report into the hands of its intended recipients in many ways — print it and deliver it by hand, fax it directly from your computer to a fax machine anywhere in the world, or export the report to a file.

If you choose the latter approach, Crystal Reports supports many output file formats, including HTML for viewing over the Web. At least one of these formats is bound to be readable by the people in your audience. The one caveat here is that if you export a report to any format other than the Crystal Reports native format (`.rpt`), you may lose some of the report's formatting in the process. You can even export directly to an application such as Microsoft Word or Lotus Domino. In such a case, Crystal Reports launches the target application and opens your report in it.

A major new distribution mechanism in Crystal 10 is the Business Views feature (actually a component of Crystal Enterprise, a companion product to Crystal Reports that enables users on client machines to view, schedule, and keep track of published reports). As discussed in Chapter 17, Business Views offer a new data-abstraction layer that simplifies the process of connecting to enterprise data sources. At that layer, you can combine data from multiple data sources of different kinds into a single data source.

Supplying Crystal Reports with data

As important as the output formats of a report are, the inputs to the report are equally important. Crystal Reports shines in this area too. It accepts data from a wide variety of data sources, including both personal computer databases such as Microsoft Access and enterprise-wide client/server databases such as Oracle, IBM's DB2, and Microsoft's SQL Server. In fact, Crystal Reports can accept data from any ODBC-compliant database or any data source that complies with Microsoft's OLE DB standard. Essentially, if your data exists in a commonly used modern data source, Crystal Reports can use it.

The Four Editions of Crystal Reports 10

Crystal Reports 10 comes in four editions that differ in their target audiences and their capabilities. The four editions are the Standard Edition, the Professional Edition, the Developer Edition, and the Advanced Edition.

The Standard Edition

The Standard Edition of Crystal Reports 10 is the least capable of the four, but that is not to say that it is deficient in any way. It is designed to be used by business professionals rather than information technology professionals. The Standard Edition contains nearly all the functionality I cover in this book. Rather than try to enumerate the features it contains, I'll save a lot of space by listing the few things it doesn't do:

- ✔ It won't create reports designed to be displayed on the Web. If you intend to develop reports for display on the Web, you need at least the Professional Edition.

- ✔ It won't integrate reports into application programs. Because the target audience for the Standard Edition consists of people who are not typically programmers, application integration tools would be more confusing than useful.

- ✔ It won't support XML or OLAP (discussed in Chapter 14), and it doesn't include the Repository (covered in Chapter 18).

- ✔ It doesn't include native drivers for client/server databases such as Oracle, DB2, Hyperion Essbase, and SQL Server. If you want to draw data from those databases, use ODBC or move up to the Professional Edition.

The Professional Edition

The Professional Edition is aimed at IT and MIS professionals, such as database administrators, report designers, and systems analysts. It's the product you need to publish reports on the Web. It also gives you more flexibility in using SQL than the Standard Edition does. The Professional Edition also allows you to draw data from client/server databases. The Repository is available in the Professional Edition and above.

The Developer Edition

The Developer Edition is for guru-class, heavy-duty application developers. It is designed to be used by programmers who want to incorporate reports in the applications they develop.

The Developer Edition has all the capability of the Standard and Professional Editions — plus the tools you need to take full control of the underlying functions of Crystal Reports. The Developer Edition is what you would use to create enterprise-wide applications that incorporate reports.

The Advanced Edition

The Advanced Edition is targeted at people who want to develop Enterprise Web applications using Java, COM, or .NET. It has essentially the same functionality as the Developer Edition, but it also has a license structure that accommodates more simultaneous users. People who receive Crystal Reports .NET as a part of Visual Studio .NET may want to upgrade to the Advanced Edition of Crystal Reports 10 when they're ready to deploy their applications on the Web.

Viewing a Report

The majority of this book tells you how to create a new report from data in a database file, using Crystal Reports. It also tells you how to modify a report so you can create a new report (similar to, but distinct from, the existing one). These are concerns of the report designer. But what if you just want to *view* a report that has already been designed?

The world has many more people viewing reports than creating such reports. You may be one of the former. No problem. Before I launch into telling you how to create reports in subsequent chapters of this book, I briefly describe the simple process of viewing reports that already exist.

Reading a printed report

Reading a report that you had Crystal Reports print on paper is the simplest (but also the most limited) way to get the information you want. It doesn't take a lot of technical sophistication to read text and view charts and maps on a sheet of paper. People were doing so long before computers came along.

For some kinds of information, however, printed reports are not as valuable as those you can view online. Printed reports are not updated when the database from which they were derived is updated. They may contain obsolete — thus misleading — information. This is a factor you must always bear in mind when basing decisions on printed reports.

Viewing a report with Crystal Reports

As you might expect, you can do more than just create or modify a report with Crystal Reports software — you can also view an existing report. This has some major advantages over reading a printed report, provided you have Crystal Reports software installed on your computer (but you knew that):

✔ **The report is connected to the source database while the report is being viewed.** That's an obvious advantage. If the data in the database has changed since the last time you viewed it, you can refresh the report before you view it again by pulling current information from the database. Crystal Reports automatically checks the database to see whether it has been updated since the last time your report was run. If so, it asks whether you want to refresh the report with current data.

✔ **You can use the drill-down capability of Crystal Reports to selectively view the detail underlying summary reports.** This enables you to get an overview of the subject by viewing the summary, and then drill down into the specific parts that interest you for more detail. (For more on drill-down, see Chapter 6.)

✔ **Viewing a "live" report gives you access to the way Crystal Reports uses hyperlinks.** You can follow a hyperlink from one part of a report to another part, from one report to another report on the same computer, or from one report to a report on another computer on your network.

✔ **You can view reports that include color graphics or text that uses font colors other than black.** For the many people who don't have high-speed color printers, this provides a way to access the full richness of a report's contents.

To view an existing report on a computer that has Crystal Reports installed on it, follow these steps:

1. **Launch Crystal Reports from your computer's Start menu.**

   Crystal Reports appears, displaying the Welcome to Crystal Reports dialog box, as shown in Figure 1-1. You can choose to create a new report or open an existing report. The dialog box lists several existing reports that may be on your system, or gives you the option of looking at more report files if you don't see the one you want in the list.

Figure 1-1:
The Welcome to Crystal Reports dialog box offers several options.

2. **Select the report that you want to view and click OK.**

   If you don't see the report you want, click More Files, click OK, and use the Open dialog box to select any report available on the system.

   Crystal Reports retrieves and displays the report, as shown in Figure 1-2.

3. **Move through the report.**

   Scroll around the report, and move back and forth among its pages. You can drill down into any summary report that supports drilldown. If the report contains hyperlinks, you can follow them to other locations in the report or in other reports

4. **When you are finished viewing the report, choose File⟳Close to close it.**

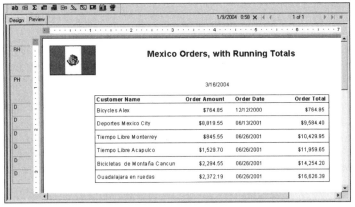

Figure 1-2: Crystal Reports report development environment, with a report displayed.

Viewing a report on your local area network or the Web

The Crystal Enterprise Web Desktop can display your reports to thousands of users on your local area network, or millions of users on the World Wide Web. Whether your users are on a local area network that's directly connected to a server running the administrative part of Crystal Enterprise, or on a remote connection via the Web, they can use the Crystal Enterprise Web Desktop to access the reports they need. The user interface is a standard Web browser, such as Internet Explorer or Netscape.

Chapter 2

Create a Simple Report Right Now!

In This Chapter

▶ Starting the program

▶ Creating your first report

▶ Troubleshooting your report

▶ Printing your report

*W*hen you start Crystal Reports, generally you want to do one of three things: create a report, modify a report, or run a report against the data in your database. Reports take data from a database, process it, format it, and then output it to a printer, computer screen, or Web site.

Crystal Reports comes with a sample database you can use for practice. It's a Microsoft Access database for a fictitious company named Xtreme Mountain Bikes Inc. You might be able to buy one of their fictitious bikes with fictitious money, if you ever find a fictitious bike shop — and the Treasury Department doesn't nab you first.

The `xtreme.mdb` database contains a number of database tables that are representative of the tables a real bike manufacturer might maintain. The tables are filled with sample data that you can manipulate and display with Crystal Reports. You can use this sample data as the basis for your first report.

To create a report, you need to know a few things:

- ✔ Which tables in the database contain the data you want

- ✔ Which data items you want in those tables

- ✔ What manipulations of the data must be performed to give you the information you want

- ✔ How you want your report to be formatted

- ✔ Whether the users of your report retrieve it from a black-and-white printer, a color printer, a local computer screen, or a Web site

For the purposes of this introduction (and for now), imagine you already know all those things.

Starting Crystal Reports 10

You've probably chosen Crystal Reports because you have a database that contains information that's important to you. In all likelihood, the data in that database changes with time, and you want to be able to keep up with its current status. You *could* retrieve the information you want by making SQL queries, but that would be too much like work. It's far better to create a report with Crystal Reports, and then run the report whenever you want the latest status of the information of interest. You have to create the report only once, but you can run it many times, getting the latest results with each successive run. You don't have to learn SQL or any other method of pulling data out of databases. Reports created with Crystal Reports are easy to build, easy to read, and easy to understand. What could be better?

SQL is the international standard language for communicating with databases. It differs from most common computer languages in that it's nonprocedural. It deals with data a set at a time rather than a record at a time. Database developers use SQL. If you're a database user (rather than a developer), Crystal Reports may give you everything you need to get what you want out of your databases.

The first step to creating a report is to launch Crystal Reports from the Windows Start menu. When you do, the Crystal Reports main window appears, displaying the dialog box shown in Figure 2-1.

Figure 2-1: Welcome to Crystal Reports!

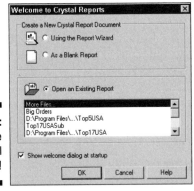

You are invited to choose from three options. You can create a Crystal Reports document using Report Wizard or by starting with a blank report. Alternatively (as I demonstrate in Chapter 1), you can open a report that already exists, either to change it or to run it.

Although Report Wizard can be a time- and labor-saver, it does constrain the form of the report. So this chapter takes you right to the point and shows you how to create a report *your* way, starting from a blank report instead of using Report Wizard.

Creating a Report with the Blank Report Option

To create a report from scratch, starting with the blank report option, follow these steps:

1. **Start Crystal Reports.**

   The Welcome to Crystal Reports dialog box appears.

2. **Select the As a Blank Report option, and then click the OK button.**

   The Database Expert dialog box appears, as shown in Figure 2-2.

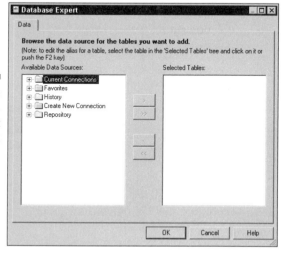

Figure 2-2: The Database Expert dialog box shows possible places to find the source of your data.

3. **In the Available Data Sources pane, click the plus sign to the left of the Create New Connection folder to expand it.**

   This is the folder you choose whenever you're creating a report from scratch. When you have connected to a database, Crystal Reports remembers where it is.

4. **Double-click the database type that matches your data source.**

   Crystal Reports recognizes a variety of different database types. You must select the right one. If you don't know which type is correct, ask someone familiar with the data source. To follow along with the example, double-click Access/Excel (DAO). The Access/Excel (DAO) dialog box appears, as shown in Figure 2-3.

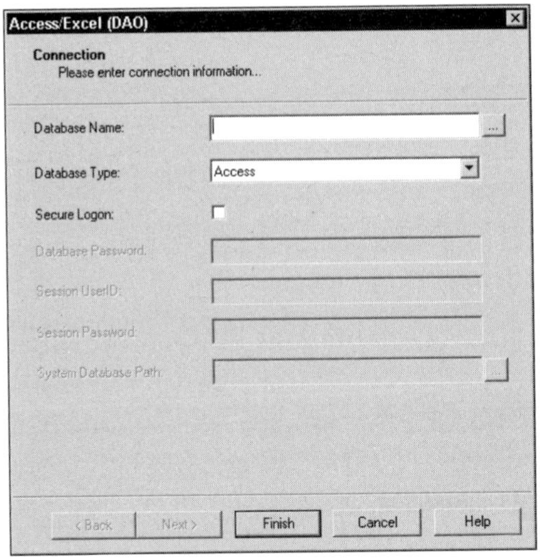

Figure 2-3: The Access/ Excel (DAO) dialog box asks how to connect to your data source.

5. **Click the ellipsis (...) button to the right of the Database Name box.**

   The Access and Excel files on your system appear. For the example, I selected an Access database file named `xtreme`. This may not be as easy as it sounds. Mine was located at `D:\Program Files\Crystal Decisions\Crystal Reports 10\Samples\En\Databases\ xtreme.mdb`.

   You may have to browse to find this file on your system.

6. **Click the Finish button.**

   Database Expert reappears, as shown in Figure 2-4, with the `xtreme` database connected.

7. **Expand the Tables node, and then double-click the table on which you want to base your report.**

The tree in the Available Data Sources pane consists of a number of nodes, some of which branch off from others. Every data source has four of these nodes branching off from it: Add Command, Tables, Views, and Stored Procedures.

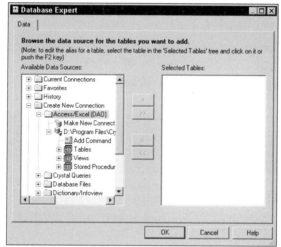

Figure 2-4:
The xtreme database is connected to the report.

8. **To follow along with the example, expand the Tables node and then double-click Product.**

   Doing so copies the Product table from the Available Data Sources pane to the Selected Tables pane.

9. **Click the OK button to close Database Expert.**

   A blank report fills the window, as shown in Figure 2-5.

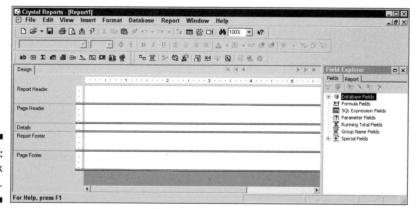

Figure 2-5:
A blank report.

The Design tab (on the left edge) shows five sections of the report:

- **Report Header:** Appears only at the top of the report and is the first thing that a viewer sees.
- **Page Header:** Appears below the report header and at the top of all the other pages in the report.
- **Details:** The actual content of the report.
- **Report Footer section:** Appears after the last detailed information in the report.
- **Page Footer:** Appears at the bottom of every page of the report.

Allocating more space to the layout

Depending on the resolution of your computer screen, the Crystal Reports window may not display the full width of your report. You can give yourself a little more width in the display by changing one of the display options. Follow these simple steps:

1. **Choose File⇨Options.**

    The Layout tab of the Options dialog box appears, as shown in Figure 2-6.

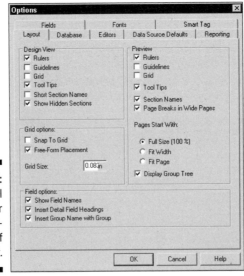

Figure 2-6: Control center for the appearance of your report.

2. **In the Design View section, click to select the Short Section Names option.**

   This reduces the section names on the left edge of the window to one- or two-letter abbreviations, freeing up a little horizontal real estate.

3. **Click the OK button.**

4. **Drag the left edge of the Field Explorer farther to the right, to allocate more horizontal space to the work area.**

   You can now view more of the report without resorting to horizontal scrolling.

Giving the report a title

The Report Header area (at the top of the first page of the report) is the ideal place to tell the reader exactly what the report contains. However, this forces you, right here at the beginning, to *decide* what the report is to contain. No problem: Start by considering who your target audience is and what they want to know.

If you are Xtreme Mountain Bikes, the target audience for your Products report is potential customers. They surely will want to know what products you carry, including information on color and size, where appropriate. They probably also want price information. They'll also need to know the stock number of an item so they can specify it properly when they decide to purchase a bike.

Placing your company logo in the report header also makes sense. The Xtreme logo is not available conveniently on the Crystal Reports distribution CD. For the purposes of this demonstration, any logo-sized image file will do. You can add one to the report header along with a title, such as *Product Price List*.

To add a logo to a report, do the following:

1. **Dismiss Field Explorer, if necessary, by clicking the X in its upper-right corner.**

2. **With the Design tab selected, click the Insert Picture icon in the Insert toolbar.**

   A dialog box appears, displaying the image files in the Databases folder. There were no image files in my database folder, so I looked around for a substitute. I found one here:

```
E:\Program Files\Crystal Decisions\Crystal Reports
        10\Samples\En\Code\RDC\Visual Basic\Pro Athlete Salaries\res.
```

Wow! That is one long URL. Perhaps you'll find a suitable image some-where else. Your organization's own logo would do fine.

3. **Click the picture's filename to select it (an outline of the logo appears on the report layout), place it in the upper-left corner of the report header with the mouse, and then click to fix it in place.**

   Figure 2-7 shows the result.

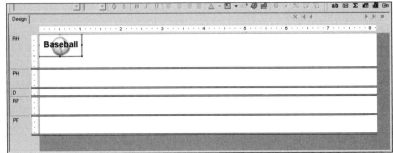

Figure 2-7:
A company
logo has
been placed
in the report.

My substitute logo was `mlb.bmp`. It is a baseball logo. I have loved base-ball ever since I played in the farm league in Belleville, New Jersey. I played in the farm league almost my whole career, only moving up to Little League a few weeks before I became too old to play in Little League any more. You can use whatever you want for your substitute logo.

You can find out the names of the toolbar icons such as the Insert Picture icon by hovering the cursor over them. After a few seconds, a tooltip appears, telling you the name of the tool you're looking at.

Next, you put a report title into the Report Header section as well. To do this, you will have to use several of the tools in the Insert toolbar.

1. **Pull down the dividing line between the Report Header section and the Page Header section so that you can place the report title below the level of the logo.**

   To pull down a dividing line, hover the cursor over it until the cursor changes shape, depress the left mouse button and drag the line to the position you want it to be in, and then release the mouse button.

2. **Click the Insert Text Object icon in the Insert Tools toolbar.**

   A text object rectangle appears.

3. **Drag the rectangle into the Report Header section, and drop it.**

   To drag and drop the rectangle: Put the mouse pointer over the rectangle, press and hold down the mouse button to select it, move it to the desired location, and then release the mouse button to drop the rectangle. A text cursor starts to blink inside the rectangle.

4. **At the blinking cursor's location, type the report title.**

   For the example, type **Product Price List**.

5. **Select the title you just typed, and then increase its size by clicking the Increase Font Size icon.**

6. **Make the title bold by clicking the Bold icon.**

7. **Move the left and right edges of the text object to the left and right edges of the report, respectively, and then click the Align Center icon to locate the title in the center of the page.**

   At this point, your report should look similar to Figure 2-8.

Figure 2-8:
The report title is now in the Report Header section.

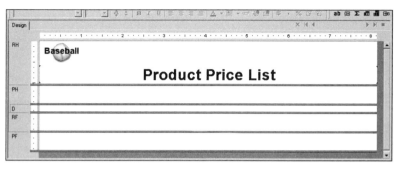

Choosing the fields that will appear in your report

The next logical step is to place in the Details section the fields you want the report to display. Simply follow these steps:

1. **If the Field Explorer is not currently visible, display it by clicking View⊅Field Explorer on the main menu.**

2. **In Field Explorer, click the plus sign to the left of Database Fields; click the plus sign to the left of Product to display its fields (because the Product table is the only available data source, it is the only one listed).**

   Field Explorer displays the fields in the Product table, as shown in Figure 2-9.

3. **Click the first field that you want to include in the report, and then drag it to the left edge of the Detail section.**

   For the example, click the Product ID field. When you drag the field, a rectangle appears. The field name appears in the rectangle in the Detail section and also above it in the Page Header section. Later, you may want to change the column titles in the Page Header section for cosmetic reasons. For now, just leave the default column titles.

Figure 2-9:
The
contents
of the
Product
table.

4. **Repeat Step 3 for any other fields that you want to include in the report.**

   For the example, place the Product Name, Color, Size, and Price (SRP) fields in order in the Detail section, leaving just a little space between them.

   Crystal Reports 10 automatically adjusts the fields displayed to match the field sizes you chose, and spaces them out proportionally. You can manually adjust the field sizes by grasping the handles on the left and right edges of the fields and moving them. You can resize the fields and move them back and forth until you arrive at a good balanced appearance. At this point, your report layout should look similar to the one shown in Figure 2-10.

Figure 2-10:
All fields
have been
placed in
the Detail
section.

Improving the readability of page headers

Everything in the Page Header section appears just below the Report Header on the first page of the report and at the top of all following pages. By default, the field names in the Page Header section are displayed in a normal font and underlined. I think they'd look better in a bold font and not underlined, so I select the Bold attribute for each of them and deselect the Underline attribute. I'll wait to see what the report looks like before deciding whether I want to change the font size as well. Figure 2-11 shows the layout with the enhanced column headings.

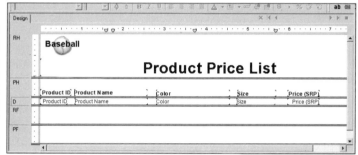

Figure 2-11: The column headings are modified to improve their appearance.

Previewing the report

So far, you've been able to see the layout of your report only in the sectioned structure of Design mode. To get a better idea of what the report looks like at this point, you can switch to Preview mode. To do so, click the Print Preview icon in the Standard toolbar. This displays the Preview tab in the upper-left corner of the work area and displays the report, complete with data pulled from the Products table. Figure 2-12 shows as much of the report as the screen can hold.

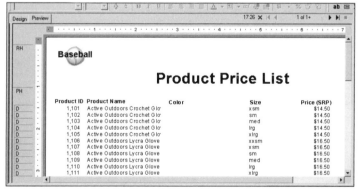

Figure 2-12: A preview of the Product Price List report.

You can notice a couple of things about the report at this point. First, Crystal Reports apparently automatically inserts commas between groups of three digits in number fields, such as the Product ID field. This is not what you want. Second, the color attribute must not apply to gloves because no color information is shown for the glove products that we can see.

The fact that gloves have no color is not a problem, but the comma in the middle of the Product ID is a problem. You can correct this as follows:

1. **Click the Design tab to return to Design mode.**

2. **In the Details section, select the field whose number format you want to change.**

   For the example, select the Product ID field.

3. **Choose Format⟶Format Field.**

   Format Editor appears.

4. **Click the numeric format that you want, and then click the OK button.**

   For the example, you want the format with no commas, as shown in Figure 2-13. This changes the format of the Product ID field to eliminate the unwanted commas.

You can verify the change by returning to Preview mode and noting that the commas are gone. By moving the sliders at the right and bottom edges of the report window, you can verify that all columns and rows are as they should be.

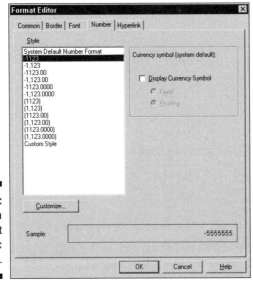

Figure 2-13:
Selecting a
different
numeric
format.

Page footers carry useful information

At the bottom of each page, you might want to display some useful information, such as the page number. If you ever drop a stack of reports off your desk, page footers can be a valuable aid to putting them back together again in the proper order.

For the Product Price List, the page number, date printed, and report title are valuable additions to the page footer. (Prices tend to change frequently in a fast moving industry such as the mountain bike business, so the date of a price list is very important.) In Design mode, follow these steps to create a page footer for your report that includes all three of these items:

1. **In the Insert toolbar, click the Insert Text Object icon.**

   You click this icon because all the items you want to place in the page footer are text items.

2. **Drag the text object rectangle to the Page Footer section and place it by clicking the left mouse button.**

3. **Drag the handles on the left and right sides of the rectangle until it spans the full width of the page.**

4. **Click the Align Center icon.**

   There isn't any text there yet, but there will be.

5. **Right-click the text rectangle and choose Edit Text.**

6. **At the blinking cursor in the rectangle, type the report title, followed by a comma.**

   Type **Product Price List,** for this example.

Next, place the current date and page number into the page footer:

1. **In Field Explorer, scroll down to Special Fields and expand it.**

   Remember, you expand a node by clicking the plus sign to its left.

2. **Click the Print Date icon or the Print Date name next to it, and drag it to the Page Footer area, right after the comma.**

3. **After the Print Date field is in position, type a comma after it, and then type** Page **followed by a hyphen.**

4. **Click the Page Number icon or the name next to it, and drag it to the right of the hyphen.**

   This gives you an arrangement that looks much like Figure 2-14.

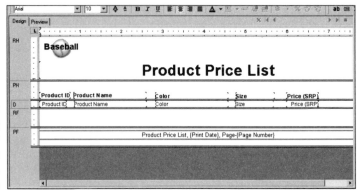

Figure 2-14:
Page footer
in Design
mode.

5. **Click the Preview tab at the top of the screen to switch to Preview mode.**

The field names are replaced by actual values, as shown in Figure 2-15.

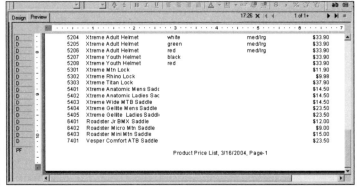

Figure 2-15:
Page footer
in Preview
mode.

Wrap things up with a report footer

For some types of reports, it's appropriate to have a final item to close out the report. This would appear after the last of the data on the last page. Items such as this go into the Report Footer section in Design mode. Remember, the report footer comes immediately after the last line of detail information and *before* the final page footer.

To illustrate this feature of Crystal Reports, put a company slogan at the bottom of the Product Price List. Place the slogan *"Xtreme Mountain Bikes Take You to the Limit"* into the Report Footer section in the same way that you put the report title into the Page Footer section. The result, in Preview mode, looks like Figure 2-16.

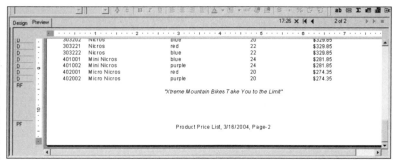

Figure 2-16:
The company slogan as a report footer.

Recording helpful information about your report

Now that the Product Price List report is essentially complete, you may want to generate some descriptive information about the report that's associated with the report but not normally printed or displayed. To do this, follow these steps:

1. **Choose File⇨Summary Info.**

   The Document Properties dialog box appears.

2. **Fill in the boxes with whatever information you want to associate with your report.**

   I added the information shown in Figure 2-17.

3. **Click the OK button.**

   The document properties you entered are stored along with the report; they can be retrieved whenever anyone views the report with Crystal Reports.

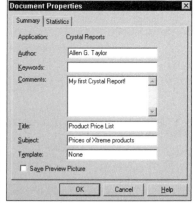

Figure 2-17:
Pertinent information about the Product Price List report.

Troubleshooting a Report That Doesn't Look Quite Right

Sometimes the vision you have in your mind is not adequately reflected in the report you produce. There are various reasons why this might be true. Perhaps your vision is not something that can be built in the real world. You can't do much about that. But you can do something about other reasons, such as not using Crystal Reports properly or not being aware of all its capabilities.

Crystal Reports gives you tremendous freedom in how you can lay out your report. It also gives you great latitude in what you include in the report. In addition to text and columns of numbers, you can include graphical images, charts, graphs, and maps. You could even crank out a full-length science fiction novel with Crystal Reports if you wanted to, although other tools are better suited to that task.

The bottom line is this: If you feel sure that a report ought to be able to include something, you can almost certainly do it with Crystal Reports. This book tells you about many of the most powerful and useful features of Crystal Reports. If I don't mention a feature or capability that you'd like to use, it may nonetheless be available. Check the *Crystal Reports User's Guide* and online help for additional information on advanced features. Crystal Reports is a product of Business Objects SA. More information on Crystal Reports can be found at www.businessobjects.com.

Printing a Report

Printing a report from Crystal Reports is really easy. Open the report in the Crystal Reports environment, and then click the Print icon or choose File⇨ Print⇨Printer. Print the report the same way you would print any document in a Microsoft Windows environment.

Chapter 3

Report Design Guidelines

*N*o book can tell you in a step-by-step manner exactly how to build the report you want. However, this book gets you into some general principles of good report design — and shows you some common types of reports. From those general principles and examples, you can decide how best to design reports that meet the needs of your organization.

An effective report design depends on many factors:

✔ The data that the report draws from the database

✔ The way the database is structured

✔ The level of detail that the users of the report require

✔ The purpose of the report

✔ The capabilities of the computer that displays or prints the report

✔ What the users of the report really need (understanding this is *critical*)

Audience

Every report should have a definite audience. Here's a key question to ask as you begin to develop any report: "Who will be reading this report?"

Some potential audience members may be familiar with the information that the report contains — and old hands at the naming conventions used for objects in the database. These people may prefer a streamlined presentation of the data. Other audience members might be unfamiliar with the report content — so you may have to translate terms, use graphical devices (such as charts), and include explanatory text. If you have two such divergent audiences, you may need to produce two reports. Both would contain the same information, presented in different ways.

Another question to ask is, "What information does the audience need and in what form should it be delivered?" If they need several unrelated things, you may serve them better by creating several reports, each one focused on one specific purpose.

Although it's best to write a report with one consistent audience in mind, sometimes you have to design a report for multiple audiences, each with its own needs. The challenge is to give the members of each audience the information they need in a form they can easily understand, without handicapping the members of other audiences by subjecting them to irrelevant material. The key is to organize the information so members of each audience can quickly and easily find and understand the information of interest to them.

Purpose

In addition to having a specific audience, the report should be restricted to one specific purpose — and accomplish that purpose by providing thorough, accurate, timely information to the target audience. This information, more often than not, is the basis for important decisions that the readers of the report will make.

Restricting a report to serving a single purpose does everyone a favor. Reports that cover multiple topics generally don't do justice to any one of them and tend to confuse readers. A good report covers a single topic and conveys a message that the reader can easily comprehend and act upon.

Knowing how important the report is to its audience may affect the amount of time and effort you put into creating it. Is the report likely to be a basis for "bet-the-business" decisions? Or does it simply make visible some facts that are nice to know but not earth-shattering?

Another consideration is how often the report will be run. Some reports are one-shot affairs — run once against the database, never to be run again. Other reports are run repeatedly — weekly, monthly, quarterly, or yearly — and need the latest information in the database every time. Reports that are run multiple times, by multiple people, deserve more attention to detail than reports run only once.

Content

After you know who the report is for, and the kinds of decisions they want to base on the information in the report, it's time to decide exactly what information should *be* in the report. Leaving out distracting, irrelevant material is just as important as including material of interest.

The best reports are succinct and to the point, offering readers the information they want right away, minus the clutter of information they don't care about. Keeping in mind the audience and the purpose of the report, also consider what level of formality or informality is most appropriate.

If your report has to meet the needs of several audiences, shape its content along these lines:

- ✔ Determine which audience is the most critical.
- ✔ Determine which information is the most important to that audience.
- ✔ Display the most important information most prominently in the report.
- ✔ Put other, less important information for the most critical audience in a nearby but subordinate position.
- ✔ For the other audiences, cluster the information in such a way that each group reading the report can find all the information it needs within a single area of the report.

Interfacing the Report to a Database

Suppose your clients have told you what they want the report to deliver — and the raw material for that information exists in the database the report will draw from. Your job as the report designer is to make the connection to the database so the needed data can flow into your report, where it will be massaged, formatted, combined, graphed, or otherwise processed to produce a finished report. The first step in that process is connecting your report to the database that will be supplying it with data. Crystal Reports has built-in interfaces that connect to a wide variety of data sources — you can get some idea of how many when you start a report design in Design view.

Connecting to Microsoft Access

Suppose you want to create a report based on data in a Microsoft Access database. Follow these steps:

1. **Start Crystal Reports.**

   You are greeted by the Welcome to Crystal Reports dialog box.

2. **Choose the As a Blank Report option, and then click OK.**

   Database Expert is displayed.

3. **Expand the Create New Connection node by clicking the plus sign (+) next to it.**

   As shown in Figure 3-1, various data sources are available.

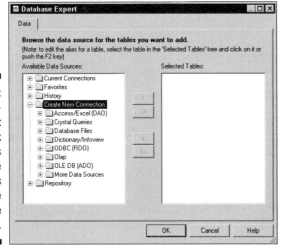

Figure 3-1:
The Database Expert dialog box shows possible locations for the database you want.

4. **Connect to the appropriate database and display its tables in the Available Data Sources pane of Database Expert, as shown in Figure 3-2.**

   For more information on this process, see Chapter 2. To follow along with this example, connect to the `xtreme1.mdb` database.

5. **Select the tables in the database that contain the data you want to include in the report.**

For the example, double-click the Customer and Orders tables in the Available Data Sources pane (to add them to the Selected Tables pane).

6. Click OK.

The Link view appears, showing how the selected tables relate to each other.

7. Click OK to exit Database Expert.

You are now connected to the database of choice and have selected from it the tables that contain the data that will be included in your report.

So, how do you connect your report to the Access database? You don't have to. It's all transparent. Crystal Reports has made the connection behind the scenes, without any help from you, beyond specifying the name of the database, finding it on your system, and choosing which tables to use from the database.

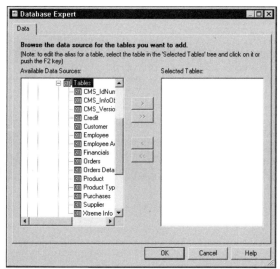

Figure 3-2:
Tables in the xtreme.mdb database are listed.

Connecting to other data sources

Access is a desktop database application; usually it resides on the same physical computer you're sitting in front of while you work with it. It also might be lurking on another computer on a small local-area network. Access is not designed to handle large databases or large numbers of simultaneous users. For those larger applications, a client/server arrangement is the preferred solution: A relational database-management system (RDBMS) resides on the *server* computer — along with the data — while users sit in front of multiple *client* machines. Because the bulk of the processing takes place on the same machine that holds the data (the server), the amount of data that must be sent over the network is minimized and good performance can stay good, even when scaled up to very large systems.

Before you can connect a report to a client/server relational database, you must log on to the database. The connection is mediated by a *database driver* program, of which there are several varieties:

- **Direct database driver:** This type of program is specifically designed and optimized to connect to a specific DBMS, such as Microsoft SQL Server, Oracle, or IBM's DB2. Crystal Reports includes direct database drivers for the most popular DBMS products, including these. In addition, Crystal Reports includes drivers for data sources that are not relational databases, such as Excel spreadsheets, Outlook folders, and Lotus Notes databases.

- **ODBC (Open Database Connectivity):** This is a second type of database connection. Unlike a dedicated direct database driver, a report can connect via ODBC to a wide variety of data sources, many more than those that are available via direct database driver. In fact, you can connect to the Access `xtreme.mdb` database via ODBC as well as by the direct route. Crystal Reports' support of ODBC means that you should be able to create a report based on the data in any data source that is ODBC-compliant, and ODBC compliance is practically universal today.

- **OLE DB:** (Pronounced "o-lay-dee-bee.") This is a newer interfacing technique similar to but more flexible than ODBC. OLE DB allows a report to pull data from multiple sources, some of which may be relational databases and others may be non-relational. OLE is an acronym for Object Linking and Embedding. DB, of course, stands for Database.

What Should the Report Look Like?

Information can be presented in a report in many different ways — narrative text, tables of numbers, and (between those two extremes) various other methods, each effective in its own way for certain kinds of display.

When you've determined your audience and what the report needs to contain, the next decision is how to present that information to that audience. If you were producing a report on video-game sales figures (for example), you would probably present the information in one format for game-industry executives and in an entirely different format for teenage video-game enthusiasts. The information in both reports might be identical — but to be effective, the presentation of data should be vastly different.

Making a good first impression

I've heard that when you meet someone for the first time, within the first 30 seconds they form a judgment of you. They decide whether they like you, trust you, or respect you. That snap judgment, based on 30 seconds of input, affects how they deal with you from then on.

Salespeople have known this truth about first impressions for a long time, which is why they "dress for success" when making a sales call. They want to make a good first impression so their prospect will be predisposed to like them, trust them, respect them, and buy from them. For all the same reasons, you want every report you create to make a good first impression so its readers "buy" (buy into) what you're selling: the information in your report.

One important way to make a good first impression is to make the appearance of your report appropriate for the audience and for the occasion. Know who your audience is and what they expect this particular report to tell them. When they look at the first page of your report for the first time, it should immediately meet their expectations. They should see a clear indication of what the report is, and an engaging presentation of the information they're most interested in seeing.

It would be a mistake to bury the most important information somewhere in the back pages of the report. For some reports, it may even be appropriate to state the conclusions that can be drawn from the data, right up front. This can encourage readers to dig deeper and digest the data pulled from the database that backs up your conclusions.

Deciding how best to present the information

The Report Creation Wizard gives you a total of six different ways to format your report: columnar, tabular, or justified layout, in either a portrait or landscape orientation. For reports that don't have to impress anybody (or for quick-and-dirty reports that you intend to run only once), one of these six options is probably fine. For more elaborate applications, your best bet is to create the report from the ground up, using Design view.

With Design view, you have complete freedom to arrange the various report elements on the page. You also can use many more different kinds of report elements than the Report Creation Wizard allows, and add functionality way beyond merely displaying data from the database. Throughout this book, I show you sophisticated ways to give your report's readers the information they want, in the most effective way.

Should the report include graphs, charts, or pictures?

If a picture is worth a thousand words, a graph is worth a lot more than a large table of numbers. Graphs and charts are valuable parts of any report that needs to show relationships between data items or trends in data. Some types of reports — such as those displaying sales figures for a product or for a family of products — have much more impact if they include graphs of the data along with the figures that back up the graphs. Other types (such as membership lists for organizations) won't benefit from graphs or charts.

Pictures such as photographs, illustrations, or line drawings can greatly increase the value of some types of report by presenting the information in an immediate, visual way. The more pathways into the brains of the readers you use, the likelier it is that they'll fully receive and appreciate your message.

When you're designing a report, ask yourself this question, "Would a graph, chart, or other illustration improve the understanding and acceptance of the content of this report?" If the answer is "Yes," then consider adding such an illustration. If an added illustration won't improve understanding and acceptance, don't include one; it could distract from the message the report is supposed to convey.

Style communicates meaning, too

The words, numbers, and graphs in a report embody the data, but the way these report elements are put together, and the judicious use of fonts, color, layout, and white space, can also make an impression on the reader. You want that impression to be favorable. Give some thought to how to use all these style elements together to create the desired effect.

You want to communicate with the reader on an emotional level as well as merely on an intellectual level. If, for instance, your report is designed to inform potential investors about the benefits of investing in your company, the report should convey an aura of professionalism, but at the same time be consistent with the business you are in. The prospectus for an investment-banking firm should have a very different style from the prospectus for a cutting-edge video-game company. Each should convey the idea that the company understands the business it's in, but the difference in industry dictates different presentation of company information. Reports should convey a style that readers would expect to see from the top organization in its field. Style adds credibility, on an emotional level, to the facts being presented.

Does the report convey the message?

Sometimes all a report needs to do is present some facts in a straightforward way. Membership lists, price lists, and inventory lists fall into this category. Another category of reports, however, must do more to be effective. These reports try not only to give the reader information, but also to change the reader's thinking. To influence a reader, the sum of what's in the report should convey a uniform and unmistakable message. To make sure that point gets across, you may want to state it explicitly at the end of the report. Crystal Reports provides a space for a report footer when you are using Design view — and it's an ideal place for any such summarizing text. If appropriate, it might also include a call to action.

Chapter 4

Reporting Overview

. . . .

. . . .

*Y*ou can start a report in any of several ways. Chapter 2, for example, shows how to create a report from scratch, starting with a blank report file. Another way is to use an existing report as a template; the new report has different content but is structurally similar to the existing report. Generally the quickest way is to use the Report Wizard, which does much of the work for you but makes some assumptions that limit your options.

This chapter follows the speediest approach: I walk you step by step through building a report with the Report Wizard. You give up some freedom and flexibility (compared to the from-scratch approach) but the wizard does much of the work for you — fast.

Creating a Report with Report Creation Wizard

The Report Wizard is often the best way to create a report that's conceptually simple and doesn't require unusual formatting or a custom appearance. The Report Wizard uses a few standard layouts, and is easy to access. When you first launch Crystal Reports, the software assumes (reasonably enough) that you want to create a report — so it displays the Welcome to Crystal Reports dialog box. If you select Using the Report Wizard and then click OK, the wizard goes into action and displays the Crystal Reports Gallery, as in Figure 4-1.

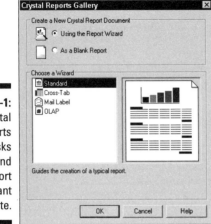

Figure 4-1:
Crystal
Reports
Gallery asks
what kind
of report
you want
to create.

The various styles of reports that the Report Wizard can produce are listed in the pane on the left. The pane on the right displays a sample layout for the currently selected report style.

Creating a standard report

You start your investigation with a standard report, which is the one most people will need most of the time. The example is from the fictitious Xtreme Mountain Bikes Inc., a business that sells mountain bikes and associated accessories. However, its information needs are much the same as the needs of any business that buys products from suppliers and sells them to customers. Thus, the kinds of standard reports that Xtreme needs are representative of the reports that many retail or wholesale businesses would find useful.

Suppose Xtreme's sales manager wants a detailed report of all orders placed in December 2000. She wants the report to include each customer's name, as well as the order date, order number, salesperson's name, items ordered, quantities ordered, and the extended price of each item ordered. To build this report, data must be extracted from multiple tables. Follow these steps to get it done:

1. **Start Crystal Reports.**

   The Welcome to Crystal Reports dialog box appears.

2. **Make sure that the Using the Report Wizard option is selected, and then click OK.**

   The Crystal Reports Gallery dialog box appears (refer to Figure 4-1).

3. **At the top of the screen, choose the Using the Report Wizard option.**

4. **In the Choose a Wizard area, select the Standard option.**

5. **Click the OK button.**

   The Standard Report Creation Wizard dialog box appears.

6. **Locate the database by using the procedures outlined in Chapters 2 and 3.**

7. **Click the plus sign to the left of the database name, and then click the plus sign to the left of the Tables item.**

   To follow along with the example, click the plus sign to the left of the Xtreme sample database, `xtreme.mdb`, and then click the plus sign to the left of the Tables icon. You see the names of the tables in the database, as shown in Figure 4-2.

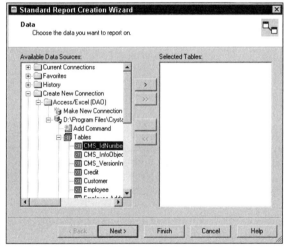

Figure 4-2:
Standard
Report
Creation
Wizard
dialog box.

8. **Select the tables that contain data that will be used by the report, moving them to the Selected Tables pane.**

   To follow along with the example, double-click the Customer table in the Available Data Sources pane and move it to the Selected Tables pane. Do the same for the `Orders`, `Employee`, `Orders_Detail`, and `Product` tables.

9. **Click the Next button.**

   Standard Report Creation Wizard displays the Link view.

The main pane of the Link view shows the tables, along with links to other tables with which they share common columns. Figure 4-3 shows what the Link view looks like at this point. The pane isn't large enough to show all the tables, but you can use the scroll bars to make sure they're all there and are all linked by common columns.

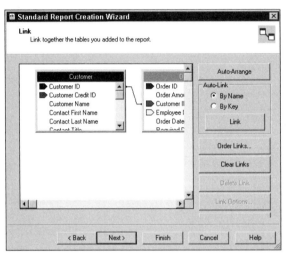

Figure 4-3:
Link view
of the
Standard
Report
Creation
Wizard
dialog box
shows the
connection
between the
selected
tables.

The Standard Report Creation Wizard has inferred that columns with the same name in different tables refer to the same objects — a valid assumption in this case, but it may not always be true. If any link that the wizard has assumed is incorrect, you can change it manually: Just click it to remove it, and then drag the pointer from one table to another to add new links.

After the tables and links are arranged to your satisfaction, do the following to continue with the example:

1. **Click the Next button in the Link view of the Standard Report Creation Wizard.**

   The Fields view appears.

2. **From the tables selected previously, select the fields you want for the report.**

   To follow along with the example, expand the Customer table node and select Customer ID and Customer Name from it. Select Last Name and First Name from the Employee table; Order ID, Order Amount, and Order Date from the Orders table; Product ID, Unit Price, and Quantity from the Orders Detail table; and Product Name from the Product table. At this point, Standard Report Creation Wizard looks like Figure 4-4.

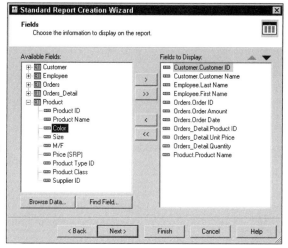

Figure 4-4:
The fields for
the report
have been
specified.

3. **Click Next.**

   The Grouping view appears.

4. **Because you don't want to do any grouping in this report, click Next.**

   The Record Selection view appears.

5. **Double-click the field that you want to filter on to move it to the Filter Fields pane.**

   For the example, you want to filter out all orders that were *not* placed during December 2000, so double-click the `Orders.Order Date` field.

6. **Pull down the list below the Filter Fields pane and select the method for filtering. Then make any secondary filtering selections, if necessary.**

   For the example, select *is between.* In the sublist, select the dates of the first and last orders that were placed during December 2000 (as in Figure 4-5). You may select any month displayed in the `xtreme` database.

7. **Click the Finish button.**

   The finished report is displayed, using the Preview tab in Crystal Reports, as shown in Figure 4-6. If the Field Explorer is still displayed, you can dismiss it to show more of the right side of the report. You can also drag the left boundary of the report area farther to the left if needed.

To fit everything on an 8½ x 11 inch sheet, the columns have been squeezed together; some information in some columns does not appear. To remedy this situation, choose File➪Printer Setup and change the orientation from Portrait to Landscape mode to get additional room.

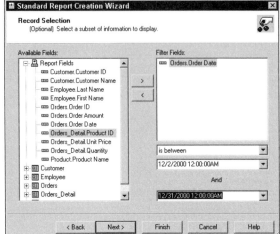

Figure 4-5:
The order
date has
been spec-
ified for
filtering.

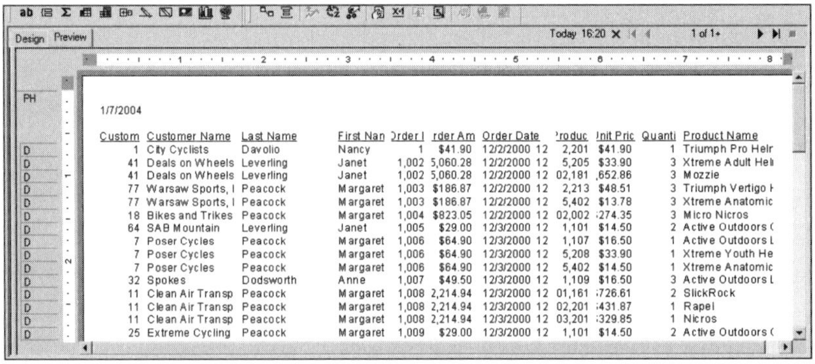

Figure 4-6:
A standard
report of
December
2000 orders.

After a little rearranging with the Design tab active, the report might look like
Figure 4-7.

Not bad, but you probably want to make it clear what this report is about by
adding a report header. You can also change column headings in the Page
Header band if you want to. In general, you can use Standard Report Creation
Wizard to do the bulk of the layout for a fairly standard report, and then fine-
tune the result using the tools available in the Design tab.

If you produce a report that's close to one of the templates used by Standard
Report Creation Wizard, it's usually quicker and easier than designing a report
from scratch.

When you're satisfied with your report, save it by choosing File⇨Save from the main menu. Later on, when you run the saved report, it reflects the state of the database at the time you saved it (the last time it was run). That's useful if you're reporting on historical data (as in the example report) or on data that changes on an ongoing basis.

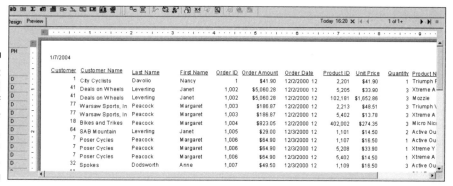

Figure 4-7:
Standard
report of
December
2000 orders,
in Land-
scape mode.

The rest of the Report Creation wizards

The Standard Report Creation Wizard gives you a good idea of how Report Creation wizards work. The other Report Creation wizards have a lot in common with the Standard Report Creation Wizard, as follows:

- **Cross-Tab Report Creation Wizard** builds a report that displays data as a cross-tab object. I cover cross-tab reports thoroughly in Chapter 10.

- **Mail Label Report Creation Wizard** automates the task of laying out a report formatted to print mailing labels. It's already set up for standard commercial label formats, but you can also design a custom label format.

- **OLAP Report Creation Wizard** displays OLAP (On-Line Analytical Processing) data as a grid. OLAP reports are similar to cross-tab reports but have different data sources and a distinctive data structure. (For more about OLAP and how to report on OLAP data, see Chapter 14.)

Starting with a Blank Report

When it displays the Gallery, Crystal Reports makes the default assumption that you want to use Report Wizard. In many cases, however, starting with a blank report is the best choice — especially if what you want is not consistent with what Report Wizard can produce.

Leveraging the work in an existing report

Few things are more frustrating than having to redo work. Some savvy report developers, when asked to develop a report similar to one that already exists, save time and effort by starting with an existing report, saving it under a new name, and modifying it to serve a new purpose. This is worthwhile if the modifications take less time and effort than building a new report from scratch.

If you foresee that a report that you've been asked to write could be the first of several similar reports, you can make those follow-on reports easier to create: Save a version of the first report containing only those elements that you believe will be common to all follow-on reports (be sure to save it under a new name). What you get is a template for the later reports — and a head start in producing them. After the template is safely stored on disk, you can add the elements to the original report that set it apart from all others that may follow.

Sometimes it may make sense to use Report Wizard to generate the basic structure of your report, and then switch to the Design tab to modify the report into the final product.

Chapter 2 leads you step-by-step through the development of a basic report from a blank report. If you go that route, look there for pointers. In the following chapters, you can design and build a variety of reports, each one starting from a blank report. Those chapters assume you've already mastered basic from-scratch report design and are ready to move on.

Connecting Your Report to Its Data Source

Crystal Reports uses several methods to accept data from a variety of data sources. The software's wide data compatibility makes it a versatile tool that has uses beyond the creation of reports from data in relational databases.

For example, Crystal Reports can accept data from direct-access database files, ODBC data sources, OLE DB data sources, Crystal SQL Designer files, OLAP files, and Crystal Dictionary/Infoview files. Each type of file is accessed in a different way; Crystal Reports makes the connections for you.

Accessing database files directly

The fastest way to pull data out of a database and include it in a report is through a direct access interface. This makes sense — the less stuff you have between the database and the report, the shorter the transit time as data goes from one to the other. Another advantage is the simple connection. As a report designer, you don't have to fuss with types of connections and middle-tier dynamic-link libraries (DLLs). You just name the data source you want to tap for data, and tell Crystal Reports to go get that data.

However, as you know, There Ain't No Such Thing As A Free Lunch (TANSTAAFL). The price you pay for the speed and simplicity of a direct connection is the need for a different, highly customized driver *for every different data source.* Usually not a problem — Crystal Reports offers a wide variety of such drivers — unless your report draws data from two or more different data sources. In such a case, you can't use direct access; you'd have to talk to each data source in its own "language," and Crystal Reports doesn't support using multiple languages in a single report.

Crystal Reports has direct access drivers for most of the popular PC database formats, including Microsoft Access, the dBase/FoxPro/Clipper triad, Paradox and the Borland Database Engine (BDE). In addition, it supports Microsoft DAO/OLE, Btrieve, ACT!, COM, Java data, Microsoft Exchange, and Microsoft Outlook. Crystal Reports has direct access drivers for the following client-server SQL databases: Oracle, Microsoft SQL Server, Sybase, Informix Online Server, and IBM's DB2 Server. Crystal Reports also talks directly to IBM's Lotus Domino, your computer's local file system, the Windows NT, 2000, or XP Event Log, the Microsoft IIS or Microsoft Proxy log file, Web or IIS log files. If it holds data, is fairly widely used, and runs on a Windows box, Crystal Reports probably had a direct access interface for it.

Linking to ODBC data sources

ODBC (Open Database Connectivity) is a standard method of connecting to a wide variety of data sources. It places a layer in the networking model between applications such as Crystal Reports and the databases they use; that layer is where ODBC-standard requests from the application are translated into the specific form required for each different data source. Practically all data sources in use today offer an ODBC interface, through which the ODBC driver connects to the database. All the application has to know is that it's communicating with an ODBC-compliant data source.

An ODBC database connection may not perform quite as well as a direct-access connection because the data has to pass through an extra layer of processing. This may or may not be a problem, depending on the implementation and the needs of the application. On the plus side, an application that communicates to its data sources through ODBC can pull data from multiple different data sources. It puts out its request in the same ODBC format, regardless of which data source it's talking to. Each such source has its own ODBC driver that translates the common ODBC commands into data-source-specific commands that the data source can understand and obey.

Data sources for which Crystal Reports has a direct access connection are also reachable through ODBC. For example, you can connect to Microsoft Access either through the direct connection or through ODBC. Direct connection may give you better performance — as long as your report requires data *only* from Access. However, if you want to include data from a data source that has no ODBC interface, you must use ODBC for both Access and that second data source. Performance may be slower, but it beats a lack of access.

Retrieving data from Crystal SQL Designer files

Crystal Reports Designer is a tool you can use to create SQL queries of ODBC data sources. The query runs on a server and returns a result set to your computer in the form of a Crystal SQL Designer file. Offloading some query processing frees up your computer to concentrate on other tasks, possibly improving performance — and that's the primary advantage of using Crystal SQL Designer. A second advantage is that you can use the full power of SQL to retrieve exactly the data you want.

But there's no free lunch here: You must be fluent in SQL to use Crystal SQL Designer. Gaining that fluency requires some effort, but may be well worth the time you put into it. Start by reading my *SQL For Dummies,* 5th Edition (published by Wiley). It gives you a painless introduction to SQL and a thorough description of all major features of the language.

Another thing to be aware of is that when you run a Crystal SQL Designer query, it returns a result to your computer in the form of a .QRY file. This file is a snapshot of the data at the time the query was run. If the data in the database is updated later, you have to rerun the query to capture the changes.

Reporting on data in OLE DB data sources

OLE DB is a connectivity methodology similar to ODBC (no surprise — both were developed by Microsoft). OLE DB adds some flexibility in the types of data sources it can communicate with (such as multidimensional OLAP sources and Web servers). ODBC communicates with relational databases that use SQL; OLE DB covers the rest, addressing data sources that don't use SQL (although it works well with relational databases too). Crystal Reports supports OLE DB data sources, which are called *OLE DB providers.*

Creating customized data access with Crystal Dictionaries

Dictionaries are filters that tailor the appearance of data for specific groups of users (or even those of individual users). Typically set up by Information Systems (IS) managers, a dictionary can offer customized access to multiple data sources. Only the database tables or other sources in the dictionary are accessible. Table and source names may be changed to make more sense to the target users. A dictionary can also manipulate data pulled from the sources without the user being aware of the manipulation. The idea is to help users bypass unneeded information, use the system effectively, and reduce the chance of errors.

Which interface should you use?

Which interface to use? It depends. (You knew I was going to say that, didn't you?) You can draw a few conclusions from the information in this chapter; here are some guidelines for openers:

- ✔ If your report draws data from only one source and there's a direct-access driver for that source, using that driver is probably your best bet for good performance.

- ✔ If your report draws data from two or more different sources, direct access is not an option.

- ✔ If you're drawing data from multiple relational databases, ODBC is designed to give you what you need.

✔ If one or more of your multiple data sources is not compatible with ODBC — but all your data sources support an OLE DB interface — OLE DB should be your connectivity choice.

✔ SQL programmers prefer Crystal SQL Designer when they want to do a complex retrieval and the connection between client and server has only limited bandwidth. Keep in mind, however, that the result set returned by a Crystal SQL Designer query is a snapshot — it shows the state of the data sources *at the instant the query was run*. It does not necessarily reflect the current state of the data.

✔ IS managers can keep their users out of trouble, protect sensitive data, and make the data sources easier to understand by building dictionaries that give users what they need in an understandable form but don't expose parts of the data sources that aren't relevant to the users' jobs.

Part II
Moving Up to Professional Quality Reports

The 5th Wave   By Rich Tennant

"You ever get the feeling this project could just up and die at any moment?"

In this part . . .

After you know how to create a report based on database data, it's time to move up to the next level. In the chapters in this part, you discover how to tease the exact data you want out of the database, unobscured by the irrelevant data that surrounds it. You find out how to arrange data in the report to maximize reader comprehension. You start to master the art of formatting a report so as to draw the reader's attention to the most important information. Finally, you preserve the valuable features that you worked so hard on, so that you can reuse them again and again in reports that you're called on to produce in the coming weeks, months, and years.

Chapter 5

Pulling Specific Data from a Database

. . . .

. . . .

*I*f your reports had no more to do than display all the data in your data sources, report creation would be easy. Organizations wouldn't need people as smart and well educated as you to design their reports. Luckily for the job security of people like you and me, report creation is not that simple. Most reports that have value to people gain that value by extracting specific information from the mass of data in the database — and *only* that information. This usually requires filtering out unwanted records, leaving behind irrelevant fields, combining data, and presenting data in a meaningful way. Database report designers are clearly valuable to any organization that depends on timely access to the information buried in its databases. With that in mind, this chapter introduces you to some of the most useful data-retrieval tools in Crystal Reports.

Get Data Quickly with Select Expert

Select Expert is an interactive tool for defining which data items to extract from a database and display in a report. Probably the best way to describe Select Expert is to give examples that show it in action.

Suppose Albert Hellstern, the business manager of Xtreme Mountain Bikes, wants to know the current inventory status and how it compares to the minimum inventory levels that the company likes to maintain for all its products. A query into the relevant tables using Select Expert will retrieve the needed information, and the Report Wizard will format it into a report. Great! This sounds like just what Albert needs, but there is a lot of preliminary work that must be done before Select Expert can be employed.

Follow along to generate this report:

1. **Choose File⇨New.**

   The Crystal Reports Gallery appears.

2. **Click, if necessary, to select the Using the Report Wizard option. In the Choose a Wizard area, select the Standard Wizard. Click OK.**

   Standard Report Creation Wizard appears.

3. **Find and connect to the** xtreme.mdb **database.**

   For more information on this process, see Chapters 2 and 3.

4. **Add the tables needed to determine the inventory status.**

   Select the Product, Product Type, and Purchases tables.

5. **Click Next.**

   The Link view of Standard Report Creation Wizard appears, as shown in Figure 5-1. You can see the links that Crystal Reports has inferred to exist between the selected tables. In this case, the inferred links are correct, so there's no need to adjust them. The icons to the left of some fields indicate that those fields are indexed (a technique that increases the speed of retrievals — there's more about it later in the chapter).

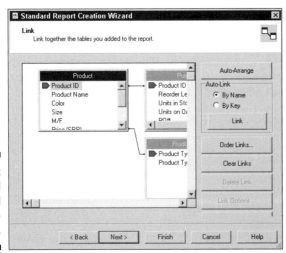

Figure 5-1:
Selected tables and their relationships.

6. **Click the Next button to move to the Fields view.**

   The tree in the Available Fields pane displays the fields that are available in the tables you have chosen.

7. **Select the fields that you want in the report, and then click the Add button to transfer them to the Fields to Display pane.**

   Figure 5-2 shows how the screen looks after the selection. I've selected `Product ID`, `Product Name`, `Color`, `Size`, and `M/F` from the `Product` table, `Product Type Name` from the `Product_Type` table, and `Reorder Level`, `Units in Stock` and `Units on Order` from the `Purchases` table.

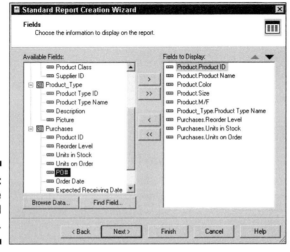

Figure 5-2:
The selected fields.

8. **Click Next to move to the Grouping view, and then click Next again to move to the Record Selection view.**

   Albert is primarily concerned with how the Reorder Level field in the Purchases table compares with the Units in Stock and Units on Order fields in that same table. Grouping is not appropriate. I discuss grouping in Chapter 6.

9. **Select the** `Reorder Level` **field, the** `Units on Order` **field, and the** `Units in Stock` **field from the tree in the left pane, and add them to the right pane.**

   The screen should look like Figure 5-3. Notice that when you add a field to the Filter Fields pane, a pull-down list appears below the pane. The list displays a number of comparison operators that allow you to compare the contents of the selected field to values that appear in that field in the table in the database. This feature, by itself, does not give Albert what he wants. He wants to compare the `In Stock` status of each product against the specific `Reorder Level` for that product, not against some fixed number. By continuing, Albert can arrive at the solution he wants.

Figure 5-3:
The filter
fields.

10. **For the present example, leave the default choice of *is any value* in place; click the Next button to display the Template view.**

    Several templates are available.

11. **Choose the No Template option, and then click the Finish button.**

    Many of the templates are fancy or colorful, but Albert doesn't care about being fancy, so he sticks with the No Template option. The report is displayed in the Preview tab, as shown in Figure 5-4.

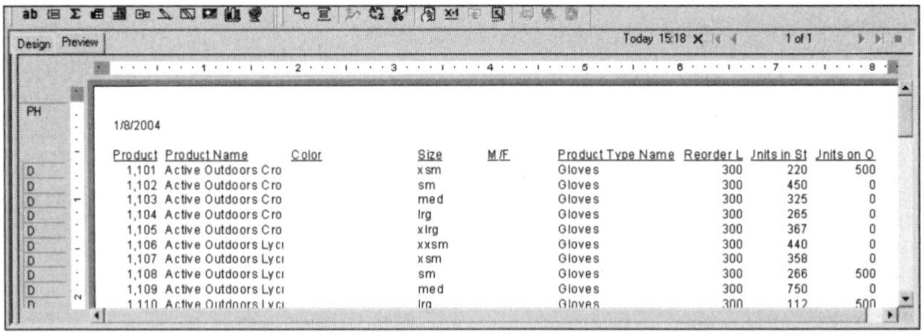

Figure 5-4:
Inventory-
level report,
created by
Standard
Report
Creation
Wizard.

The report shows the information you expect, but the formatting could be improved. Some columns, such as Color and Product Type Name, are wider than necessary to fully display the data they contain. Other columns are too narrow to fully display their headings. Switch to the Design tab and make manual adjustments to these layout features. Figure 5-5 shows one result.

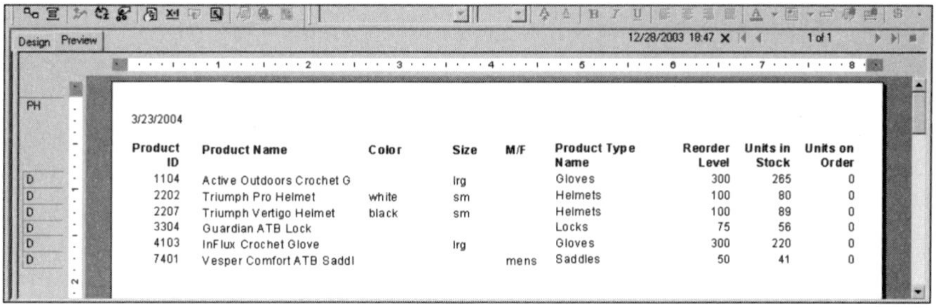

Figure 5-5:
Reformatted
inventory
level report.

Product ID	Product Name	Color	Size	M/F	Product Type Name	Reorder Level	Units in Stock	Units on Order
	3/23/2004							
1104	Active Outdoors Crochet G		lrg		Gloves	300	265	0
2202	Triumph Pro Helmet	white	sm		Helmets	100	80	0
2207	Triumph Vertigo Helmet	black	sm		Helmets	100	89	0
3304	Guardian ATB Lock				Locks	75	56	0
4103	InFlux Crochet Glove		lrg		Gloves	300	220	0
7401	Vesper Comfort ATB Saddl			mens	Saddles	50	41	0

This is pretty good. It displays all the products and shows their inventory levels compared to their reorder levels. However, the report doesn't emphasize the products in critically short supply. What Albert would really like to see is a report that lists only those products whose inventory is at or below reorder level. To get that, you have to go beyond what a straightforward use of Crystal Reports can provide.

Suppose an emergency crops up before you can figure out how to get the report that Albert wants. A worker comes in from the warehouse and tells him that some of the helmets are in short supply. Keeping a full line of helmets in stock is difficult because they come in several different sizes and colors. Albert knows that the reorder level for helmets is 100 units, so he asks you to modify the report you have just created to show only items where fewer than 100 units are in stock.

Your job now is to quickly give Albert the information he needs, and this is where Select Expert comes in:

1. **With the inventory report open, choose Report⇨Select Expert.**

   The Choose Field dialog box appears.

2. **In the** Purchases **table, select** Purchases.Units in Stock **and then click OK.**

   Be sure to select the field from within the Report Fields category, not from the actual tables. Your screen should appear as shown in Figure 5-6.

   Select Expert appears, with the pull-down list that you can use to specify a condition for the Purchases.Units in Stock field.

3. **Choose *is less than or equal to* and enter 100 in the comparison field, as shown in Figure 5-7. Click OK.**

   A dialog box appears, asking whether you want to use data that was saved earlier or refresh the data by querying the database again.

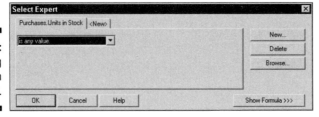

Figure 5-6:
Selecting
the Units in
Stock field.

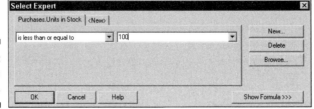

Figure 5-7:
Selecting a
condition.

This question has major performance implications. For a large database with many records, refreshing the data could take a significant amount of time. On the other hand, saved data is available instantly. If you have reason to believe that the database has not changed since it was saved, you can speed up your task by using saved data. In Albert's case, that's not a good idea because someone may have just bought a *lot* of helmets.

4. **Albert wants to know what the inventory status is right now, so click the Refresh Data button.**

   Figure 5-8 shows the report that appears.

Figure 5-8:
Inventory
report
showing
only prod-
ucts for
which the
quantity
in stock is
less than or
equal to 100.

The report shows all products where quantities in stock are less than or equal to 100. This includes some helmets, some locks, and some saddles. All listed helmets are below their reorder quantities and should be ordered immediately. Some of the locks and saddles are below their reorder quantities and some are above, because locks and saddles have lower reorder quantities than helmets. Albert can quickly tell from this report which helmets he needs to order. However, the report would be better if it weren't cluttered with data about locks and saddles (not his present concerns). To have that level of specificity, you have to use a formula.

When your comparison is on a numeric field, such as Units in Stock, the available comparison operators, such as *is less than or equal to,* are appropriate for making numeric comparisons. Likewise, for date type data, comparison operators appropriate for dates are available. The types of comparisons you can do depend on the type of data you're looking at.

Using Formulas to Retrieve Data

In Chapter 11, I give formulas extensive coverage. For now, you'll see how you can use formulas to help Albert. Suppose he decides that it *is* helpful to know about products other than helmets that are also below their reorder levels — but without having to wade through rows of products that are *not* below their reorder levels. You can help.

The current selection criterion specifies that Units in Stock be less than or equal to 100; you can replace it with a new, more complex selection criterion: that Units in Stock be less than or equal to Reorder Level. In the original selection, you're comparing against a fixed quantity (100). In the new selection, you're comparing against a quantity that varies, depending on the type of product you're examining.

These steps get you there:

1. **Choose Report⇨Selection Formulas⇨Record.**

   Formula Workshop's Record Selection Formula Editor window appears, as shown in Figure 5-9. It displays the formula that governs the current selection that resulted in the report shown in Figure 5-8. The formula is

   ```
   {Purchases.Units in Stock} <= 100
   ```

   This is the formula that Select Expert created in response to the choices you made.

Figure 5-9:
Record
Selection
Formula
Editor,
showing
original
selection
formula.

But now you're creating a new formula, replacing the 100 to the right of the <= sign with {Purchases.Reorder Level}, and adding a plus sign (+) and {Purchases. Units on Order} to the left of the <= sign. If an item is below its Reorder Level, but an order for more has already been made, you probably don't want to order it again.

2. **To create this new formula, select the 100 and delete it, and then double-click** Purchases.Reorder Level **in the** Report Fields **tree (the tree in the upper-left corner of the Record Selection Formula Editor window). Next add a plus sign and then add** {Purchases.Units on Order} **to the left side by typing them or by double-clicking as you did with** {Purchases.Reorder Level}.

Figure 5-10 shows the result.

3. **Click the Save and Close button in the upper-left corner of the Record Selection Formula Editor.**

Formula Workshop disappears.

Figure 5-10:
New selec-
tion criterion
restricts
retrieval to
items whose
stock level
is below
the reorder
level and
which have
not been re-
ordered.

4. **When asked whether you want to refresh the data or use saved data, choose Refresh Data.**

   The modified report appears, as shown in Figure 5-11. This report displays inventory items where the quantity in stock is less than or equal to the reorder level for that item. This gives Albert a good idea of what to order.

Figure 5-11:
The inventory report, showing items in quantities below reorder level.

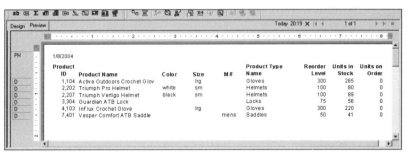

Product ID	Product Name	Color	Size	M.F	Product Type Name	Reorder Level	Units in Stock	Units on Order
1,104	Active Outdoors Crochet Glov		lrg		Gloves	300	265	0
2,202	Triumph Pro Helmet	white	sm		Helmets	100	80	0
2,207	Triumph Vertigo Helmet	black	sm		Helmets	100	89	0
3,304	Guardian ATB Lock				Locks	75	56	0
4,103	InFlux Crochet Glove		lrg		Gloves	300	220	0
7,401	Vesper Comfort ATB Saddle			mens	Saddles	50	41	0

Using Parameter Fields to Retrieve Data at Runtime

To show one of the many things that you can do with parameter fields, suppose Xtreme's Vice President of Sales, Andrew Fuller, wants a report that he can run from time to time to show him major purchases and who's made them. To help focus the company's sales efforts, he wants to identify customers who have placed large orders — and to specify what constitutes a "large" order at the time he runs the report.

The first step in this process is to create a report that lists customers and the orders they've made. The next step is to place a condition on the report that restricts the rows displayed to orders that have a higher dollar value than the value Andrew enters at runtime. A fixed value or a value from a database table field won't do the job. The report requires a parameter field.

To create the first version of the report that Andrew needs (the Big Orders report), follow these steps:

1. **Choose File⇨New to display the Crystal Reports Gallery.**

2. **Use the Report Wizard, and select the Standard Wizard option. Click OK.**

   3. **When Standard Report Creation Wizard appears, make sure that the** xtreme.mdb **database is connected.**

   For more information on this process, see Chapters 2 and 3.

   4. **Transfer Customer and Orders to the Selected Tables pane, using the drag and drop technique.**

   5. **Click Next.**

   The Links view displays a graphical representation of the tables and the links between them, as shown in Figure 5-12.

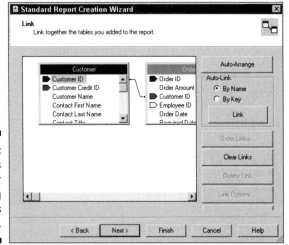

Figure 5-12:
Tables
needed for
the Big
Orders
report.

   6. **Click the Next button to display the Fields view.**

   7. **Select the following fields to display on the report:** Customer ID, Customer Name, Contact First Name, Contact Last Name, **and** Phone **from the** Customer **table and** Order Amount **from the** Orders **table.**

   Figure 5-13 shows the Fields view after you make these selections.

   8. **Move all the way to the Template view by clicking the Next button three times.**

   No need to do anything with the Grouping or Record Selection view at this time.

   9. **In the Template view, retain the No Template option, and then click the Finish button.**

   The report looks like Figure 5-14.

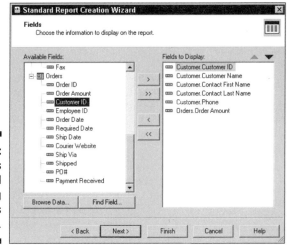

Figure 5-13:
Fields
needed
for the Big
Orders
report.

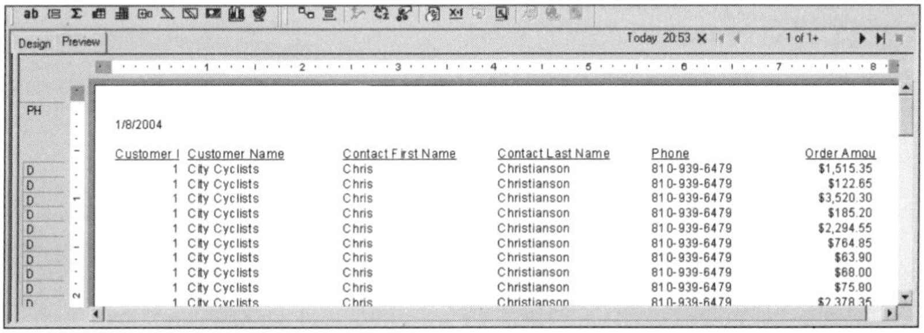

Figure 5-14:
First version
of the Big
Orders
report.

The spacing of the columns isn't the greatest, but you can adjust them manually and do some other formatting. With a bit of tweaking, you can get something like the report shown in Figure 5-15.

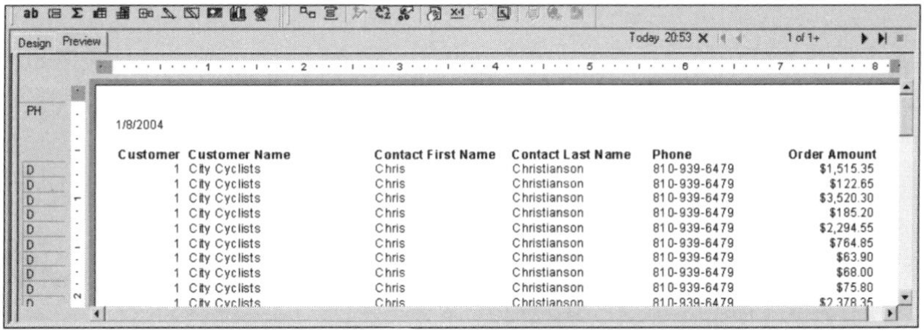

Figure 5-15:
Second
version of
the Big
Orders
report.

Speed retrievals with indexes

Remember those icons in Figure 5-1? The ones that look like overturned Monopoly houses? They indicate which fields in the tables are associated with indexes. Records in a database table are generally not arranged in any useful order. Usually they're still in the order in which they were first entered into the table.

To make a selective retrieval (such as Andrew's that finds all orders over $5000), every single record must be examined — unless you sort 'em beforehand. If you sort those records by Order Amount in descending order, only the records that equaled or exceeded $5000 would have to be checked. This could save some serious retrieval time, especially for a large table in which relatively few orders had values of more than $5000.

Not surprisingly, a lot of overhead is associated with maintaining a data table *in sorted order.* In addition, sorting it on one field also *unsorts* it on any other field that you might want to use as a retrieval key. The answer is to create indexes for the fields you'll be using as retrieval keys. The icons in Figure 5-1 show which fields are indexed. As you can see, Order Amount is not one of them. If the Orders table grows to hundreds of thousands of rows, and if people are going to be making frequent retrievals based on Order Amount, Andrew might want to ask Xtreme's database administrator to create an index field for Order Amount in the Orders table of the company's database.

The report has almost 2,200 records. Each record represents a single order by one of Xtreme's customers. The next step is to pare down those records to just the ones Andrew wants to see. To get there, create a parameter field so Andrew can enter a dollar amount as the minimum value for those records:

1. **If you can't see Field Explorer on the right edge of the screen, choose View⇨Field Explorer.**

   Field Explorer appears.

2. **In the Field Explorer tree, right-click the Parameter Fields option and choose the New command.**

   The Create Parameter Field dialog box appears.

3. **Enter a name for the parameter field, some prompting text to tell the user what to enter, and the data type of the entry the user is to make.**

   For the example, you can name the parameter field *Lower Limit*, use *Lower limit for a big order:* as the prompting text, and choose the Currency data type from the pull-down list. Figure 5-16 shows the Create Parameter Field dialog box after you make these entries. The choices in the Options area are left at their default values: Multiple values aren't allowed and the value entered must be discrete.

Figure 5-16:
Create
Parameter
Field dialog
box, speci-
fying the
lower limit
parameter
field.

4. Click OK.

The parameter field is ready to add to the Big Orders report as the selection criterion, specifying which records to retrieve from the two-or-so-thousand in the Orders table. Select Expert is the tool for this job; here's how to put it to work:

1. **Click the Select Expert icon in the toolbar.**

   The Choose Field dialog box appears.

2. **Select the field you want to compare against and then click OK.**

   For the example, select the `Order Amount` field in the `Orders` table. Crystal Reports displays the `Orders.Order Amount` tab of Select Expert.

3. **In the pull-down list, select *is greater than or equal to.***

   A data entry field with a pull-down control appears to the right of the list.

4. **Pull down the list and select** `{?Lower Limit}`.

   Crystal Reports denotes a parameter field by enclosing it in curly braces and preceding the parameter field's name with a question mark.

5. **Click OK.**

   The Enter Parameter Values dialog box appears, with the cursor blinking in the Discrete Value text-entry box.

6. **Enter** 5000 **as an initial value, and then click OK.**

   The by-now familiar Change in Record Selection Formula Detected dialog box appears, asking whether you want to use saved data or refreshed data.

7. If there's any possibility that the data has changed since the last time it was saved, choose Refresh Data.

Figure 5-17 shows the result. The report looks much as it did in Figure 5-16 — but only a few hundred records (instead of thousands) appear, every one of them with an Order Amount of at least $5000.

Figure 5-17: Big Orders report run with a $5000 lower limit.

8. Save this report with the name Big Orders.rpt.

Andrew can now see at a glance which customers make a large number of orders valued at over $5000 as well as which ones occasionally make orders that large. He can now formulate sales promotions targeted at these customers. (Imagine him saying thanks. Hey, no problem, Andrew.)

Suppose that now, after seeing the hundreds of entries in the report in Figure 5-17, Andrew wants to see a list containing only the customers who have made *really* big orders — those that exceed $9000. All you have to do is rerun the report and then follow these steps:

1. Click the Refresh icon in the toolbar to rerun the report.

The Refresh Report Data dialog box appears, asking whether you want to use the current parameter values or prompt for new parameter values.

2. Choose the Prompt for New Parameter Values option, and then click OK.

The Enter Parameter Values dialog box appears.

3. Enter 9000 **in the** Discrete Value **field, and then click OK.**

Now the report contains only 43 records. Only orders of at least $9000 are included in this version of the Big Orders report.

You can rerun the report as many times as you want, changing the Lower Limit parameter each time, to get a precise idea of which customers make large buys, regardless of how you want to define a large buy. (Gotcha covered, Andrew.)

Troubleshooting Tips

Three basic problems might arise when you try to retrieve specific data from a database:

- You don't retrieve all the data you want.
- You retrieve data you don't want.
- You retrieve all the data you want and none of the data you don't want, but the retrieval takes an unacceptably long time.

The first two problems sometimes have an easy explanation:

- **Failing to specify all the tables you need.** Some of the tables may not contain a single field you want to display, but they're needed anyway to provide a link between the tables that *do* contain fields you want displayed.

- **Failing to specify all the fields you need from the tables you select.** Make sure you understand exactly how the tables relate to each other — and to the information you're asking for. If what you need depends on multiple fields in multiple tables, be sure to select all of those fields.

- **Specifying your selection condition incorrectly with Select Expert.** You must choose from a number of comparison operators and must apply the operator to the correct constant value, field value, or parameter value. You can verify that you're comparing against the correct constant value or field value when you create the report. However, if the user enters an incorrect parameter value at runtime, it could cause incorrect results that might slip by undetected.

Slow retrievals are another matter; they can cause problems when you have to deal with large data sets. Often a careful analysis — followed by indexing the fields that serve as retrieval criteria — can speed up retrieval time tremendously. This is a job for the database administrator, however, not the report designer.

Chapter 6

Sorting, Grouping, and Totaling Result Sets

● ●

In This Chapter

▶ Putting report data in a logical order by sorting

▶ Clustering similar data items with grouping

▶ Figuring out percentages

▶ Adding drill-down functionality

▶ Adding things with running totals

▶ Solving sorting, grouping, and totaling problems

● ●

*T*he primary goal in creating a report is to put database data into a meaning-ful and easily understandable form. To achieve this goal, you must extract only the data you want, from the specific rows and columns of the relevant tables. However, if you don't present the information in the report in a logical manner, meaning and understanding can suffer.

You can greatly enhance the value of a report by arranging the retrieved data in a way that clearly conveys what that data means and emphasizes its important features. Sort the records, and group related records in such a way that the significant information is emphasized. Crystal Reports has powerful tools to help you sort report data in a variety of ways, group related data, and summarize data within groups.

Sorting Report Data

In most cases, the original order of the data in a database is not the most help-ful order, so you must reorder the data for your purposes. The sort function in Crystal Reports does this for you.

The way in which data is sorted depends on how you specify the sort and on the type of data that you want to sort. You can sort data in ascending order or descending order. In general, *ascending* means lowest to highest, and *descending* means highest to lowest. What ascending and descending mean for any given sort, however, depends on the type of data you're sorting.

The data types you might want to sort include the following:

- ✔ Single-character string fields
- ✔ Multiple-character string fields
- ✔ Currency fields
- ✔ Number fields
- ✔ Date fields
- ✔ Date-time fields
- ✔ Time fields
- ✔ Boolean fields

Assuming an ascending sort order, Table 6-1 shows how data types will be sorted. For descending order, just reverse the sequence.

Table 6-1	Ascending Sort Order for Various Data Types
Field Type	**Sort Order**
Single-character-string field	Blank
	Punctuation mark
	Numeral
	Uppercase letter
	Lowercase letter
Multiple-character-string field	First character, then second, then third, and so on; for example: mm comes before mmm, and ALLEN comes before Abe
Currency field	Numeric order
Number field	Numeric order
Date field	Chronological order
Date-time field	Chronological order, first by date and then by time
Time field	Chronological order
Boolean field	False, and then true

TIP

If a sort is based on a field that contains null values, the null values are sorted before non-null values. A field is said to have a null value when it has nothing in it. In contrast, zero is not a null value. It is a definite value. A blank space is also a definite value, not a null value.

Sorting based on multiple fields

When you sort data items based on the value of one field, the outcome is straightforward. If the sort is ascending, it proceeds according to the rules in Table 6-1. If the sort is descending, the sorted order is the reverse of an ascending sort. Sometimes, however, you want to sort data based on the contents of more than one field.

Consider, for example, the `Customer` table in the Xtreme database. Xtreme's Sales Manager wants a list of customers sorted first by country, then by region within a country, and finally by customer name within a region. Crystal Reports can perform such a nested sort. In fact, it can do so for as many levels of nesting as you want. To build such a report, follow these steps:

1. **In Crystal Reports Gallery, click the Using the Report Wizard option. Under Choose a Wizard, select Standard. Click OK.**

2. **Add the `Customer` table from the `xtreme.mdb` database to the Selected Tables pane.**

3. **Click the Next button in the Standard Report Creation Wizard to display the Fields view.**

4. **Add the `Customer ID`, `Customer Name`, `Region`, and `Country` fields to the Fields to Display pane.**

5. **Click the Next button three times to display the Template view.**

    At this point, you don't want to group records or select specific records, so skip those pages.

6. **Retain the No Template option, and then click the Finish button.**

    The report shown in Figure 6-1 appears.

Figure 6-1:
The first draft of the Customer report, sorted by Customer ID.

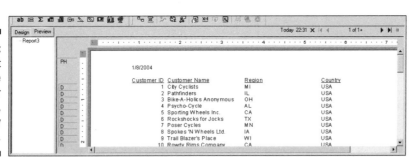

At this point, the report has the data you want, but it's sorted by Customer ID because that's the first field you specified in the Fields view. Furthermore, the columns are not centered, and the report needs a title. To correct these problems, do the following:

1. **Switch to Design view.**

   The report appears like that shown in Figure 6-2.

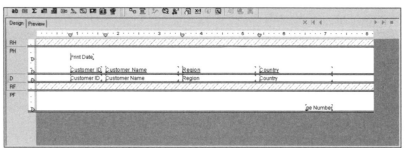

Figure 6-2: Design view of the first draft of the Customer report.

2. **Change the justification of all fields to *center* by using the Align Center button in both the Page Header and Data sections.**

   This balances the appearance of the report.

3. **Right-click in the area to the left of the Report Header section and choose Don't Suppress from the shortcut menu that pops up.**

4. **Pull down the border between the Report Header section and the Page Header section to make room for the report title in the Report Header.**

5. **Click the Insert Text Object icon in the Insert toolbar, and then drag the text box that appears and drop it into the Report Header.**

6. **In the text box, type** Customer List, Sorted by Country and Region.

   This is the report title.

7. **Expand the text box to the left and right so that it spans the entire width of the report. Expand it vertically as well so that it can accommodate a large font.**

8. **Center the report title in the text box, make it bold, and increase its font size by clicking the Increase Font Size icon.**

   Figure 6-3 shows what Design view looks like after you make these modifications.

Figure 6-3:
Design
view of the
modified
Customer
report, still
sorted by
customer ID.

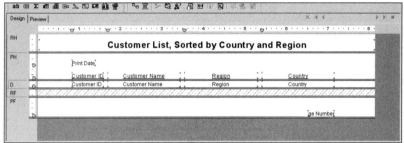

This design produces the report preview shown in Figure 6-4.

Figure 6-4:
A preview of
the modified
Customer
report,
sorted by
country and
region.

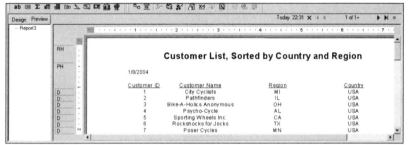

The report looks nice, but it is not sorted by country and region. To remedy that problem, follow these steps:

1. **Choose Report⇨Record Sort Expert.**

   The Record Sort Expert appears, as shown in Figure 6-5.

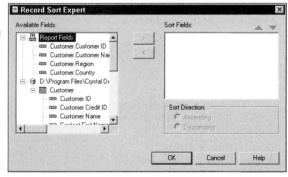

Figure 6-5:
Use the
Record Sort
Expert to
specify how
the report
will be
sorted.

2. **In the Available Fields pane, select Customer.Country, and then click the > button. Do the same for Customer.Region and then for Customer. Customer Name.**

3. **Make sure that the Sort Direction is Ascending for all three fields, and then click OK.**

   The report's records are sorted first by country, then by region within a country, and finally by customer name within a region. Figure 6-6 shows the properly sorted report.

Figure 6-6:
The Customer report, sorted by country, region, and customer name.

Notice in the figure:

✔ The first record is for a customer in Argentina, and the second is for a customer in Aruba. The first sort key is Country.

✔ Within Australia, New South Wales comes before Queensland, which precedes Tasmania and Victoria. The second sort key is Region.

✔ Within Victoria, Bruce's Bikes comes before Kangaroo Trikes. The third sort key is Customer Name.

The report meets the objectives of the development effort in terms of both information content and ease of understanding.

Sorting and performance

How long it takes Crystal Reports to produce a report can depend, to a large measure, on the sorting that the report requires. For databases with tables consisting of many records, sort times often account for a major portion of the total time it takes to produce a report.

The sort time is affected by the fields on which you sort. In most cases, you can sort a large table on an indexed field orders of magnitude faster than you can sort the same table on a nonindexed field. The lesson here is to sort on indexed fields whenever possible. If you regularly run reports that include sorts on nonindexed fields, consider talking to your database administrator (DBA) about adding indexes to those fields. A performance penalty is associated with maintaining an index (it can be significantly time consuming), but if you don't update the data table often and run reports frequently, the updating overhead may be insignificant compared to the ability to generate reports more quickly.

It does *not* make sense to index a field in a table with few records, or a table with many records if the index field can take on only one of a small number of values. The cost of maintaining the index exceeds the benefit you would gain from it.

Grouping Related Items

A simple sort, such as the one in the preceding section, works fine when all you want to do is put a list of items in some order. Often, however, you want to do more with your data, such as displaying subtotals, counts, averages, or other summary information along with each group. Crystal Reports offers great flexibility in specifying groups as well as a wide variety of summarization facilities. These grouping and summarization capabilities are among the most advanced of any reporting tool.

To demonstrate a small fraction of the power of Crystal Reports' grouping facilities, take another look at the Xtreme Mountain Bikes database. Suppose that the Vice President of Sales wants to get a better idea of where customer orders are coming from. Focusing on Mexico, he wants a report that shows order totals grouped by state and sorted by customer name within each state. Follow these steps to build that report:

1. **In Crystal Reports Gallery, click the Using the Report Wizard option. Under Choose a Wizard, select Standard. Click OK.**

2. **In the Available Data Sources pane, add the** Customer **and** Orders **tables to the Selected Tables pane.**

3. **Click Next.**

    The Link view appears, as shown in Figure 6-7.

4. **Click Next.**

    The Fields view is displayed.

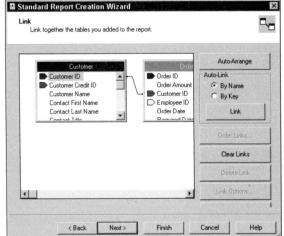

Figure 6-7:
The
Customer
and Orders
tables, con-
nected by
Customer ID.

5. **Select the** Customer Name **and** Region **fields from the** Customer **table and the** Order Amount **field from the Orders table.**

6. **Click Next.**

   The Grouping view appears.

7. **To meet the Vice President's needs, group by Region.**

   To do so, move Customer.Region to the Group By pane.

8. **The default sort order (in ascending order) is fine, so click the Next button.**

   The Summaries view appears. Crystal Reports has assumed that the field you want to summarize is the Order Amount field because it's the only numeric field in the report. This is a good assumption, as is the assumption that the type of summary you want is a sum rather than an average or some other kind of summary.

   Even though the default summary type of Sum is the one you want for this report, several other options are available. Average gives you the average value for the group, Maximum displays the maximum value for the group, and Minimum displays the minimum value. Statistical functions and a simple count of the number of records in the group are available as well.

9. **Click Next three times.**

   You don't need to change anything on the Group Sorting view, and you don't want a Chart, so skip these views.

10. In the Record Selection view, include in the report the records for Mexico customers only.

In the Available Fields pane, select Country from the `Customer` table and add it to the Filter Fields pane. In the pull-down list below the Filter Fields pane, select Is Equal To, and from the pull-down list that pops up below it, select Mexico.

11. Click Next.

The Template view appears.

12. Retain the No Template option and then click the Finish button.

The report shown in Figure 6-8 appears.

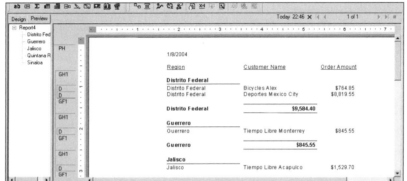

Figure 6-8:
The
Customer
report,
grouped
by region.

As with most reports created by the Standard Report Creation Wizard, this one could use some tuning. Here are some problems you may want to fix:

✔ The customer region names appear too often.

✔ The region summaries should be located under the Order Amount column.

✔ The report could use a bold, centered title.

Switch to the Design tab and make the adjustments that will correct these problems. After you make the adjustments, the Design view appears as shown in Figure 6-9, and the Preview tab view appears as shown in Figure 6-10.

The Vice President of Sales can now easily see which states in Mexico are producing orders and which customers in those states are placing orders. Thanks to the group subtotals and a Grand Total at the bottom of the report, he can also see the total value of orders in each state and in the entire country.

Save the report as Customer Report Grouped by Region (Mexico). Every time you run the report, it will show the updated results based on the current database contents.

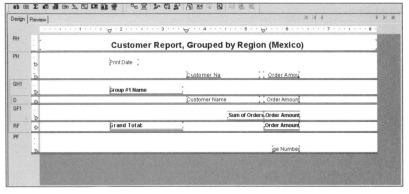

Figure 6-9:
The Design view of the reformatted Customer report.

Figure 6-10:
A preview of the reformatted Customer report.

Calculating Percentages

Suppose Xtreme's Vice President of Sales feels it would be more instructive to know the percentage rather than the dollar value of Mexico's order total coming from each state. Simply modify the existing report to include percentage summary fields rather than the sum field:

1. **In Design view, right-click the** `Sum of Orders.Order Amount` **field in the GF1 band and choose Edit Summary.**

   The Edit Summary dialog box appears, as shown in Figure 6-11.

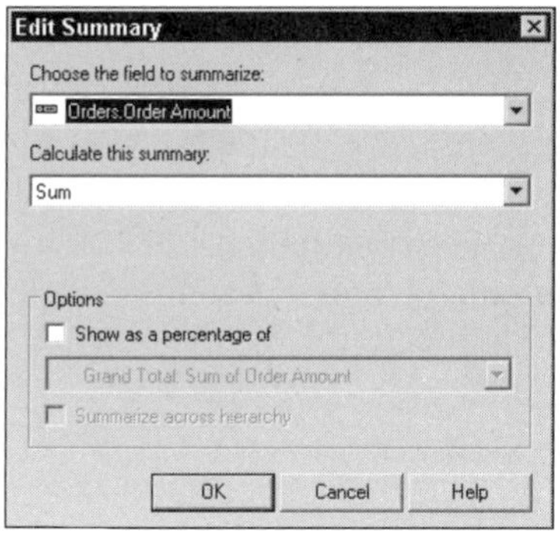

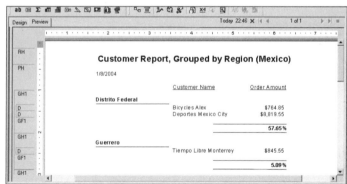

Figure 6-11:
The Edit
Summary
dialog box,
showing
the Orders.
Order
Amount
field.

2. **Select the Show as a Percentage Of check box.**

   This activates the drop-down list that shows the default choice, Grand Total: Sum of Order Amount.

3. **You want to display the group totals as percentages of the Grand Total, so click OK.**

4. **Switch to the Preview tab.**

   The report looks like Figure 6-12.

Figure 6-12:
The
Customer
report
showing
state totals
as a per-
centage of
the country
total
(Mexico).

This report makes it immediately obvious that more than half of Mexico's orders are coming from Distrito Federal. This information may cause the company to change its marketing strategy to encourage orders in other parts of the country.

Drilling Down for Detail

In the report you just prepared for Xtreme's Vice President of Sales, it's easy to see where most sales are coming from because the company doesn't have many customers in Mexico. The same report would not be as informative if it were run for the United States, where many more customers are located. The first page of the same report for the United States would look like Figure 6-13.

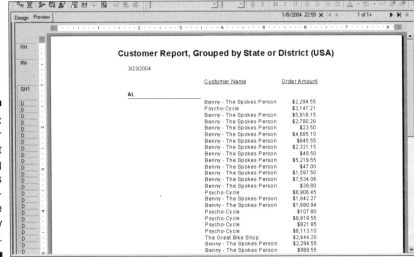

Figure 6-13:
A Customer report showing state totals as a percentage of country total (USA).

To change the Mexico report to a report on U.S orders, follow these steps:

1. **Choose Report➪Select Expert.**

   The Select Expert dialog box appears.

2. **Select Customer.Country is equal to USA in place of the existing Customer.Country is equal to Mexico.**

3. **Click OK and then, when prompted, click Refresh Data.**

4. **Edit the text in the report header to say Customer Orders, Grouped by State or District (USA).**

5. **Save this report as Customer Orders Grouped by State or District (USA).**

This report is not very helpful. The first page tells you that Benny – The Spokes Person, Psycho-Cycle, and The Great Bike Shop in Alabama have made a lot of orders, but that's about it — unless you're willing to riffle through a lot a pages.

You can hide specific customer information to present a more general picture of orders. If report viewers then want the specific information about any particular state, they can drill down by double-clicking that item. When users hover the cursor over the group header of interest, it changes to a magnifying glass icon. At that point, double-clicking displays the hidden detail data about individual orders.

To add drill-down functionality to this report, do the following:

1. **Switch to Design view.**

2. **Right-click the D designator to the left of the Detail band and choose Select Hide (Drill-Down OK).**

   The Detail band appears dimmed.

3. **Switch back to Preview mode.**

   You see the report shown in Figure 6-14.

4. **Save this report as Customer Orders Grouped by State or District with Drilldown.**

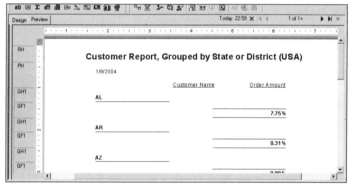

Figure 6-14: The Customer report with the details hidden.

This information is much more helpful for strategic decision making. You can easily see which states are contributing to Xtreme's bottom line and which are not. If report viewers want to see the detail for a specific state, they can double-click the group header or group footer for that state. Figure 6-15 shows what this looks like.

The drill-down capability of Crystal Reports provides tremendous flexibility to online report viewers. Different viewers can see different levels of detail, even though they're all viewing the same report. Be sure that you save this report before moving on to the next section.

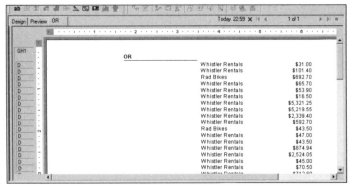

Figure 6-15:
Customer
report with
details
shown for
Oregon.

Don't try drilling down on a report that has been printed on paper. You can click all day. You can even place your mouse directly on top of the paper. It is no use; the details will not be displayed. Drill-down works only for online report viewing.

Keeping Track of Things with Running Totals

Reports with summarized group totals, like those in the preceding section, are valuable for many purposes, but they don't satisfy all needs. Sometimes it's helpful to see how the status of an item changes with time. Crystal Reports' running total facility gives you that kind of information.

To see how that might work, construct a variant of the Orders report for Mexico where the total value of all orders is tracked as a function of the order date:

1. **Select Standard Report Creation Wizard and the** `xtreme.mdb` **database.**

2. **Select the** `Customer` **and** `Orders` **tables and make sure they're linked by the** `Customer ID` **field.**

3. **Add the** `Customer Name` **field from the** `Customer` **table and the** `Order Amount` **and** `Order Date` **fields from the** `Orders` **table to the Fields to Display pane in the Standard Report Creation Wizard.**

4. **For this report, skip the Grouping view and move to the Record Selection view.**

5. **Add the Customer table's** `Country` **field to the Filter Fields pane. In the pull-down lists that appear below, select the is equal to and Mexico options.**

   This means the report will display results only for Mexico.

6. **Retain the No Template option, and then click the Finish button.**

   You're not really finished, as you can see by looking at the report preview shown in Figure 6-16.

Figure 6-16:
A Customer
report
with an
incomplete
running
total.

The running total column is not on the report, the Order Date column shows times, and the report title is missing. Switch to the Design tab to put the report into final form. You can add the title — *Mexico Orders, with Running Totals* — in much the same way that you did for the previous examples.

You can change the format of the `Order Date` field to eliminate the time information. Just right-click the `Order Date` field to display the shortcut menu. Select Format Field from the menu, and then when the Format Editor appears, use it to change the date format.

For the running total, you want to place a fourth column to the right of the Order Date column. To do that, follow these steps:

1. **Make sure that the Design tab is displayed, and then if Field Explorer is not currently displayed, choose View⇨Field Explorer.**

   Field Explorer appears.

2. **Select the Running Total Fields option.**

3. **Click the New icon at the top of Field Explorer.**

   The Create Running Total Field dialog box appears, as shown in Figure 6-17.

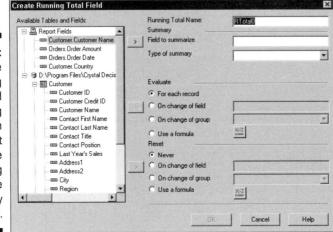

Figure 6-17: The Create Running Total Field dialog box, with a default name in the Running Total Name text entry field.

4. **In the Running Total Name box, replace the default name with** Order Total.

5. **In the Available Tables and Fields pane, select Orders.Order Amount from the Report Fields area. Then click the arrow button pointing to the Field to Summarize box.**

   The default *sum* appears in the Type of Summary pull-down list. This is what you want, so proceed to the next step.

6. **In the Available Tables and Fields pane, select Orders.Order ID from the** Orders **table. In the Evaluate area, click the On Change of Field option, and then click the arrow button pointing to the Evaluate area.**

   The report will display all the orders for Mexico, so you want the running total to be updated for each order (each time the Order ID changes).

7. **Because you want the running total to be cumulative for the entire report, leave the Reset option set to Never and then click OK.**

   The Create Running Total Field dialog box disappears, once again showing Field Explorer.

8. **Drag the running total field from Field Explorer onto your report, just to the right of the** `Order Date` **field.**

9. **Dismiss Field Explorer, and in the Report Header section, center the title Mexico Orders, with Running Totals. Drag the page number object to the right.**

   Your Design view should look similar to Figure 6-18.

10. **Switch to Preview mode.**

    The report preview looks similar to Figure 6-19.

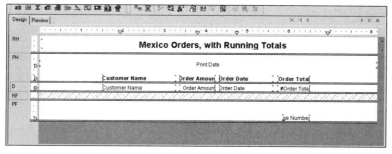

Figure 6-18: The Design view of the report with a running total column.

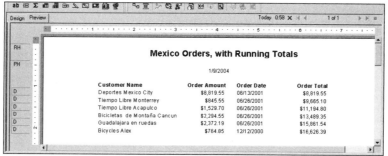

Figure 6-19: A preview of the report with a running total column.

The report is now nicely laid out and balanced, but it's not sorted in chronological order. To remedy that situation, follow these steps:

1. **Click the Record Sort Expert icon in the Expert Tools toolbar.**

   The Record Sort Order dialog box appears.

2. **Add Orders.Order Date to the Sort Fields pane.**

  3. **Leave the Sort Direction at Ascending, and then click OK.**

  4. **Switch to Preview mode, if necessary.**

     You can see that the report is sorted in chronological order.

  5. **Save the report as Mexico Orders with Running Totals Sorted by Date.**

Troubleshooting Sorting, Grouping, and Totaling Problems

What can go wrong when you try to include sorting, grouping, or totaling in a report? In this section, I take each case in turn.

Sorting problems and how to solve them

Crystal Reports gives you many options for sorting, so many things can go wrong. Crystal Reports will always do exactly what you tell it to do. The problem is that it's not always clear what you should tell it. You can sort on one field or multiple fields. You can sort an entire report or within each group in the report.

The main solution to any sorting problem is to have a clear idea of how you want the report to be sorted:

  ✔ Decide which fields you want to sort on and which should be specified first. For a field with multiple sort keys, the second sort key comes into play only when multiple records have the same value for the first sort key.

  ✔ Decide whether you want the sort to be ascending or descending.

After you decide exactly how you want your information to be sorted, choose Report➪Record Sort Expert or click the Record Sort Expert icon to display the Record Sort Order dialog box. The left pane shows all the fields you might want to sort by; the right pane (Sort Fields) is waiting for you to add them.

You must add the fields to the Sort Fields pane in the correct order. First add the field that you want as your primary sort key; next add the field that you want as the secondary sort key, and so on. After you choose the appropriate sort direction (ascending or descending) for each sort key, click OK to execute the sort.

In the Sort Fields pane, the letter *A* precedes fields that will be sorted in ascending order. Similarly, the letter *D* precedes fields that will be sorted in descending order. A field with multiple sort keys might be sorted in an ascending direction for one key and a descending direction for another.

Unusual grouping options

Separating report records into groups of related items is not difficult, but the rich array of options for grouping might be confusing. For example, you can sort not only individual records but also groups. You can sort the groups in ascending order, descending order, the original order in which they appear in the database, or in some other specified order. To place a new level of grouping into an existing report, choose Insert⇨Group and specify the options you want in the Insert Group dialog box that appears.

You can choose to include some groups in the report and exclude others. Select Expert is the tool you use to do that job. With Select Expert, select the groups to display by specifying a field to select on or by specifying a formula that determines which groups to include.

If you've created groups in a report but later decide that the grouping you've created is not the best, you can change it. Choose Report⇨Group Expert to display the Group Expert dialog box, shown in Figure 6-20.

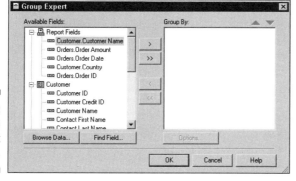

Figure 6-20:
Group
Expert
dialog box.

Use this dialog box to change the field that the group is sorted by, the sort order, and the name of the group. You can specify whether you want to keep the group together after the change, and whether you want to repeat the group header at the top of each page.

Getting the right totals

Crystal Reports enables you to print subtotals in group footers as well as a grand total at the end of the report. You can also print running totals. With all these possibilities, you might specify your subtotals incorrectly. It's a good idea to run your report with a few records of sample data, for which you know what the correct subtotals should be. If what you get isn't what you expect, check how you specified the subtotals to be computed. If you find an error in how you've specified a subtotal, you can delete the erroneous specification and replace it with the correct one.

Chapter 7

Mastering Report Sections

. . . .

In This Chapter

▶ Resizing sections

▶ Controlling group placement

▶ Creating summary and drill-down reports

▶ Generating mailing labels

. . . .

As you may have seen in other chapters, Crystal Reports divides a report document into sections, including the Report Header, Page Header, Details, Report Footer, and Page Footer sections. What you perhaps have not seen is the tremendous flexibility this architecture provides. A report can have multiple copies of each section, each one serving a different purpose.

You have a lot of leeway in how you format a section. You can vary the height, the color, and even the number of columns in each section. By using Crystal Reports tools creatively, you can give your report the appearance you want.

Changing the Size of a Section

The width of a section is the same as the width of the report that the section is in. You determine this value when you set your margins.

The height of a section begins at some default value. If that value gives you the appearance that you want, you can leave it the way it is. If you want a different height for a section, it's easy to change, as described next.

Vertical spacing between lines

Consider the vertical spacing between the lines of a variant of the Mexico Orders, with Running Totals report that I show you how to create in Chapter 6. This version of the report has a box around the fields and vertical lines between the columns. You can add this effect to your reports by using the Insert Box and Insert Line icons on the Insert Tools toolbar.

As shown in Figure 7-1, the horizontal lines are quite close. This arrangement allows the maximum number of lines to be displayed on each page.

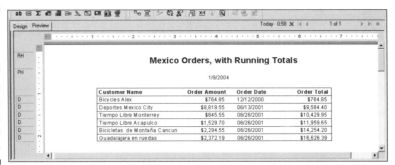

Figure 7-1: An enhanced version of the Mexico Orders, with Running Totals report.

Because this report has only a few lines, placing the lines close together provides no real advantage. To make it easier to read the report, you can give each line a little more room. Make this easy adjustment by following these steps:

1. **Switch to the Design tab.**

2. **Move the cursor to the bottom of the Details section.**

   The cursor changes shape, as shown in Figure 7-2. When the cursor takes on the appearance of the sizing cursor, you can use it to drag the section boundary up or down to give you the vertical height you want for the section in question.

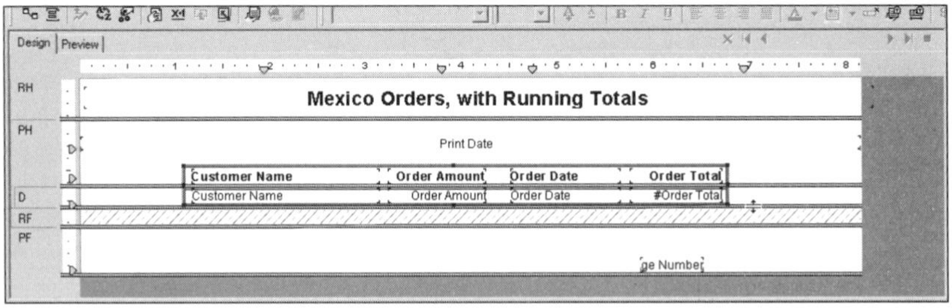

Figure 7-2: The cursor has changed to the sizing cursor.

3. **Drag the Details section boundary down, as shown in Figure 7-3.**

   Note that the box edge below the Detail fields has not moved.

4. **To maintain an appearance similar to the original report, click the box edge to select it.**

   This highlights the border box and displays drag handles at the corners and the middle of the box.

Design
Preview
RH
Mexico Orders, with Running Totals
PH
Print Date
Customer Name
Order Amount
Order Date
Order Total
D
Customer Name
Order Amount
Order Date
#Order Total
RF
PF
ge Number

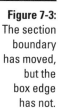

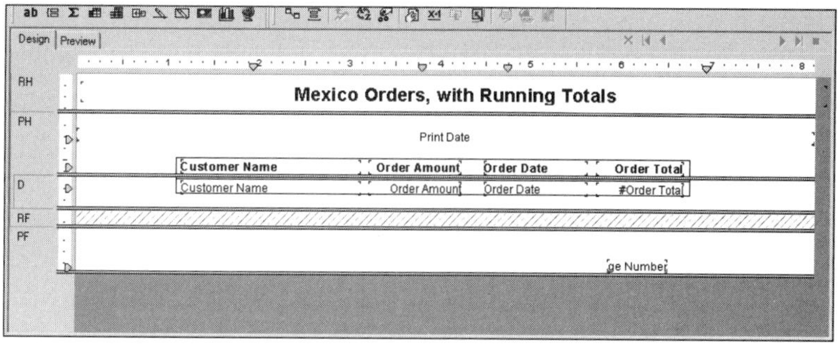

Figure 7-3: The section boundary has moved, but the box edge has not.

5. **Grab the center-bottom handle and drag the box's bottom borderline down to the section boundary.**

   The result should look like Figure 7-4.

Design
Preview
RH
Mexico Orders, with Running Totals
PH
Print Date
Customer Name
Order Amount
Order Date
Order Total
D
Customer Name
Order Amount
Order Date
#Order Total
RF
PF
ge Number

Figure 7-4: The bottom box border-line is now on top of the bottom boundary of the Details section.

6. **Switch to the Preview tab.**

   The report now looks like Figure 7-5.

Design
Preview
Today 0:58
1 of 1
RH
PH
Mexico Orders, with Running Totals
1/9/2004
Customer Name
Order Amount
Order Date
Order Total
Bicycles Alex $764.85 12/12/2000 $764.85
Deportes Mexico City $8,819.55 06/13/2001 $9,584.40
Tiempo Libre Monterrey $845.55 06/26/2001 $10,429.95
Tiempo Libre Acapulco $1,529.70 06/26/2001 $11,959.65
Bicicletas de Montaña Cancun $2,294.55 06/26/2001 $14,254.20
Guadalajara en ruedas $2,372.19 06/26/2001 $16,626.39

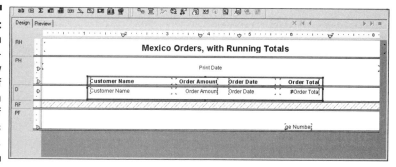

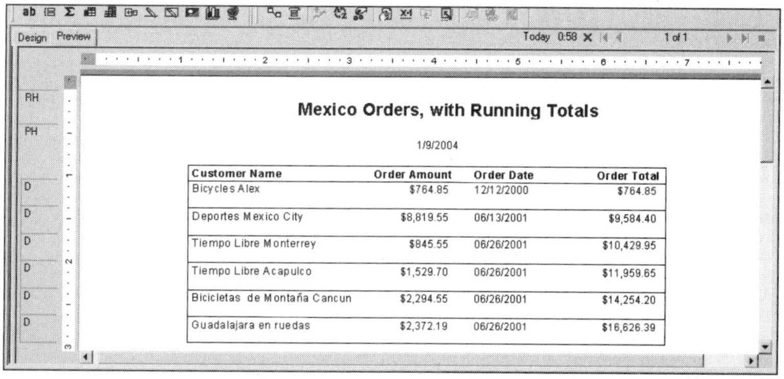

Figure 7-5: A preview of the report.

The report is more readable, but it would look even better if the detail lines were centered vertically within each box. This problem is easy to correct.

To center the records vertically within their boxes, follow these steps:

1. **Switch back to the Design tab.**

   Notice that the left margin has a little triangle pointing towards the lower edge of the fields in the Details section. This is a horizontal guideline indicator used to align fields on a single horizontal line.

2. **Use the mouse to grab the triangle (the horizontal guideline indicator) and then drag it down to just below the center of the section.**

   The fields move down with it. If the line jumps to a location lower than what you want, the Snap to Grid feature is probably enabled. To disable it, right-click the triangle. In the pop-up menu, uncheck Snap to Grid and then position the triangle where you want it.

   This completes the modification of the report, as shown in Figure 7-6.

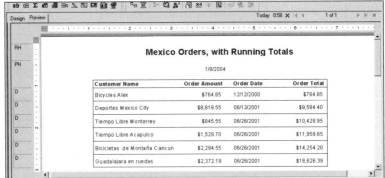

Figure 7-6: The formatted report.

The Section Formatting menu

To create a summary report in Chapter 6, you use the Hide (Drill-Down OK) function in the Section Formatting menu. Right-clicking in the area to the left of a report section displays the menu. The menu contains other useful functions in addition to the Hide function, as shown in Figure 7-7.

Figure 7-7 is the menu for the Details section, as seen in Preview mode. The following list provides a brief description of each option in this menu:

✔ **Hide (Drill-Down OK):** Doesn't display this section of the report but allows the user to drill down to view it.

✔ **Suppress (No Drill-Down):** Doesn't display this section of the report and doesn't allow the user to view it by drilling down.

✔ **Section Expert:** Displays Section Expert.

✔ **Hide Section Names:** Toggles between showing and hiding section names.

✔ **Insert Line:** Adds an additional horizontal guideline to the section. If there's not enough room for an additional line, the section is automatically expanded to accommodate the additional guideline.

✔ **Delete Last Line:** Deletes the bottom guideline from the section and raises the bottom of the section up to just below the next higher guideline.

✔ **Arrange Lines:** Arranges guidelines vertically so that they're evenly spaced. Adds more guidelines if there aren't enough.

✔ **Fit Section:** Brings the bottom of the section up to the bottom of the lowest object, removing any guidelines that are lower.

✔ **Insert Section Below:** Adds another section of the same type as the current section, just below it.

✔ **Select All Section Objects:** Selects all objects in the section.

✔ **Cancel Menu:** Removes the menu from the screen.

The options on the Section Formatting menu provide a convenient way to make basic formatting changes to a section.

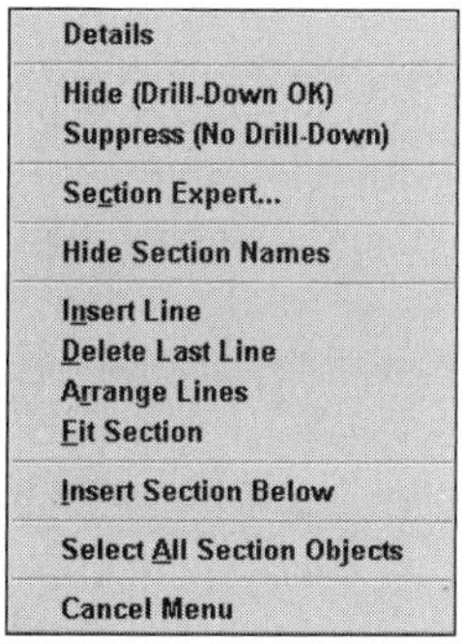

Figure 7-7:
Things you
can do in
the Details
section.

Details
Hide (Drill-Down OK)
Suppress (No Drill-Down)
Section Expert...
Hide Section Names
Insert Line
Delete Last Line
Arrange Lines
Fit Section
Insert Section Below
Select All Section Objects
Cancel Menu

Common tab of Section Expert

Section Expert is the primary tool for changing the formatting of a section. With it, you can set a number of options to determine what is displayed, how it's displayed, and what color the display is. Section Expert has two tabs: the Common tab and the Color tab.

Figure 7-8 shows the default settings for the Report Header section of the Common tab. (Each section has different default settings.)

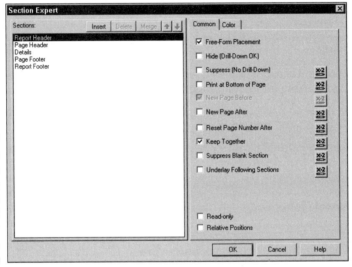

Figure 7-8:
The
Common
tab for the
Report
Header
section.

Here is a short description of the options on the Common tab:

- ✔ **Free-Form Placement** allows you to place objects anywhere in the section without snapping to horizontal guidelines. If this option is unchecked, horizontal guidelines are functional.

- ✔ **Hide (Drill-Down OK)** hides the section. However, drilling down displays the section's contents.

- ✔ **Suppress (No Drill-Down)** hides the section, and drilling down does not override the suppression.

- ✔ **Print at Bottom of Page** prints the section at the bottom of the page. This option doesn't make much sense for a Details section, but it's useful when applied to a Report Footer that otherwise would be printed near the top of the last page of a report.

- ✔ **New Page Before** prints the section at the top of a new page instead of immediately after the previous section. You would probably not use this option for a Details section, but it could come in handy for a Group Header section.

- ✔ **New Page After** prints the next section after the current one at the top of a new page. This is similar to the New Page Before option but is more appropriate in a Group Footer section.

- ✔ **Reset Page Number After** resets page numbering to the beginning of the sequence. If you apply this setting to a Group Footer, the first page of the next group is numbered 1 rather than the last page number of the current group being incremented.

- ✔ **Keep Together** prevents a page break in the middle of a section. This option is useful if a section contains a small number of detail lines that should be viewed together, regardless of where they happen to fall on a page.

- ✔ **Suppress Blank Section** closes the gap between the preceding and the following sections if a section is blank. If this option is not checked, the empty space assigned to the section is on the report.

- ✔ **Underlay Following Sections** prints the section and then prints all the following sections right on top of this one. The function is often used to apply a faint watermark to a page. It can also be used to overlay two types of content, such as text and a chart.

- ✔ **Read-only** locks the formatting and position of all objects in the section. In the process, it disables all the foregoing options, as well as those that are normally available on the toolbars and shortcut menus.

- ✔ **Relative Positions** freezes the relative positioning of objects in a section. If one object moves, its spacing relative to an adjacent object is retained.

The X+2 icon to the right of most of the options on the Common tab displays Format Formula Editor. With this editor, you can write a formula that tests a condition. For true/false conditions, if the condition is satisfied (true), the chosen formatting option is applied; if false, the formatting option is not applied. For multivalued conditions, an If-Then-Else structure is used, which defines which one of several formatting options to apply. For more on formulas, see Chapter 11.

Color tab of Section Expert

With the Color tab, you can specify a background color for a report section. You can give each section a different background color, or you can have multiple colors within a section by using Format Formula Editor. With the editor, you write a formula that specifies which lines within a section will have a specific background color. Figure 7-9 shows the Section Expert's Color tab.

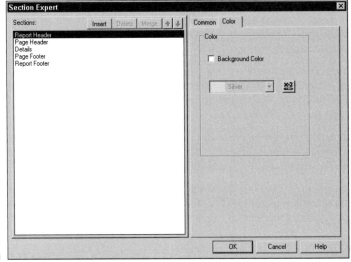

Figure 7-9:
You can change the background color of a report section.

If you don't check the Background Color option, Crystal Reports doesn't give the background any color. If you select the option, the pull-down list becomes active, as shown in Figure 7-10.

Quite a few colors are available. If the standard choices don't meet your needs, you can select the More option, which displays the Color palette. As shown in Figure 7-11, you can define thousands of colors from the Color palette.

Using different colors for different sections

Using the Color tab of Section Expert, you can specify a background color for each section of the report. Depending on the effect you want to convey, you might leave all section backgrounds uncolored or create a rainbow effect, with each section a different color. A more conservative approach is to use colored backgrounds sparingly but tastefully.

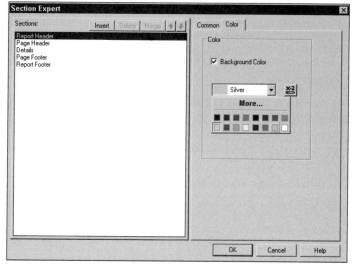

Figure 7-10:
Color tab,
with pull-
down list
activated.

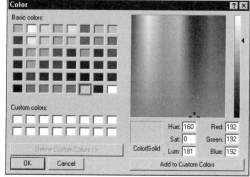

Figure 7-11:
Select any
hue, satura-
tion, and
luminance
you want,
as well as
fractions of
red, green,
and blue.

Be aware of how your users will view your report. If the report will be printed on a black-and-white printer, it's not a good idea to go overboard with color. However, if users will be viewing the report on computer screens or as the output of a color printer, take advantage of the expanded possibilities that color gives you.

Giving reports a classic banded look

Back in the early days of computing (the 1950s and 1960s), computers printed reports on wide paper that was sprocket-fed through electromechanical line printers. The paper had sprocket holes on the left and right edges and alternating green and white horizontal bands. Each band was high enough to hold two printed lines. The bands helped you focus on a single line.

You can simulate that classic banded look in your reports. Doing so requires the use of a conditional formula. To demonstrate this, add silver bands (or bands of any other color) in the background of the Big Orders report that I show you how to build and save in Chapter 5, as follows:

1. **Open the report and switch to the Design tab.**

2. **Right-click the margin to the left of the Details section and choose Section Expert.**

   Section Expert appears.

3. **Switch to the Color tab.**

4. **Select the Background Color option.**

5. **In the pull-down list, select a color and then click the Formula (X+2) icon.**

   For the example, select Silver. Formula Workshop appears in Format Formula Editor: Background Color mode.

6. **In the text area in the bottom half of the editor, enter the following formula, replacing** *color* **with the color you selected:**

   ```
   If Remainder (RecordNumber, 4) In [1,2] Then color Else NoColor
   ```

   If you follow along with the example, the formula should be the same as the one shown in Figure 7-12.

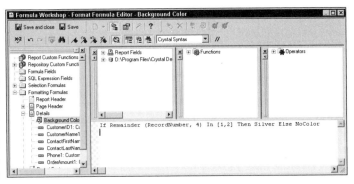

Figure 7-12:
Adding
the color
banding
formula.

7. **Click the Save and Close button.**

8. **Click OK in Section Expert to dismiss it.**

9. **Switch to the Preview tab.**

   You can see the effect of this change on the single-month Orders report, as shown in Figure 7-13.

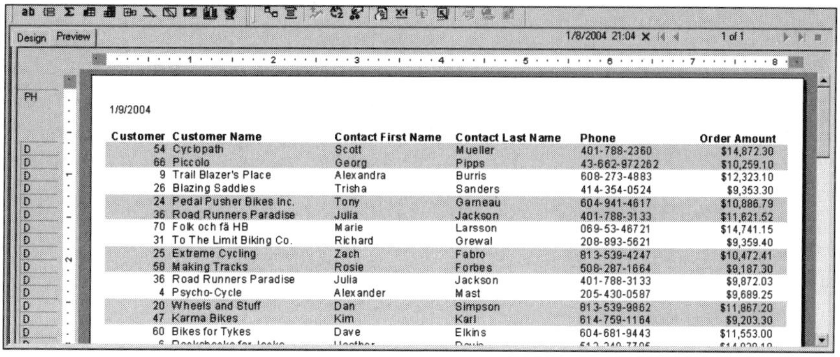

Figure 7-13:
The report
on simulated
banded
paper.

This report brings back memories of the good old days and makes it easy to correlate the Order Amount on the right with the Customer Name on the left.

Placing Groups Where You Want Them

Depending on the type of report you're creating, you might want to depart from the default position of groups within the Details section or of an entire section. You can do so in several ways, as shown next.

Starting each group at the top of its own page

Suppose that you have a number of groups and each group includes a large number of detail lines. Each group will end at some random place in the middle of a page, with the next group following immediately. For large groups, you might want to start each group at the top of a new page, to provide a proper separation between groups.

Figure 7-14 shows the top of one page of Xtreme's Customer Report Grouped by State or District (USA). It has the last of many records for California, followed by the Colorado group.

For branch managers responsible for single states, it makes sense to have each state's records start on a new page. This makes it easier to distribute the appropriate information to the appropriate manager, while not revealing what is happening in other states.

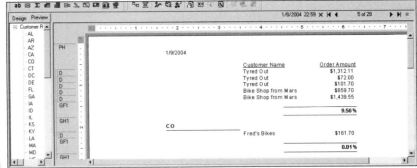

Figure 7-14:
The
Customer
Report page
showing
California
and
Colorado
records.

To make each group start on a new page, follow these steps:

1. **Right-click the GH1 area to the left of the first group header on the report and choose Section Expert.**

   Section Expert appears (refer to Figure 7-8).

2. **On the Common tab, select the New Page Before option.**

   On a report such as this one, which has a report header, checking this option will cause a page feed after the report header is printed on the first page, and the first group will appear at the top of the second page. To avoid this problem, when you check the New Page Before option, also click its Formula Editor button to display the Format Formula Editor. In the formula entry area, type **Not OnFirstRecord**. This ensures that the first group always prints on the first page of the report.

3. **Click the Save and Close button to close the Format Formula Editor and then click OK in Section Expert.**

Printing totals at the bottom of a page

For a multipage report with subtotals for each group and a grand total at the end, you might want to print the grand total at the bottom of the last page. This is not the default format in Crystal Reports, which puts the grand total immediately after the subtotal for the last group, as shown in Figure 7-15.

Xtreme did not have many sales from West Virginia, so the grand total prints near the top of the last page. Printing the total at the bottom of the page is another job for Section Expert:

1. **Right-click in the area to the left of the Report Footer section and choose Section Expert.**

2. **On the Common tab, select the Print at Bottom of Page option.**

   This puts the grand total at the bottom of the page, where it's traditionally located.

Figure 7-15:
The grand total is near the top of the last page of this report.

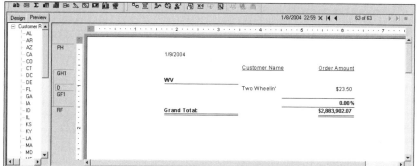

Restarting page numbering at the beginning of each group

If you're starting each group on a new page and the group extends for multiple pages, it might make sense to restart the page numbering every time you start a new group. This would cause less confusion to people who receive a distribution consisting of only one group. To restart page numbering at the beginning of each new group, access Section Expert from the Group Footer, and select the Reset Page Number After option in the Common tab.

Hiding Details with Summary and Drill-Down Reports

In Chapter 6, I give you a brief look at summary reports and how to drill down into them to see the hidden detail they contain. By making a simple selection from the Section Formatting menu, you can choose to either display or hide a report's detail information. You can print a detailed report for one client, and then print a summary that hides the detail but shows the summary information in the group footer for another client.

For example, aside from the full detailed report that you might give to the branch manager responsible for a single state and the drill-downable summary report that you might produce for the national sales manager, you can also produce a summary report for which drill-down is not possible. You can produce all three types of reports from the same basic report. To create the drill-downable report, use the Hide (Drill-Down OK) option from the Section Formatting menu. To create a similar summary report for which drill-down is not enabled, use the Suppress (No Drill-Down) option instead. With one report, you can satisfy the needs of three classes of users.

Creating Mailing Labels

You'll use multicolumn reports in a variety of situations. One example is a report for printing three or four columns of mailing labels on 8½ by 11-inch label stock. Crystal Reports recognizes that people frequently want to print mailing labels, so it provides a wizard for that specific task.

To create a report that prints mailing labels in multiple columns, follow these steps:

1. **In the Crystal Reports Gallery, select Mail Label and then click OK.**

   The Mailing Labels Report Creation Wizard appears.

2. **Connect to the `xtreme.mdb` database and add the Customer table to the Selected Tables pane.**

   For more information on this process, see Chapter 2.

3. **Click Next to display the Fields view.**

4. **Add the following fields from the Available Fields pane to the Fields to Display pane: Contact First Name, Contact Last Name, Customer Name, Address 1, Address 2, City, Region, and Postal Code.**

5. **Click Next to display the Label view.**

   The Label view enables you to select a standard label type or specify the dimensions and margins of nonstandard labels. You can also specify the direction in which they will be printed: across the page and then down, or down and then across.

   The standard labels include not only labels that you might put on envelopes, but also disk labels, audiocassette labels, videotape labels, and Rolodex cards.

6. **Select a standard label type.**

   For this example, choose Avery 5160.

7. **Click Next to display the Record Selection view.**

8. **Specify which records you're printing labels for.**

   For this example, suppose you want to write to customers only in the United States. You can restrict the label printing to those customers by specifying that the Country field from the Customer table is equal to USA.

9. **Click the Finish button.**

   If you followed along with the example, you get the report shown in Figure 7-16.

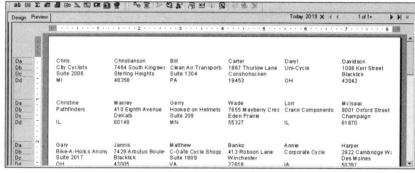

Figure 7-16: Mailing labels produced by Mailing Label Expert.

The three columns of labels are not laid out in the most readable way. To correct that, follow these steps:

1. **Switch to the Design tab to move things around a little.**

   Figure 7-17 shows the Design tab view of the report.

2. **Concatenate the Contact First Name field and the Contact Last Name field on the first line.**

   To do so, move the fields into the Page Header temporarily. Next, click the Insert Text Object icon and drag a text box down to the Da section. Expand the text box to the full width of the label. Now drag the Contact First Name and Contact Last Name fields into the text box, with one blank space separating them. You have to right-click in the Da section and choose Edit Text from the pop-up menu to insert the blank space.

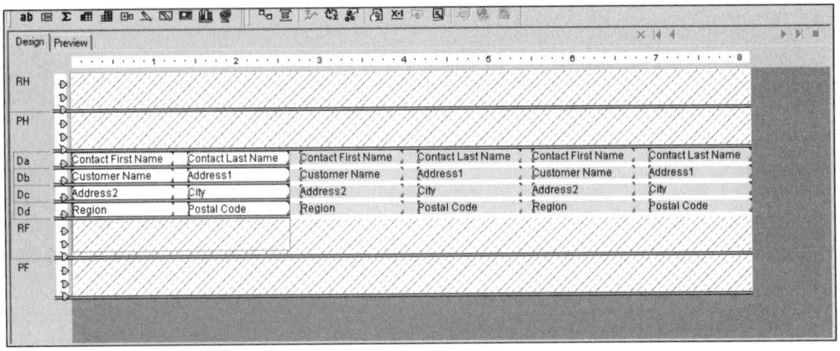

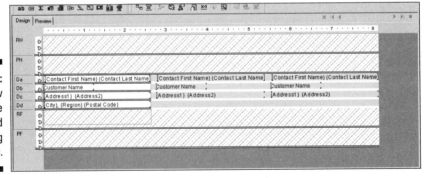

Figure 7-17:
Design view
of the
mailing
labels.

3. **Concatenate the Address1 and Address2 fields on the third line, putting a couple of spaces between them.**

   To do so, move Address2 and City out of the way temporarily. Next, click the Insert Text Object icon and drag a text box into the Dc section. Now drag the Address1 and the Address2 fields into the text box. Insert the editing cursor between the two fields, and press the spacebar twice.

4. **Move Region and Postal Code out of the Dd section, and then drag a text box down into that section. Move City into the text box in Dd.**

5. **Type a comma and a space after the City field, and then move the Region field after that. Follow Region with a space, and then drag Postal Code into the text box after the space.**

   The result should look similar to Figure 7-18.

Figure 7-18:
Design view
of the
modified
mailing
labels.

6. **Switch to the Preview tab.**

The screen should look similar to Figure 7-19. These labels look great and will fit nicely on the Avery label stock you chose previously.

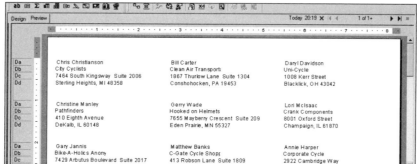

Figure 7-19:
A preview of
the modified
mailing
labels.

Saving Money on Postage by Doing a Zip Sort

Figure 7-19 shows an example of how the addresses would print on label stock. The labels look great but are in the order in which they were entered into the database, which means no particular order at all. The United States Postal Service gives a postage discount on mass mailings of first class letters if the letters are sorted by zip code when you bring them to the post office.

It's a lot easier to apply the labels to envelopes in Zip sorted order if the labels are in Zip sorted order in the first place. Start with the report shown in Figure 7-19 and then follow these steps:

1. **In Design mode, click the Record Sort Expert icon.**

The Record Sort Order dialog box appears.

2. **Add Customer.PostalCode to the Sort Fields pane.**

3. **Leave the sort direction as Ascending and then click OK.**

4. **Switch to Preview mode.**

The report shown in Figure 7-20 appears. The labels are now sorted in zip code order.

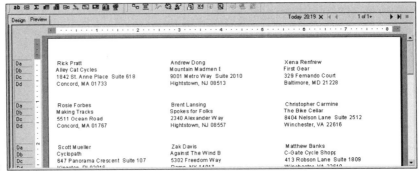

Figure 7-20:
Mailing
labels,
sorted by
zip code.

Chapter 8

Formatting Your Reports

- -

In This Chapter

▶ Comparing absolute and conditional formatting

▶ Enhancing readability with Highlighting Expert

▶ Inserting a picture into a report

▶ Working with preprinted forms

▶ Importing text-based objects from a file

▶ Using the Formatting Options dialog box

▶ Adding special fields to a Report

▶ Emphasizing important information with Report Alerts

▶ Speeding development with Report Templates

- -

*F*ormatting is the primary reason for the existence of Crystal Reports —
or any report-writing software, for that matter. Any database-management
system (DBMS) can retrieve results from a database and display or print them.
The primary purpose of a DBMS, however, is to maintain data. Putting retrieved
results in the most understandable form isn't the DBMS vendor's job.

Crystal Reports excels at transforming the raw data retrieved from a DBMS
into a report that communicates. To achieve that goal, Crystal Reports provides tools you can use to shape the appearance of any report you generate.
It gives you the means to create the desired impression for your readers.

Absolute Formatting and Conditional Formatting

Absolute formatting is the regular kind of formatting that you can apply to text
and fields with Crystal Reports in your quest to present data the best way.
After you apply absolute formatting, the format is fixed, regardless of the
values of the data making up the content of the report. With *conditional formatting,* you can vary the appearance (or even the presence or absence) of a

particular field, depending on the value contained in the field. The result is greater flexibility and a way to help your report's audience focus on relevant details. Each approach has its advantages and best uses.

Absolute formatting overview

Before you get into the intricacies of conditional formatting, take a look at the power and versatility of absolute formatting. In this section, you have some fun with the Customer Report, Grouped by Region (Mexico), one of the reports in Chapter 6. The report is shown in Figure 8-1.

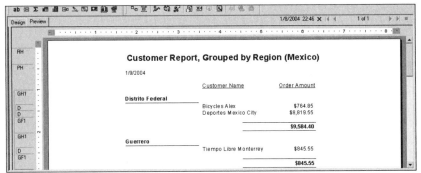

Figure 8-1: The Customer Report, Grouped by Region (Mexico) from Chapter 6.

This isn't bad, but you might want to give the report more visual appeal by changing the fonts of various report elements. To alter the report title, follow these steps:

1. **In Design view, click the report title. Right-click the text to activate Edit Text mode, and then select the entire title.**

2. **In the Formatting toolbar, choose one or more of the fonts available on your machine to give the report title a different look.**

   Make sure that whatever font you choose is also available on all the computers and printers used by the people who view the report.

3. **Select the style, size, and color of the font.**

   In the present case, the style and size are fine, but you might want to experiment with font color to get the look you want.

I chose the Bookman Old Style font face for the report title. It's a distinctive font, available on Windows XP machines. I also chose green as the color for the report title, date, grand total in the report footer, and the group headers.

The color change adds some contrast to the report and grabs more of the reader's attention. Changing the color of the text in the date, grand total, and group header fields is pretty simple: Right-click them, choose Format Text to display the Format Editor, and then (on the Font tab) choose green as the font color. Figure 8-2 shows the report at this point (in black and white).

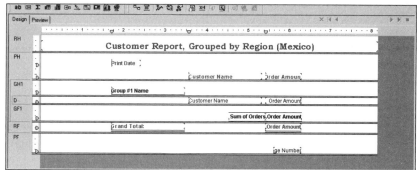

Figure 8-2: Selected font and color changes.

Centering the date would be a good idea. You might also want to change the date format. Crystal Reports provides a presentable default format, but there are many others. Figure 8-3 shows the Date tab of Format Editor with a longer date format selected.

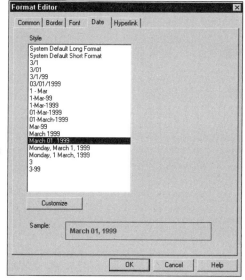

Figure 8-3: Format Editor's Date tab, with Month Day, Year selected.

Another technique you can use to improve the visual appeal of your reports is to add graphical elements (such as lines and boxes) for emphasis. For example, you could set the report title off from the rest of the report by enclosing it in a box. Follow these steps to see how it changes the visual impact of a report:

1. **Give the title some more vertical space, to make room for the box.**

   To do this, you have to expand the Report Header section. In Design view, drag down the lower border of the Report Header section about ¼ inch. Center the report title vertically in the Report Header section.

2. **Switch to Preview mode, then in the Insert Tools toolbar, click the Insert Box icon.**

   The cursor changes to a pencil.

3. **Draw a box around the title by clicking and holding over one corner, dragging to the diagonally opposite corner, and releasing the mouse button.**

   After you've drawn the box, you can format it.

4. **Click the box to select it, and then right-click it and choose Format Box.**

   Format Editor appears, as shown in Figure 8-4. The Box tab allows you to select a line thickness and a color, among other options.

5. **Choose a line thickness and color.**

   To follow along with the example, choose a medium thickness for the line and green as the color.

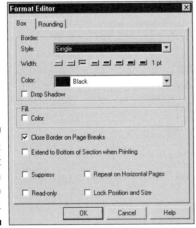

Figure 8-4:
Format
Editor with
Box tab
selected.

6. **Click the Rounding tab, and then choose the amount of rounding.**

   The Rounding tab enables you to round the corners to whatever extent you like, all the way from a rectangle to a circle. I selected a little bit of rounding (4%), as shown in Figure 8-5.

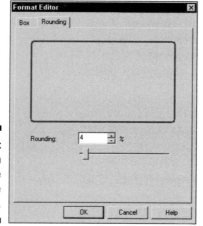

Figure 8-5:
You can change the appearance of the box.

The result is the report shown in Figure 8-6. It's a substantial improvement over the first version, which was created automatically by Report Wizard.

After you set a format with absolute formatting, the format is fixed unless you change it with the Design tab or Format Editor. Every time you run the report, the formatting is the same. Sometimes, however, you want different formatting, depending on the data that you're displaying. For that, you use the extensive conditional formatting capabilities of Crystals Reports.

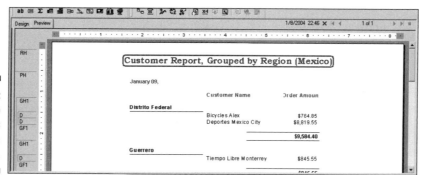

Figure 8-6:
The Mexico Orders report, with a boxed title.

Conditional formatting

In contrast to absolute formatting (which is fixed after you complete a report's design), *conditional formatting* allows the appearance of a report to change each time it's run, depending on the data it contains.

For example, Xtreme might want to draw attention to underperforming regions by coloring group totals red for all states or districts that have cumulative orders below $2,000. A state might qualify for a red group total one month but (through additional sales) earn the right to a black group total the following month.

To demonstrate how to add conditional formatting to a report, use the Mexico Orders report from the preceding section and add the condition that group totals less than $2,000 should show as red rather than black:

1. **Switch to Design view.**

2. **In the Group Footer section, right-click the** Sum of Orders.Order Amount **field and choose Format Field.**

   Format Editor appears.

3. **Click the Font tab.**

   The default color is black, which is the color you want most of the time, but not this time.

4. **To add a condition for low order totals, click the Format Formula Editor button to the right of the Color menu.**

   The Format Formula Editor dialog box appears, as shown in Figure 8-7.

5. **Expand the Report Fields node in the first of the three panes above the work area, so the items shown in Figure 8-7 are visible.**

Figure 8-7:
Format
Formula
Editor,
showing the
formula that
displays all
totals of less
than $2,000
in red.

6. **Build the formula shown in Figure 8-7.**

   To do so, type the keyword **If**. Then double-click the @@sig Group #1 line in the Report Fields window (in the upper-left pane above the work area). Complete the formula by typing the following:

   ```
   ) < 2000 Then Red Else Black
   ```

   The final formula should look like this:

   ```
   If Sum ({Orders.Order Amount}, {Customer.Region}) < 2000 Then Red Else
        Black
   ```

7. **Click the Save and Close button in Format Formula Editor.**

8. **Click OK in Format Editor.**

9. **Preview mode now displays the report in Figure 8-8.**

   State totals of less than $2,000 are displayed in red, and all totals greater than $2,000 are shown in black.

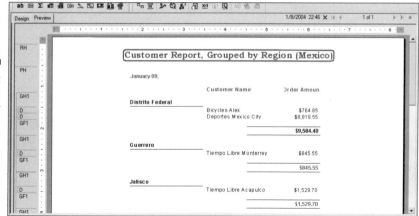

Figure 8-8:
The Customer Report, with group totals of less than $2,000 displayed in red.

Format Formula Editor is a powerful tool for creating complex conditions that govern (a) what's printed on a report and (b) how it's printed. To make it work, however, you need to know either the default formula-language syntax used in Crystal Reports or the BASIC language syntax. You can type a formula by hand or build it up by selecting fields, functions, and operators from the panes in the top half of the Editor. There is, however, an easier way to get some of the features of Format Formula Editor — without learning formula syntax: Use Highlighting Expert, coming up next.

Highlighting Expert Creates Emphasis

Highlighting Expert is one of the easiest-to-use formatting tools in the Crystal Reports repertoire. Compared to Format Formula Expert, Highlighting Expert has limited flexibility, but you could have used it instead of a formula to get the same red group total in the preceding section. Highlighting Expert operates only on number and currency fields; Format Formula Editor works on any type of field.

To see Highlighting Expert in action, follow these steps:

1. **Click the Design tab of the Customer Report shown in Figure 8-8.**

2. **In the Group Footer section, right-click the** Sum of Orders.Order Amount **field and choose Highlighting Expert.**

   The Highlighting Expert dialog box appears, as shown in Figure 8-9.

   You can change the font color, the background color, or the border of the selected item. For this example, you'll put a single-line box around all state or district order totals that are equal to or greater than $5,000.

3. **Click the New button.**

4. **In the Value of This Field box, select** is greater than or equal to. **In the text box below Value of, enter** $5000.00.

5. **In the Border box, select Single box.**

   The Highlighting Expert dialog box now appears as shown in Figure 8-10.

6. **Click the OK button.**

   These settings produce the report shown in Figure 8-11. The total for Distrito Federal is enclosed in a box because its value is greater than $5,000. The other group totals are unchanged.

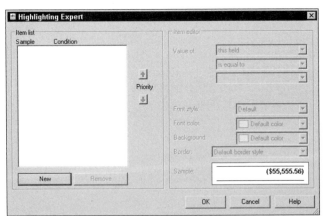

Figure 8-9:
Highlighting
Expert
dialog box.

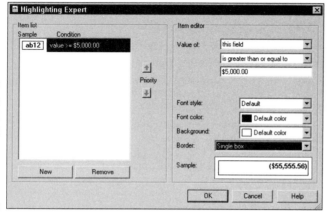

Figure 8-10:
Highlighting
Expert
dialog
box with
formatting
condition.

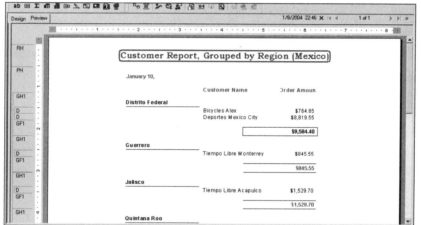

Figure 8-11:
Report
based on
modification
done with
Highlighting
Expert.

Adding Pictures to a Report

You can add bitmapped graphic images to a report to further enhance its
visual appeal. To add a picture to your report, follow these steps:

1. **In the Insert Tools toolbar, click the Insert a Picture from a File icon.**

   A dialog box appears, from which you can select the image file that you
   want to add to the report.

2. **Select the appropriate image file.**

   On the report, a rectangle appears that you can move around with the
   mouse.

3. **Position the rectangle where you want the image to be located, and then click.**

    The image appears on the report. Figure 8-12 shows the result of placing a Mexican flag in the report.

4. **Save the report as Customer Orders by State or District (Mexico).**

You now have a report fit for the eyes of a Vice President of Sales!

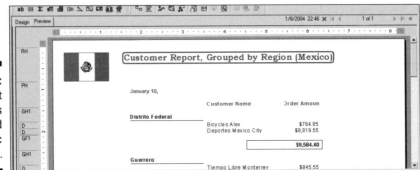

Figure 8-12: The report includes bitmapped graphic images.

A Trick for Aligning Preprinted Forms

Preprinted forms are designed to be filled out by hand or run through a sprocket-fed line printer. With a laser printer or inkjet printer, it's devilishly hard to line up text with the lines and boxes on the form that are supposed to hold that text. Most people are likelier to have a laser printer or an inkjet printer than a sprocket-fed printer these days, so alignment can be a problem.

Crystal Reports offers a clever solution to aligning text to preprinted forms. Because a report can have both text and graphical elements, and one can overlie the other, you can align text perfectly to a preprinted form by following a few simple steps involving a scanner:

1. **Scan the preprinted form and save it as a bitmapped file.**

2. **Place the scanned form in the Page Header section of the report as a bitmap.**

3. **Click to add a check mark to the Underlay Following Sections property on Section Expert's Common tab.**

4. **Add text fields in the appropriate places of the Details section to line up with the form.**

5. **Both the form and the data print out in one operation.**

Adding Text from a File

Crystal Reports is primarily designed to take data from a database, process it, format it, and then display it to the user. In addition, however, it can display blocks of text stored in document files.

To insert a block of text into a report, follow these steps:

1. **Create a text object and insert it into the report at the location where you want the text to appear.**

2. **Right-click the object and choose Insert from File.**

    An Open dialog box appears, listing files in whatever directory was accessed last.

3. **Change to the directory that has the file you want to insert (if necessary), and then specify the file in the File Name field of the Open dialog box that appears.**

4. **Click the Open button.**

    The text file is transferred to the text object.

Formatting Options

Report developers can customize the development environment by choosing File⇨Options. The Options dialog box appears, as shown in Figure 8-13.

The Options dialog box has eight tabs, with the Layout tab on top by default. As you can see in Figure 8-13, you can change many options. They all have to do with what gets displayed and how it gets displayed. Most options are self-explanatory. Following is a quick rundown of each tab:

✔ The Layout tab enables you to select what will be displayed on the work surface in both Design and Preview modes.

✔ The Database tab, which is a little more interesting, can be used to view system's tables and any synonyms or stored procedures that the database may have. You can look for approximate matches in table names, and decide how tables and fields are listed. The default values of the Advanced Options, shown in Figure 8-14, are better left as they are unless you have a compelling reason to change them.

✔ With the Editors tab, you can customize the formatting options for the text you create with any of the editors, such as the Formula Editor.

✔ The Data Source Defaults tab enables you to specify not only where to look for databases, but also how to recognize them.

✔ The Reporting tab gives you the opportunity to set a number of miscellaneous options.

✔ The Smart Tag tab enables you to define the Web server and viewing page you want to use when selecting Office XP smart tags for Crystal report objects.

✔ The Fonts tab allows you to set default fonts for fields, charts, and text objects.

✔ With the Fields tab, you can customize the formats of the various field types.

Crystal Reports' broad array of formatting options gives report developers a lot of latitude in the way their reports present information. Those options make the developer's job of communicating much easier. However, Crystal Reports offers other modes of communication that are just as effective. One of the most powerful is Crystal Reports' charting capability, which is the subject of Chapter 15.

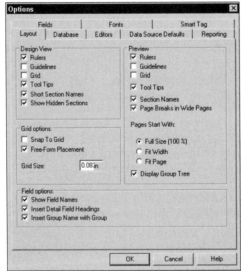

Figure 8-13:
Options
dialog box,
with Layout
tab selected.

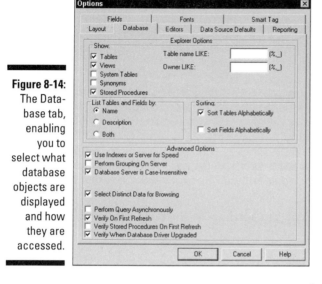

Figure 8-14:
The Data-
base tab,
enabling
you to
select what
database
objects are
displayed
and how
they are
accessed.

Special Fields Contain Report Metadata

Metadata is data about data. Report Metadata is descriptive data about a report. Crystal Reports enables you to include report metadata within the report that the metadata is describing. For many kinds of reports, there are metadata items that you might want to include in the report itself. For example, readers might want to know the date on which the data in the report was last refreshed. They might want to know the name of the author of the report. You can display such things in your reports as special fields — which are accessible from the Special Fields list in the Field Explorer. Well over a dozen special fields are available in the list, each holding pertinent information about the report. You can drag them onto your report and drop them wherever you like.

Raising a Red Flag with Report Alerts

Sometimes the data in a report indicates a condition that requires urgent attention on the part of the report reader. The urgency may not be immediately obvious just from perusing the report. To make sure the message gets across, Crystal Reports provides the Report Alerts facility.

Report Alerts are custom messages that appear when certain conditions are met by data in the report. A Report Alert may merely inform the reader of the condition, or it may specify a course of action to take.

You can create a Report Alert by entering a formula, as described in Chapter 11, using the Formula Workshop. The formula evaluates conditions that you specify. If the overall condition evaluates to TRUE, the alert is triggered and its message is displayed. The message may be a text string, either by itself or combined with one or more report fields.

As an example, suppose Xtreme's sales manager wants to be alerted whenever a customer in Mexico orders more than $5,000 worth of merchandise. A Report Alert added to the Customer Orders by State or District (Mexico) report will do the job. Here's how to add it:

1. **With the target report active, select Report⇨Alerts from the main menu, and from the submenu that appears, click Create or Modify Alerts.**

   The Create Alerts dialog box appears, as shown in Figure 8-15.

Figure 8-15: Create Alerts dialog box lists alerts by name and tells whether they are enabled or disabled.

2. **Click the New button to display the Create Alert dialog box (different from the Create Alerts dialog box).**

3. **In the** Name **field of the Create Alert dialog box, enter** BonusTime.

4. **Click the Formula (x+2) button to the right of the Message Field to display the alert Message Formula Editor version of the Formula Workshop.**

   You will now build a formula to create the message that will be displayed.

5. **From the Report Fields pane, drag down** Customer.Customer Name, **and drop it in the upper-left corner of the formula area that fills the lower half of the Workshop.**

6. **Type a space, a plus sign, and then another space to the right of the** Customer.Customer Name **field in the formula area.**

7. **To the right of the plus sign and space, type the text string,** " has made a BIG order!"

   Be sure to include the double quotes in the string that you type. The formula should appear as shown in Figure 8-16.

Figure 8-16:
Report Alert message as constructed by a formula.

8. **Click the Save and Close button to return to the Create Alert dialog box.**

9. **In the Create Alert dialog box, click the Condition button.**

   The Alert Condition Formula Editor version of the Formula Workshop appears. Now you must specify what condition must occur that will trigger the display of this Report Alert.

10. **From the Report Fields pane, drag the** Orders.Order Amount **field down into the formula area and drop it in the upper-left corner.**

11. **In the Operators pane, expand the Comparisons node and drag the Greater than operator down. Drop it just to the right of the** Orders. Order Amount **field.**

12. **To the right of the Greater Than symbol, type** 5000.

   This produces the formula shown in Figure 8-17.

Figure 8-17:
Condition formula for Orders that exceed $5,000.

13. Click Save and Close to once again return to the Create Alert dialog box.

14. Ensure that the Enabled condition is checked, then click OK.

This puts your new Report Alert into the Create Alerts dialog box shown in Figure 8-18.

15. Click the Close button to return to your report.

Figure 8-18:
The
BonusTime
alert is
present and
enabled.

That's how you create a Report Alert. To see it in action, just click the Refresh icon in the Standard toolbar. If any of the customers have orders that exceed $5,000, a Report Alert will pop up to let you know. Figure 8-19 shows what one looks like.

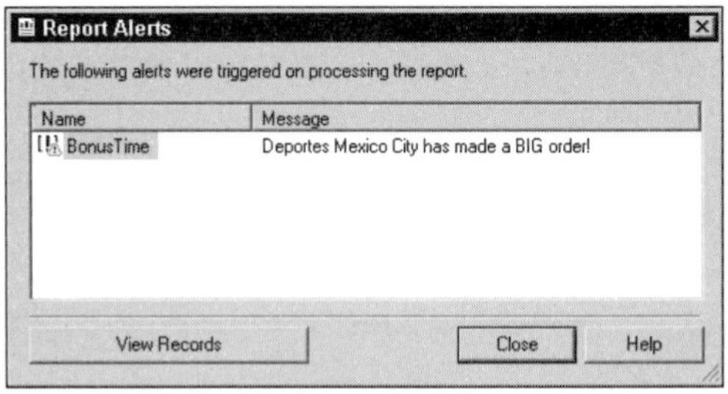

Figure 8-19:
BonusTime
Report Alert,
showing a
customer
whose order
exceeds
$5,000.

You can click the View Records button if you want to see exactly how big the order total is.

Report Templates Save Time and Effort

Crystal Reports makes the task of report creation much easier than it would be without such a powerful tool. However, it still takes considerable thought and work to come up with reports that are well proportioned, presented with an attractive choice of fonts, drawing elements, colors, and layout. If you make that investment in time for one report, it would be nice if you could recycle the work on a similar report later. Not only can such recycling of general report features save you time and effort, it creates a visual consistency from one report to the next that conveys professionalism. You can achieve that consistency and save that time and effort by using templates.

What's a template?

A *template* is an existing report, complete with formatting, that you can use as a starting point for a new report that you create. You don't have to create the new report from scratch; you have to change only the things that are different between the template report and the new report you are creating. Sometimes you don't have to change anything. Apply the template as the last step in your report creation process and you are finished, with a polished, professional report in a fraction of the time it would normally take to create one.

How do you use a template in a report?

There are several ways to apply a template to a report. They are:

- ✔ In the process of creating your report, select a template from the Template view in the Standard Report Creation Wizard.

- ✔ Select a template using the Template Expert after you have created your report.

- ✔ Use an existing report as a template for your new report. Once you use a report as a template, it is added to the list of available templates for possible use in the future.

- ✔ Create a report specifically for use as a template. It can serve as a formatted skeleton for a variety of reports you build in the future.

Applying a template to an existing report

Applying a template to an already existing report is easy. To see just how easy, look again at the Big Orders report in Chapter 5. It is shown in Figure 5-17 (with a $5,000 lower limit) and again here in Figure 8-20 (with a $9,000 lower limit).

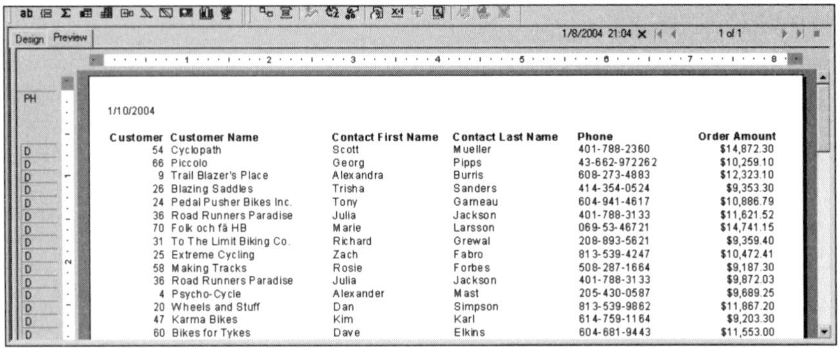

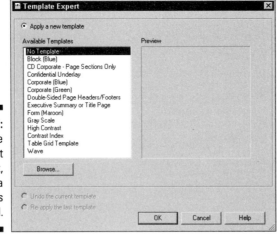

Figure 8-20: Big Orders report, run with a $9,000 lower limit.

It looks pretty plain. You can spruce it up with one of the Crystal Reports standard templates. Here's how:

1. **Click the Template Expert in the Expert Tools toolbar.**

   This launches the Template Expert shown in Figure 8-21.

Figure 8-21: Template Expert dialog box, before a template is selected.

2. In the Available Templates pane, select Block (Blue), then Click OK.

The Template Expert disappears, and after a few seconds, the Block Sample formatting is applied to your report. In this example, the result looks like Figure 8-22.

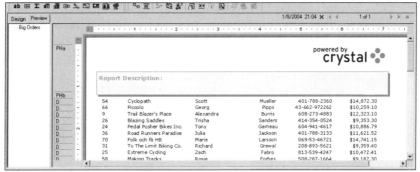

Figure 8-22: Big Orders report with Block Sample (Blue) formatting applied.

In this case, the template's headings have overridden the original headings. The detail rows are unchanged. If the formatting that the template has given you is close to what you want, but it's not exactly perfect, you can now change to design mode and make any needed changes. This should be much less work than would be needed to apply all the formatting from scratch.

Applying a template to a report you're creating

When you create a report, using the Standard Report Creation Wizard, the wizard steps you through a series of views:

- First comes the Data view, where you select tables to include in your report.

- Second comes the Links view (if you're including more than one table), where you can specify how the tables are linked to each other.

- Third comes the Fields view, where you specify which fields from the selected tables you're going to use.

- Fourth, you specify Grouping, which separates records into groups in the report (for example, grouping customers by country).

✔ Fifth, you specify any summaries that you want to include in the report, such as totals or averages of numerical data.

✔ Sixth in Group Sorting view, you specify the order in which you want groups to be sorted.

✔ Seventh in Chart view, you specify what kind of chart you want to create to give a graphical representation of your data.

✔ Eighth, in Record Selection view, you can filter out records that you don't want, so that you can concentrate on the records that you do want.

✔ Ninth and finally, you specify the Template you want to use from the Template view of the Standard Report Creation Wizard. This wizard, shown in Figure 8-23, looks very similar to the Template Expert shown in Figure 8-21. This is not surprising because they serve similar purposes.

If some of the listed views aren't relevant, they don't appear, depending on the choices you've made.

Figure 8-23: Standard Report Creation Wizard's Template view, showing the templates currently available for use in a report.

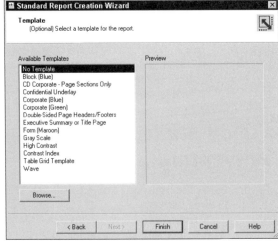

Part III
Advanced Report Types and Features

The 5th Wave   By Rich Tennant

"I'm not sure — I like the mutual funds with rotating dollar signs although the dancing stocks and bonds look good too."

In this part . . .

This part introduces you to the major leagues of report creation. With the knowledge you gain here, you'll be able to produce reports that are the ultimate in sophistication. You uncover ways to select the data that your report will include and sort it for maximum understandability. You make reports that use formulas and almost think for themselves. Cross-tab reports expose correlations in your data. OLE enables you to include data from nontraditional data sources. OLAP introduces you to multidimensional reporting. Charts and graphs tell your story in a way that words can't express.

Chapter 9

Displaying Your Favorite Hit Parade with Group Sort

An old saying in the sales business is that you get 80 percent of your sales from 20 percent of your customers. It's called the Pareto Principle or the 80/20 rule, and it's not restricted to sales. Some people or things are more productive than others doing the same work. If you identify the most productive salespeople, machinery, or whatever, you can analyze the factors that make them so effective and perhaps apply what you learn to increase productivity overall.

In Chapter 6, I cover how to sort records and group them. A valuable extension of these capabilities is producing a report that shows only the top producers. In this chapter, you find out how to do just that.

Sorting Groups Based on Performance

In Chapter 6, I discuss the creation of a report for Xtreme Mountain Bikes that shows the dollar totals of individual sales orders, sorts the orders by customer name, groups records by state, and sorts the groups by state. That report (shown back in Figure 6-13) isn't very helpful to the Vice President of Sales, who is trying to get a feel for which customers are buying the most.

Summary fields do more than just compute sums

The Insert Summary dialog box in Figure 9-6 specifies the `Sum` summary. Many other summary functions appear in the pull-down list, some of which you might want to use, depending on your application.

For numeric fields, the summary options are as follows: `Sum; Average; Sample variance; Sample standard deviation; Maximum; Minimum; Count; Distinct count; Correlation with; Covariance with; Median; Mode; Nth largest; Nth smallest; Nth` `most frequent; Pth percentile; Population variance; Population standard deviation; Weighted average with.`

For text fields, you choose from a smaller range of possibilities: `Maximum; Minimum; Count; Distinct count; Mode; Nth largest; Nth smallest; Nth most frequent.`

These choices give you just about any type of summary you'd ever want.

Adding *drill-down* capability to the report (refer to Figure 6-14 for a look) shows which states are responsible for the most sales (on a percentage basis) but doesn't show which customers are the best. To get the information you want, in the form that's easiest to understand, a Top N report is probably your best choice. To build one, follow these steps:

1. **Choose File⇨New. In Crystal Reports Gallery, select Standard, and then click OK.**

   The Standard Report Creation Wizard appears.

2. **Find the** `xtreme` **database, and then select the** `Customer` **and** `Orders` **tables, as shown in Figure 9-1.**

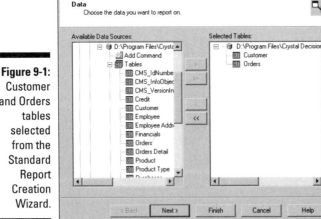

Figure 9-1: Customer and Orders tables selected from the Standard Report Creation Wizard.

3. **Click Next to display the Link view.**

   You see the Customer table connected to the `Orders` table by the `Customer ID` field.

4. **Click Next to display the Fields view.**

5. **Move** `Customer Name`, `Region`, **and** `Order Amount` **to the Fields to Display pane.**

6. **Click Next to display the Grouping view.**

   The Vice President of Sales wants to list the five top U.S. customers, along with their states and the total amount of their orders. The easy way to do this is to group the records by `Customer ID`, hide order detail, sort by the sum of the order amount for each customer, and include the top five customers in the report.

7. **Move** `Customer.Customer Name` **to the Group By pane and specify descending order.**

   This puts the customer with the highest total first.

8. **Click Next to display the Summaries view.**

9. **In the Summarized Fields pane, specify** `Sum of Orders.Order Amount`. **In the pull-down list below that pane, specify Sum.**

10. **Click Next to display the Group Sorting view, which is shown in Figure 9-2.**

11. **Select Top 5 Groups. In the Comparing Summary Values for the Top or Bottom Groups pull-down list, select** `Sum of Orders.Order Amount`.

12. **Click Next to display the Chart view, and then click Next again to display the Record Selection view.**

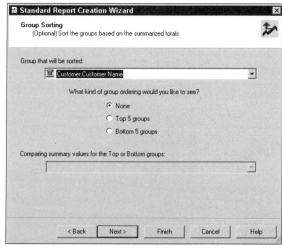

Figure 9-2:
Group
Sorting view
of the
Standard
Report
Creation
Wizard,
showing the
Top 5 Groups
option.

13. You're interested in only U.S. sales at present, so fill out the Record Selection view, as shown in Figure 9-3.

Figure 9-3:
Record Selection view of the Standard Report Creation Wizard with USA selected.

14. Click Next to display the Template view.

15. Select a template for the report.

To follow along with the example, select the Block (Blue) template. (I cover templates in Chapter 8.)

16. Click the Finish button.

Crystal Reports builds your report and it appears on-screen, as shown in Figure 9-4.

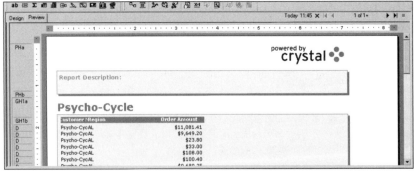

Figure 9-4:
Top Five USA Customers report, as created by the Standard Report Creation Wizard.

It's not exactly what the Vice President of Sales had in mind. You need to make the following adjustments:

- ✔ Give the report a title.
- ✔ Delete the *Powered by Crystal* line, which appears at the top of every page.
- ✔ Change the Region column heading to State, and center the state data under it.
- ✔ Delete the repeated customer name entries in the detail lines.
- ✔ Space the columns out horizontally.
- ✔ Hide the individual entries for each order.
- ✔ Display the sum of the orders for each displayed customer.

To make the needed adjustments, follow these steps:

1. **Switch to Design mode.**

2. **Right-click the Powered by Crystal graphic in the page header and choose Cut.**

3. **On the Insert Tools toolbar, click the Insert Text Object icon, and drag the rectangular placement frame to the page header area above the shaded rectangle that says *Report Description*.**

4. **Type** Top Five USA Customers **inside the newly placed text field.**

5. **Expand the text field and center it. Increase the font size of the text to 22 to make the heading easier to read.**

6. **In the Report Description area, drag a text object from the Insert Tools toolbar to the line after the words *Report Description*.**

7. **In the text object, type** The Top Five USA Customers.

   Things are going well.

8. **Change the Region column heading to State and center the two-character state abbreviations below it.**

   Make the change to the column heading in group header. To center the state abbreviation, click the Region field in the Details section, and then click the Align Center icon on the Formatting toolbar.

9. **Spread out the group headers and details columns for State and Order Amount on the page, while eliminating the Customer Name column.**

   Because the customer name appears in the group header, there is no need to repeat it in the detail area.

   At this point, the report looks like Figure 9-5.

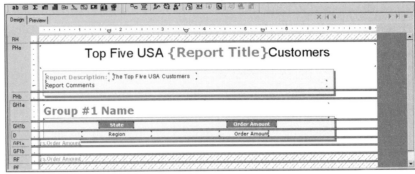

Figure 9-5:
The page
header,
column
headers,
and details
lines have
been
modified.

The next thing to do is display a group total in the Group Footer section:

1. **Pull down the lower boundary of the shaded rectangle drawing object from Group Footer 1a to Group Footer 1b.**

   This enables you to put a group sum lower in the Group Footer 1a space.

2. **Drag the** `Group Sum` **field to the bottom edge of the Group Footer 1a space.**

3. **Click the Insert Summary icon.**

   The Insert Summary dialog box appears.

4. **Make the selections as shown in Figure 9-6.**

   These selections are: summarize the `Orders.Order Amount` field; use the Sum summary operator; and choose Group #1 for the summary location.

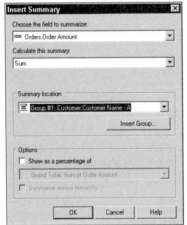

Figure 9-6:
The Insert
Summary
dialog box
specifies the
summariza-
tion of Order
Amount for
each group.

5. Click OK.

Crystal Reports displays the sum field in the appropriate place in the Group Footer 1a section, below the Order Amount heading.

The next thing you might want to do to produce a summary report for a top executive is to hide all the detail lines:

1. Right-click in the area to the right of the Details section and choose Hide (Drill-Down OK).

The report now looks like Figure 9-7. This is still not quite what you want. The customer name is bigger and bolder than it needs to be for a one-line entry. The state information has been hidden, and you still have only one customer per page. These defects are easy to correct.

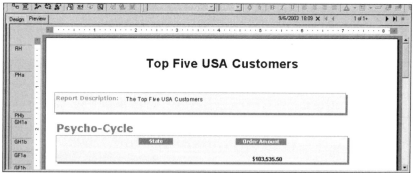

Figure 9-7:
Report with details hidden.

2. Click the Insert Summary icon.

The Insert Summary dialog box appears.

3. Make the selections as shown in Figure 9-8.

These selections are as follows:

- Summarize the Customer.Customer Name field.
- Use the Maximum summary operator.
- Choose Group #1 for the summary location.

Crystal Reports automatically places the Customer Name field in the appropriate place in the Group Footer 1a section, below the Customer Name heading. You may have to move the summary vertically to line it up with the numerical sum on the right side of the report.

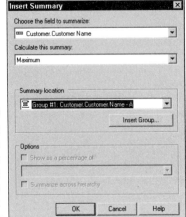

Figure 9-8:
Putting the
Customer
Name in
the Group
Footer.

4. **Repeat Step 3 for the** Customer.Region **field to insert it below the State heading.**

5. **With the Region still selected, click the Align Center icon to center the state abbreviation below the** State **heading.**

6. **Delete the** Customer.Customer Name **field from Group Header 1a.**

   This leaves each group with all the information you want and none of the extra stuff you don't want to display.

Now all you have to do is remove the page breaks between groups. The page breaks were set by a formula in the Group Footer #1 specification. To delete the formula, follow these steps:

1. **Right-click in the area to the left of the Group Footer #1a section and choose Section Expert.**

   The Section Expert dialog box appears, as shown in Figure 9-9. Group Footer #1a is selected.

2. **Move the Group Footer #1a selection up one row to Group Footer #1.**

   Note that for the Group Footer #1 section, the New Page After box is checked, and a color change in the formula icon for that selection indicates that this action is controlled by a formula.

3. **Click the formula icon.**

   Formula Format Editor appears, as shown in Figure 9-10.

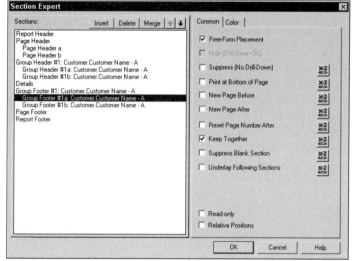

Figure 9-9:
You want
to remove
page breaks
between
groups.

Figure 9-10:
You want to
delete this
formula.

4. **Delete the** `not onlastrecord` **formula (in the lower part of the screen).**

5. **Click the Save and Close icon.**

6. **Uncheck the New Page After box, and then click OK.**

   This gives you the five top customers, their states, and the amount each has purchased, as shown in Figure 9-11.

7. **Save this report as** `Top5USAfinal.rpt`.

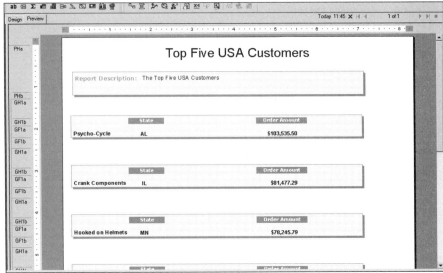

Figure 9-11:
The
completed
report.

Going with the Percentages

Sometimes it's more helpful to know who is responsible for the largest *percentage* of an organization's total sales rather than the specific dollar amount. The Group Sorting screen of the Standard Report Creation Wizard handles summaries expressed as percentages as well as straight numbers. You could build a report from scratch, similar to the one you built in the preceding section, by following most of the same steps, with just a slight difference at the summarization step.

Rather than going through all that again here, though, you can modify the completed report (refer to Figure 9-11) to display percentages rather than group totals. Just follow these steps:

1. **In Design mode, right-click the** Sum of Orders.Order Amount **field in the Group Footer #1a section.**

   The menu shown in Figure 9-12 appears.

2. **Choose Edit Summary.**

   The Edit Summary dialog box appears.

3. **Select the** Orders.Order Amount **field to summarize; calculate the** Sum **summary, and select the box to the left of** Show as a Percentage of.

   The drop-down list below the Show as Percentage of line holds the value you want (Grand Total: Sum of Order Amount).

Figure 9-12:
Menu for
Orders.
Order
Amount
field.

Field: Sum of Orders.Order Amount
Format Field...
Format Painter
Edit Summary...
Highlighting Expert...
Select Expert...
Move ▶
Size and Position...
Cut
Copy
Paste
Delete
Cancel Menu

4. Click OK.

Now when you switch to Preview mode, you see the report shown in Figure
9-13. The five top customers are listed along with their percentage of Xtreme's
total sales. This report tells you something that you didn't get from the previous report: The top five customers combined account for less than 15 percent
of Xtreme's orders. Looks like Xtreme is in the healthy position of not depending too much on a small number of customers. Sales volume is distributed
over a large customer base.

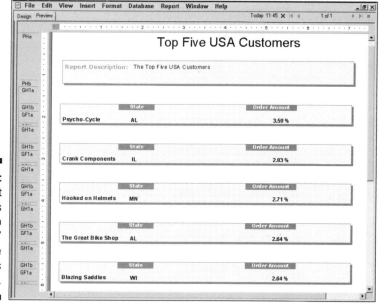

Figure 9-13:
This report
shows
the top
customers'
percentage
of Xtreme's
total orders.

What if you want the top seventeen instead of the top five?

The group sort used here to produce the latest reports happened to ask for the top five customers. Okay, that's suspiciously convenient; the Standard Report Creation Wizard gives you the option of selecting the top five or bottom five — but not the top ten, top seventeen, and so on. If you want your report to return some number of groups other than five, use Group Sort Expert.

 When you click the Group Sort Expert icon on the Expert Tools toolbar, the Group Sort Expert dialog box appears, as shown in Figure 9-14.

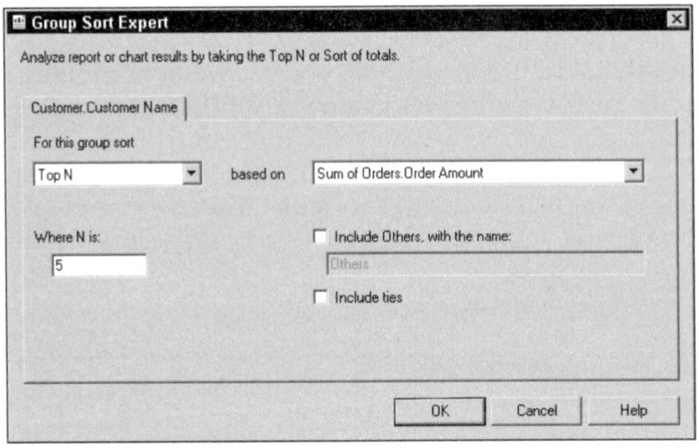

Figure 9-14: You can sort in several ways.

The default values for the current report are shown. The type of sort is Top N, based on Sum of Orders.Order Amount, where N is 5. If you want to see the percentage sales of the top 17 customers instead of the top 5, just replace the 5 with a **17** in the Where N Is box, and then click OK. The only task that remains to make this a complete report is to change the references to *Five* in the page header to *Seventeen*. Figure 9-15 shows the result.

Hmmm. Maybe you're not finished after all. Now the report extends over two pages, and it seems redundant to repeat column headings above each customer line. Also, the space between records is excessive. You can tighten up the report as follows:

1. **In Design mode, right-click the area to the left of Page Header b and choose Insert Section Below.**

One way to tighten up your report is to move the column headings from the Group Heading section to the Page Heading section. This means you have to expand the Page Heading section by adding a new subsection, in this case, Page Header c.

2. **Drag the column headings up from Group Header 1b to Page Header c, placing them at the top of the Page Header c space.**

3. **Drag the bottom of the section up to the bottom of the column headings.**

4. **Drag the bottom of the shaded box Drawing Object that provides the background color down into the Page Footer section.**

5. **Drag the top of the box down to the bottom of the Group Header b section.**

6. **Right-click in the area to the left of Group Header a to display the pop-up shortcut menu, and then use it to suppress Group Header a.**

This eliminates Group Header a, which is doing nothing but taking up space. At this point, the report looks like Figure 9-16.

7. **Save the report as Top17USA.**

Figure 9-15: Top Seventeen report.

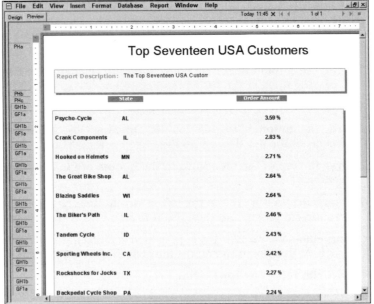

Figure 9-16:
The
revised Top
Seventeen
report.

A Choice of Group Sorts

You have probably guessed from what you have seen so far, that everything you can do for the top performers, you can also do for the bottom. Take a closer look at the Group Sort Expert dialog box. Figure 9-17 shows it with the group sort list pulled down. The options on this menu are No Sort, All, Top N, Bottom N, Top Percentage, and Bottom Percentage.

You have already seen what Top N does. Bottom N does the same thing, but for the tail-enders rather than the leaders. The other four options require a little explanation.

The No Sort option does what it says: nothing. It leaves the lines of the report in the order in which the corresponding groups appear in the database. You might wonder why this option even exists. One reason might be that you want to build a new report based on an existing one, but the existing report is sorted. If you want your new report to reflect the order of the records in the database rather than the sort order of the old report, one way to get what you want is to use the No Sort option.

The All option sorts and displays all the groups, not restricting the display to any given number. A report built according to this option would contain all the data of a Top N report, plus all the data of a Bottom N report, plus data on all the groups not included in either of those.

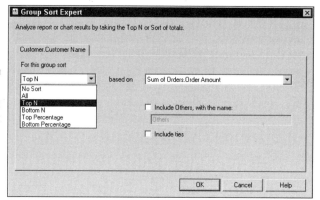

Figure 9-17:
Group Sort
Expert
dialog box,
showing
group
sort list.

With the Top Percentage group sort, you specify the top percentage that you want to see in the report. For example, if you wanted to see whether the 80/20 rule applies to your organization, specify a Top Percentage group sort, and enter **80** in the Where Percentage Is box. If you have, for example, 90 customers, the 80/20 rule holds if the report lists about 18 customers (representing 20 percent of the total).

To report on the customers who order the least amount of product, use the Bottom Percentage group sort. For Xtreme Mountain Bikes, the companies in this report need help or should be replaced by companies that can do a better job.

Troubleshooting Group Sort Problems

Because Group Sort Expert walks you through the process of sorting and summarizing group data, there aren't many ways for you to get into trouble. However, you should keep a few things in mind when adding group sort capability to a report:

- ✔ You can't perform a Top N, Bottom N, or other type of group sort unless your report contains a summary value. If you have trouble creating a Top N or Bottom N report, make sure the sort is based on a summary value.

- ✔ Creating a subtotal for a group may not work if the report data is drawn from tables linked in a one-to-many relationship. For such a case, you may have to use a running total instead of a subtotal. If you're not getting the summary values you want, and your report is drawing data from multiple tables, check to see whether the tables have a one-to-many relationship. If such a relationship exists, try using a running total rather than a subtotal for each group. (Chapter 6 explains the use of running totals.)

✔ Sometimes you'll want to shrink the size of a section by dragging up its lower boundary. If you find that the section will shrink only so much and no more, an invisible object might be in the section. You can't shrink a section past the border of an object that the section contains, even if you can't see the object. Check carefully to see whether the border of a drawing object or an empty text object is hidden under the boundary line that you're trying to drag up.

Chapter 10

Making Correlations with Cross-Tab Reports

*F*or some people, a summarization of one sort or another is far more valuable than reams of detailed data. However, reports with summaries in group footers or the report footer don't always display summaries in a form that is good for comprehension and decision-making. In some of these cases, a *cross-tab* object can present the data in a form that's both easy to understand and capable of conveying the *significance* of the data.

The main advantage of a cross-tab is that it can put multiple summaries together in a compact form. You can draw inferences from a single cross-tab on a single page, that displays separate summaries that are nonetheless related.

Creating a Cross-Tab Object to Summarize All Report Data

Suppose that the Sales Manager at Xtreme Mountain Bikes would like to see how the various product categories are contributing to total sales volume in Canada. A cross-tab report is ideal for presenting that information in a way that can be easily viewed and comprehended. Follow these steps:

1. **In Crystal Reports Gallery, select Cross-Tab, and then click OK.**

   Cross Tab Report Creation Wizard appears.

2. **Select the** `Customer, Orders, Orders Detail, Product,` **and** `Product Type` **tables from the** `xtreme` **database.**

3. **Move the tables to the Selected Tables pane.**

4. **Click Next to display the Link view.**

   The display should show the five tables connected to each other by the fields that they have in common.

5. **Click Next to display the Cross-Tab Report Creation Wizard, which is shown in Figure 10-1.**

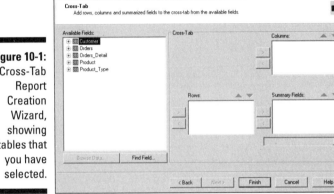

Figure 10-1:
Cross-Tab
Report
Creation
Wizard,
showing
tables that
you have
selected.

6. **In the Available Fields pane, expand the Customer node and select Region. Then click the right-facing arrow to the left of the Rows pane.**

   Each row of the cross-tab now corresponds to a region (in this case, a province of Canada).

7. **In the Available Fields pane, expand the Product_Type node, and drag Product Type Name to the Columns pane.**

   Each column of the cross-tab now corresponds to a product type.

To get the report to make the specific summaries you want, follow these steps:

1. **In the Available Fields pane, expand the Orders node. Drag Order Amount to the Summary Fields pane.**

   The default value in the pull-down list below the Summary Fields pane displays `Sum`, which is the type of summary you want for this report.

2. **Click Next to display the Chart view.**

   You can add a bar, line, or pie chart to the report, if you want.

3. **Select Bar Chart to check what it will give you.**

When you select a chart type, the wizard suggests a chart title that you can override if you want. It also asks that you verify several other assumptions it has made about what you want the chart to show.

4. Change the Chart Title to Sales by Province and Product Type, as shown in Figure 10-2.

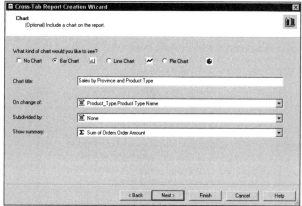

Figure 10-2:
Chart view
of Cross-
Tab Report
Creation
Wizard, with
descriptive
chart title.

5. Click Next to display the Record Selection view.

For this report, you want to deal with records only from Canadian customers.

6. In the Available Fields pane, expand the Customer node and move Country to the Filter Fields pane. In the pull-down lists that appear below the Filter Fields pane, select is equal to **and** Canada.

7. Click Next to display the Grid Style view, which is shown in Figure 10-3.

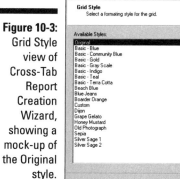

Figure 10-3:
Grid Style
view of
Cross-Tab
Report
Creation
Wizard,
showing a
mock-up of
the Original
style.

A good assortment of styles is available, some more appropriate than others for various kinds of reports.

8. **Retain the Original style, and then click the Finish button.**

The report is displayed in Preview mode. The upper part of the report is shown in Figure 10-4.

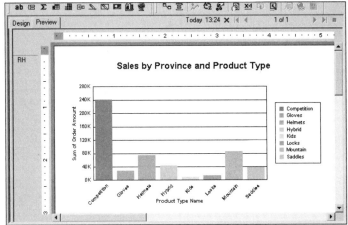

Figure 10-4:
The top of the cross-tab report.

This chart should be of interest to the Sales Manager. It shows that competition bikes are outselling mountain bikes by a factor of almost three to one. It also shows that Xtreme is deriving almost as much revenue from the sale of helmets as it is from the sale of mountain bikes. This kind of information can be a great help to decision-makers.

Moving down the page to the actual cross-tab report shown in Figure 10-5, you can see that most sales are coming from British Columbia. This information might also be important to the Sales Manager.

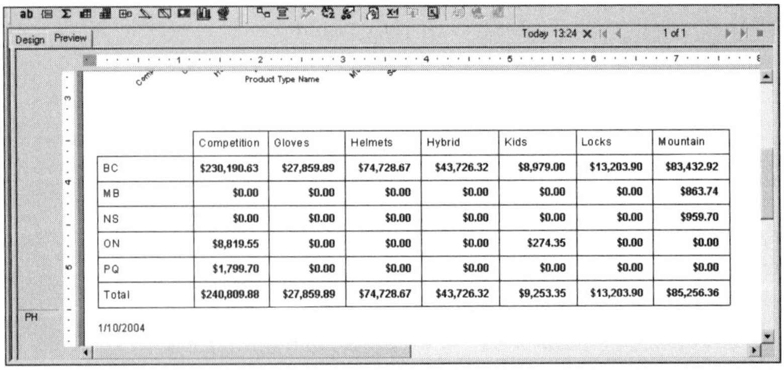

Figure 10-5:
Main part of the cross-tab report.

	Competition	Gloves	Helmets	Hybrid	Kids	Locks	Mountain
BC	$230,190.63	$27,859.89	$74,728.67	$43,726.32	$8,979.00	$13,203.90	$83,432.92
MB	$0.00	$0.00	$0.00	$0.00	$0.00	$0.00	$863.74
NS	$0.00	$0.00	$0.00	$0.00	$0.00	$0.00	$959.70
ON	$8,819.55	$0.00	$0.00	$0.00	$274.35	$0.00	$0.00
PQ	$1,799.70	$0.00	$0.00	$0.00	$0.00	$0.00	$0.00
Total	$240,809.88	$27,859.89	$74,728.67	$43,726.32	$9,253.35	$13,203.90	$85,256.36

1/10/2004

The overall totals for each province are off the screen on the right edge of the report, with a grand total in the bottom-right corner. With this cross-tab object and its accompanying chart, the manager can quickly see the relevant facts and make decisions based on those facts.

9. **Save the report.**

   For this example, save the report as `Sales by Province`. You'll use this report later.

Summarizing the Contents of a Group with a Cross-Tab

The section in which a cross-tab object is located in a report is related to the data it contains. For example, if the cross-tab should include all the data in the database for customers in Canada, as in the preceding section, the cross-tab must be located in either the report header or the report footer. This makes sense — the displayed data is a summary of data from all the Canadian provinces, so it must appear in a report section that encompasses data from all those provinces.

It's also possible to create individual cross-tab objects for each group in a report. For example, you could create a report similar to the preceding one, but with summaries for each province rather than one overall summary for all of Canada. Follow these steps:

1. **In Crystal Reports Gallery, select Standard and then click OK.**

   Because there's more to this report than just a cross-tab, you use the Standard Report Creation Wizard (rather than Cross-Tab Wizard) to create the report.

2. **Place the Customer, Orders, Orders Detail, Product, and Product Type tables in the Selected Tables pane.**

3. **Click Next to display the Link view.**

   The links between these tables are straightforward, so the wizard has assumed them correctly.

4. **Click Next to display the Fields view.**

   Your report won't include any fields other than those in the cross-tabs, so there's no need to select any fields here.

5. **Click Next to display the Template view.**

   You won't use a template either.

  6. **Leave the default choice (No Template) intact; click Finish.**

     This creates a report with nothing in it but a date and a page number.

To continue building the report:

  1. **Switch to Design mode.**
  2. **Expand the Print Date field in the Page Header to make it big enough to display a date.**
  3. **Add a text field in the Report Header to hold the report title.**

     Here's how:

       a. Right-click the area to the left of the Report Header section and choose Don't Suppress.

       b. On the Insert Tools toolbar, click the Insert Text Object icon and drag the text rectangle down into the Report Header.

       c. Expand the rectangle across the entire width of the page, and then type the report title.

          To follow along with the example, type **Sales of Product** Types by Province.

       d. On the Formatting toolbar, click the Align Center icon to center the text.

       e. Enlarge the font and give the text the Bold attribute to make it more readable.

  4. **On the Expert Tools toolbar, click the Group Expert icon.**

     The Group Expert dialog box appears.

  5. **Expand the Customer node and then move Region over to the Group By pane. Click OK.**

     This creates Group Header 1 and Group Footer 1.

  6. **Drag the bottom boundary of the Group Header section down to make room for the cross-tab you place there.**

  7. **On the Insert Tools toolbar, click the Insert Cross-Tab icon.**

     Cross-Tab Expert appears.

  8. **In the Available Fields pane, drag Customer Name from the** Customer **table to the Rows pane, Product Type Name from the** Product Type **table to the Columns pane, and Order Amount from the** Orders **table to the Summarized Fields pane, as shown in Figure 10-6.**

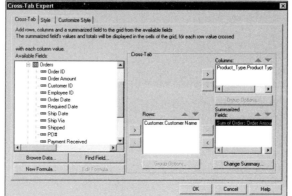

Figure 10-6:
Cross-Tab
Expert,
with fields
selected.

9. **Click OK.**

The dialog box disappears and the cursor becomes a rectangle.

10. **Drag the rectangle from the left edge of the Group Header section to just below the** Group Name **field. Click the mouse button to place the rectangle.**

11. **Switch to Preview mode.**

The report now looks like the one shown in Figure 10-7.

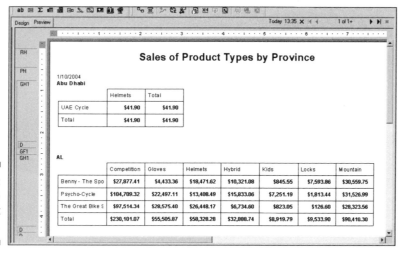

Figure 10-7:
Cross-tab
report, first
version.

You have cross-tabs all right, but they're not the ones you want. The first is for the customer in Abu Dhabi, and the second is for customers in Alabama. There are over 3,000 records. You want the report to show only customers in Canada. To do that, you have to work on the report just a little bit more:

1. **On the Expert Tools toolbar, click the Select Expert icon.**

   The Choose Field dialog box appears.

2. **Expand the Customer node, and then select Country. Click OK.**

   The Select Expert dialog box appears, with the Customer.Country tab on top.

3. **In the pull-down lists, select** is equal to **and** Canada. **Click OK.**

   You want to select only Canadian customers.

4. **When the dialog box asks whether you want to use saved data or refresh the data, click one of the options.**

   In this case, it doesn't matter which you choose because the database has not changed since the last time you ran the report.

   The report, which is shown in Figure 10-8, now contains only Canadian customers, but there's a formatting problem. Below the cross-tab for British Columbia, you can see a large number of detail lines — all empty. Get rid of them so the cross-tabs for all provinces are displayed one below another.

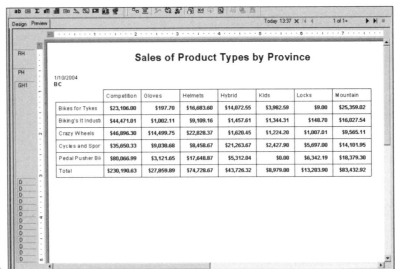

Figure 10-8: Cross-tab report, second version.

5. **Right-click in the area to the left of the Details section and choose Suppress (No Drill Down).**

   The report shown in Figure 10-9 appears. The data for Manitoba is right below that for British Columbia, and the data for Nova Scotia is right below Manitoba's. This is what we want.

6. **Save this report as Sales of Product Types by Province.**

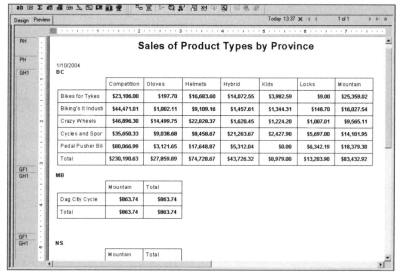

Sales of Product Types by Province

1/10/2004
BC

	Competition	Gloves	Helmets	Hybrid	Kids	Locks	Mountain
Bikes for Tykes	$23,106.00	$197.70	$16,683.60	$14,072.55	$3,982.59	$9.00	$25,359.02
Biking's It Indust	$44,471.01	$1,002.11	$9,109.16	$1,457.61	$1,344.31	$148.70	$16,027.54
Crazy Wheels	$46,896.30	$14,499.75	$22,828.37	$1,620.45	$1,224.20	$1,007.01	$9,565.11
Cycles and Spor	$35,650.33	$9,038.68	$8,458.67	$21,263.67	$2,427.90	$5,697.00	$14,101.95
Pedal Pusher Bi	$80,066.99	$3,121.65	$17,648.87	$5,312.04	$0.00	$6,342.19	$18,379.30
Total	$230,190.63	$27,859.89	$74,728.67	$43,726.32	$8,979.00	$13,203.90	$83,432.92

MB

	Mountain	Total
Dag City Cycle	$863.74	$863.74
Total	$863.74	$863.74

NS

	Mountain	Total

Figure 10-9:
Cross-tab report, final version.

As you saw in the preceding section, you can add cross-tabs to a report header or report footer. This section showed you how to add cross-tabs to group headers or group footers. You can't put a cross-tab in page headers, page footers, or details sections.

Enhancing the Appearance and Readability of a Cross-Tab Object

You can do a number of things to enhance the appearance of a cross-tab report. This section experiments with achieving different effects in the reports you just created.

Changing the width and height of cross-tab cells

The width and height of cross-tab cells are easy to change in Design mode. Merely select the cell you want to change and drag its width or height handle in the direction you want. If you drag a width handle, all the cells in that column are changed along with the cell you're dragging. If you drag a height handle, all the cells in the same row are changed in the same way. This retains size consistency across columns and rows. It's not uncommon to need to enlarge cells to display all that they contain because the default size assigned by the Cross-Tab Wizard is often not adequate.

Formatting entire rows and columns

You can apply formatting to an entire cross-tab object by right-clicking the blank area at the top-left corner of the object and choosing Format Cross-Tab from the menu that pops up. The Format Editor dialog box appears, as shown in Figure 10-10.

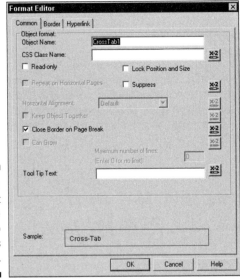

Figure 10-10:
Format entire cross-tab objects here.

You can specify various attributes such as Read-only and Lock Position and Size. By switching to the Border tab, you can also specify refinements such as border lines, drop shadows, and foreground and background colors. Click the Hyperlink tab and you can associate your cross-tab with a Web site, an e-mail address, or a disk file.

Formatting individual fields

To format an individual field, right-click it and choose Format Field. This displays a version of the Format Editor tailored to the data type of the field you're formatting. For example, a currency field displays font options and currency format options in addition to the Common, Border, and Hyperlink options that appear when you're formatting an entire cross-tab.

You can give multiple cross-tab cells the same formatting by selecting them simultaneously using shift-click, and then applying formatting in the same way you would for a single cell.

Suppressing selected cross-tab data

Sometimes the cross-tab objects you create may contain empty rows or columns because no data is available to fill them. For readability, you may want to suppress these empty rows and columns. To do so, right-click the blank area in the upper-left corner of the cross-tab object and choose Cross-Tab Expert. One of the tabs for this Expert is Customize Style. Click that to display the dialog box shown in Figure 10-11.

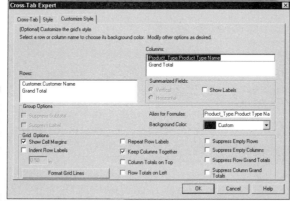

Figure 10-11: Suppress the display of empty rows and columns.

The figure shows that you can suppress not only empty rows and columns, but also row and column grand totals. — even subtotals if your report has them. A variety of other customizations are also available.

Printing cross-tabs that span multiple pages

It's not uncommon for a cross-tab object to be wider or longer than the specified page size. Crystal Reports automatically formats the report on as many extra (extension) pages as needed. Column headings are repeated on all such extra pages. By default, row labels are not repeated. If you want row labels to be repeated on extension pages, select the Repeat Row Labels option on the Customize Style tab of Cross-Tab Expert (refer to Figure 10-11).

Chapter 11

Adding Formulas to Reports

· ·

· ·

*Y*ou can create a report by dragging database fields onto a blank report, adding text and images, and performing a variety of summaries. Such reports are fine for many applications, but sometimes you want to do more than merely summarize data. You might want to process it in some way before displaying it. Crystal Reports has a formula capability that gives you much more latitude in creating the report you want. If you're already a programmer, using formulas won't be tough. If you're not a programmer, you may be surprised to see how soon you can do useful things with formulas.

Formula Overview and Syntax

You can use formulas in a number of ways. One common use is to perform a calculation that modifies the contents of a database field. Suppose you have a database table named `Product` that holds data (including price) on all the products you sell. To calculate a 10 percent discount from your normal price, you could use a formula such as

```
{Product.Price} * .9
```

This formula follows one of two Crystal Reports syntaxes, either one of which you can use to write formulas. The two syntaxes are equivalent, so you can use whichever you find easier. The preceding formula (for example), written with Basic syntax, looks like this:

```
formula = {Product.Price} * .9
```

Crystal Reports Basic syntax is similar to Visual Basic syntax. If you're a Visual Basic programmer, you may be most comfortable using Basic syntax — and it'll work. If you're not particularly biased toward Visual Basic, you may want to use Crystal Reports syntax (unchanged since the early versions of the product). Although Crystal Reports syntax can do a few things that Basic syntax can't, neither has a universal advantage over the other. In the example formulas in this book, I use Crystal Reports syntax.

Lessening the Workload with Functions

Crystal Reports has a number of predefined functions that you may find useful. You can include these functions in formulas to reduce the size and complexity of the formula code that you have to write yourself. For example, suppose that you have a database application with a data entry form in which users enter a customer's name and address information. In the Region field, users should enter a two-letter state or province code, in uppercase. If the user accidentally fails to use uppercase, you can correct the problem with the Crystal Reports UpperCase function:

```
UpperCase ({Customer.Region})
```

This formula converts whatever is in the Region field of the Customer table. If the contents are already in uppercase, no change occurs. If any of the letters are lowercase, they're changed to uppercase. By using this function, you don't have to bother with checking the case of an entry, and then correcting it if necessary. I discuss functions in greater detail when I talk about the Formula Editor component of Formula Workshop, later in this chapter.

Creating a Custom Function Using Formula Workshop

You can access Formula Workshop from the Expert Tools toolbar. When you click the Formula Workshop icon, the screen shown in Figure 11-1 is displayed.

The Workshop tree in the left pane of Formula Workshop displays several folders: Report Custom Functions, Repository Custom Functions, Formula Fields, SQL Expression Fields, Selection Formulas, and Formatting Formulas.

Figure 11-1:
The main
categories
of functions
and for-
mulas for
inclusion in
your report.

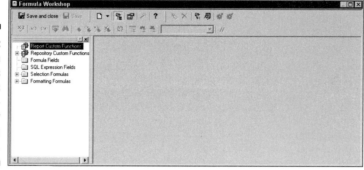

After you create a formula, you can give it a name and save it as a custom function. You can then use the custom function again — in the same report or in other reports. To create a custom function, follow these steps:

1. **Open the report where you want to use the function.**

   To follow along with the example, open the Top5USAfinal.rpt report file from Chapter 9.

2. **On the Expert Tools toolbar, click the Formula Workshop icon to open Formula Workshop.**

3. **Right-click the** Report Custom Functions **branch on the** Workshop **tree and choose New.**

   The Custom Function Name dialog box appears, asking you to enter a name for the custom function you are about to create.

4. **Enter a meaningful function name.**

   Name the function ConcatWith1Space. You'll use this function to con-catenate a customer contact's first and last name, with one blank space in between.

5. **Click the Use Editor button.**

   The Custom Function Editor appears, as shown in Figure 11-2. On the right is a Functions pane, with various predefined functions that you can include in your custom function, and an Operators pane. You can use the operators to combine function elements or operate on function elements. There is a collection of predefined functions in the Functions pane on the left and an array of operators in the Operators pane on the right.

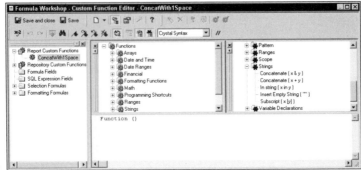

Figure 11-2:
Custom
Function
Editor is
waiting
for you to
specify what
the function
will do.

6. **Expand the Functions and Operators nodes to see the functions and operators if they are not already displayed.**

   You can drag these down to the formula entry area, to build up a custom function, or you can type the function into the formula entry area directly.

7. **Either drag the elements you need down from the Functions and Operators panes or type your function in directly.**

   To follow along with the example, expand the Strings branch in the Operators pane (because concatenation is a string function). You could specify concatenation in two ways: (x + y) and (x & y). Drag either one down into the formula-entry area.

   In many cases (as in this example), it's easier to just type the formula rather than drag pieces of it from the trees in the panes above the formula-entry area.

8. **In the pane below the Tree panes, type the parameter declarations and the body of the function. Note that the word** `Function ()` **is already there.**

   The parentheses are to enclose any parameters that the function might use. If the function has no parameters, the parentheses remain, enclosing nothing.

   For the example, you want to concatenate the contact first name and the contact last name from the `Customers` table, with one blank space between them. The two parameters, x and y, represent the two names you want to concatenate. Both are declared as string variables. Type the following:

```
Function (StringVar x, StringVar y)
(x + " " + y);
```

This function concatenates a string with a blank space, and then concatenates the result with a second string.

9. **Click the Save and Close button to save the custom function** `ConcatWith1Space`.

This is just what you need to create a full name for customer contacts. It may also be useful in a number of other contexts. After you create a custom function, you can use it in many places and with any two string arguments.

Formula Editor

You can't use a custom function directly in a report; you must wrap the function in a formula. Therefore the next order of business is to create a formula that applies your general concatenation function — specifically to concatenating the first and last names of customer contacts:

1. **Click the Formula Workshop icon.**

2. **In the Workshop tree on the left edge of Formula Workshop, right-click Formula Fields and choose New.**

   The Formula Name dialog box appears.

3. **Enter a name, such as** `ContactFullName`.

4. **Click the Use Editor button.**

   Formula Editor appears, as shown in Figure 11-3. It looks a lot like Custom Function Editor, with some differences.

Figure 11-3:
Use Formula Editor to create a formula.

In the Workshop tree on the left, expand the Report Custom Functions node and notice that ConcatWith1Space is listed under it. Note also that ContactFullName is listed under Formula Fields, even though you haven't added functionality to it yet. The formula exists; it just doesn't do anything yet.

As with the Custom Function Editor, you get useful things to include in your formula: A Functions tree contains standard functions and an Operators tree contains operators. You can drag these functions and operators down to the appropriate spot in the formula you're building, or you can type them by hand. Often it's easier to type them than to drag them. Formula Workshop also has a Report Fields tree, which Custom Function Editor doesn't have. You can drag fields from the Field tree into the appropriate spot in the formula you're building.

If you've been following along, then you don't need these handy tools just now — though they're good to know about — because you already did most of the work of building this formula when you created the ConcatWith1Space custom function. In that case, all you need do next is the following:

1. **Click on your custom function under the Report Custom Functions node in the Workshop tree down to the formula pane.**

   To follow along with the example, click ConcatWith1Space. It will appear in the formula pane.

2. **Click the Save and Close icon.**

The next step is to add the contact's full name to the report. You do that with the help of Formula Expert.

Formula Expert

Currently, the Top Five USA Customers report lists the customer name, state, and order total for the five U.S. customers who have purchased the most merchandise from Xtreme Mountain Bikes. Suppose that — at each of these customer sites — you want to insert the full name of the contact person between the Customer Name and the State columns:

1. **Switch to Design view.**

2. **Move the State and Order Amount columns in all the appropriate sections to the right to make room for the new column that will contain the contact's full name.**

3. **On the Expert Tools toolbar, click the Formula Workshop icon.**

4. **Expand the Formula Fields node in the Workshop tree, and then click the ContactFullName formula.**

Formula Expert appears in Formula Workshop. The Custom Function Supplying Logic pane offers two entries: Report Custom Functions and Repository Custom Functions.

5. **Expand the Report Custom Functions node, and then click** ConcatWith1Space, **which appears as shown in Figure 11-4.**

   In the Function Arguments pane, the x and y arguments from the ConcatWith1Space custom function await values. For this report, you want x to be Customer.ContactFirstName and y to be Customer. ContactLastName.

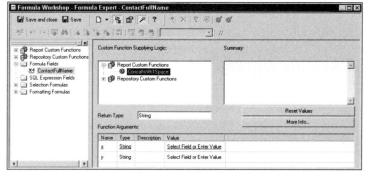

Figure 11-4: Details of the ContactFull Name formula.

6. **Click the** Value **field of the** x **row and then select Choose Other Field from the drop-down menu that appears.**

   The Choose Field dialog box appears.

7. **In the** Customer **table, select** Contact First Name, **and then click OK.**

   The selected field appears in the Value column for the x row.

8. **Click the** Value **field of the** y **row and then select Choose Other Field from the drop-down menu.**

9. **In the** Customer **table, select** Contact Last Name, **and then click OK.**

   The selected field appears in the Value column for the y row.

10. **To finish up, add Contact as a heading to section GH1b, above the full name field.**

    An easy way to do this is to copy the State header, paste it above the ContactFullName column, and then edit it to read Contact instead of State.

11. **Click the Save and Close button.**

    The formula is saved and Formula Workshop closes.

Next, add the full name of the contact to your report:

1. **On the Insert Tools toolbar, click the Insert Text Object icon, and drag the resulting placement frame to a spot in Group Footer 1a, between the Customer column and the State column.**

2. **Drag** ContactFullName **from the Formula Fields node of the Field Explorer to the placement frame.**

3. **On the Formatting toolbar, click the Bold icon.**

   Now the font in this column matches the font in the other columns.

4. **Switch to Preview mode to confirm that the names of the customer contacts appear where you want them.**

   You can always switch back to Design mode and adjust the position of the new column. Figure 11-5 shows the result.

5. **Save the report as** Top5USAwithContact.

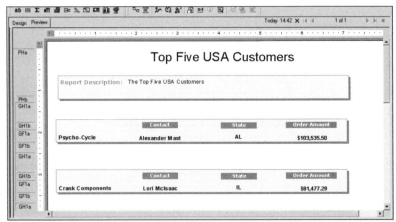

Figure 11-5:
The report
with a
column
created by
formula
rather than
by data-
base field.

SQL Expression Editor

The SQL Expression Editor is another incarnation of the Formula Workshop. It is very similar to the Formula Editor, but is used to build SQL expressions from tables, functions, and operators. With an SQL *expression,* you can issue commands to the database that underlies your report — but you can retrieve no more than one database record at a time. With an SQL *statement,* you can retrieve multiple records in a single operation. Chapter 24 covers the use of SQL statements, but to really handle SQL properly, you have to know more about it than this book has space to cover. For a thorough treatment, read my *SQL For Dummies* (also from Wiley).

The SQL Expression Editor view of the Formula Workshop looks exactly like the Formula Editor view of the Formula Workshop, except for the name in the title bar. You operate on it the same way too. The only difference is that the expression you build must adhere to legal SQL syntax. The SQL Expression Editor is an advanced feature; you probably won't use until you have gained considerable experience with both Crystal Reports and with SQL.

Selection formulas

Crystal Reports offers two kinds of selection formulas: group selection and record selection. By applying a group selection formula to a report, you can restrict retrieval to a single group or to specific desired groups. With a record selection formula, you can restrict retrieval to specific records. For example, in a report that groups sales figures by state, you can use a group selection formula to pull out the sales for a specific state. Similarly, you can use a record-selection formula to retrieve selected records (of specific customers and so on).

Group selection

To see an example of a group selection formula in action, start by opening the Customer Orders, Grouped by State or District (USA) report (described in Chapter 6 and shown in Figure 6-13). Note that the first page shows sales for Benny the Spokes Person, Psycho-Cycle, and The Great Bike Shop in Alabama, because Alabama is the first state or district in an alphabetical sort on Region. Note also that the right side of the tab bar indicates that the report has multiple pages (1 of 1+).

This is the full report, with results for all Xtreme customers in the United States. Suppose that you wanted to print a report for only a single state, North Carolina. Follow these steps:

1. **On the Expert Tools toolbar, click the Formula Workshop icon.**

2. **Expand the Selection Formulas node in the Workshop tree to display the Group Selection and Record Selection options. Select Group Selection.**

   Group Selection Formula Editor appears in the Workshop. You want to retrieve the records where the value of the Region field is NC.

3. **Drag** Customer.Region **from the Report Fields pane down to the blank pane at the lower right of Group Selection Formula Editor.**

   You want to set that field equal to NC.

4. **After the** Customer.Region **field, type an equals sign (=).**

   You could instead expand the Comparisons node in the Operators pane and drag down an equals sign.

5. **Finish the formula by typing (after the equals sign) the two-letter state abbreviation, surrounded by single quotes.**

   Type **'NC'** to follow along with the example. The resulting formula is shown in Figure 11-6.

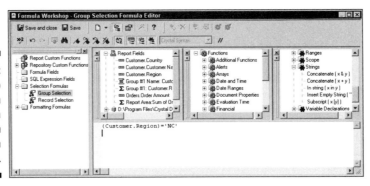

Figure 11-6:
The group selection formula for North Carolina customers.

6. **Click the X+2 Check icon to check your formula for syntax errors.**

7. **Click the Save and Close button to save the formula and close Formula Workshop.**

   Now when you look at the report, it consists of only a single page, showing information for only North Carolina.

8. **Close the report without saving.**

   The North Carolina report is a one-shot report that you probably won't have to run again.

Record selection

For record selection, you follow substantially the same procedure as for group selection. Suppose you want to see all transactions in Customer Report, Grouped by State or District (USA) in which the order amount was greater than $10,000. After opening the report, follow this procedure:

1. **On the Expert Tools toolbar, click the Formula Workshop icon.**

2. **Expand the Selection Formulas node in the Workshop tree to display the Group Selection and Record Selection options. Select Record Selection.**

   Record Selection Formula Editor appears in Workshop. The formula pane already contains a formula ({Customer.Country} = "USA"). To add an additional constraint to retrieve records where the value of the Orders.Order Amount field is greater than 10,000, you must add a new clause to the formula.

3. **To the existing formula, append the keyword AND, then Drag** `Orders.` `Order Amount` **from the Report Fields pane down into the formula pane below the existing formula.**

4. **Type > (greater than sign) after the** `Orders.Order Amount` **field.**

5. **Finish the formula by typing an amount after the greater than sign.**

   Type **10000** to follow along with the example. The resulting formula is shown in Figure 11-7.

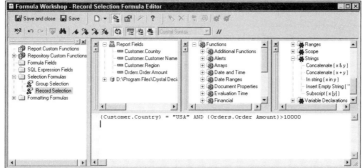

Figure 11-7: Record selection formula for orders greater than $10,000.

6. **Click the Check icon to check the formula for syntax errors.**

7. **Click the Save and Close button to save the formula and close Formula Workshop.**

   Presumably this is the type of information that management will want to see more than once while making decisions.

Now, when you refresh the data and look at the report, only orders greater than $10,000 are shown. Only ten states have customers with orders in excess of $10,000.

Formatting formulas

You can use formatting formulas to change various aspects of the format of a report. In this section, you take another look at the Customer Report, Grouped by State or District (USA) report (used in the previous section):

1. **Open Formula Workshop.**

2. **Expand the Formatting Formulas node in the Workshop tree.**

   Several subnodes appear, including the Report Header node.

3. Expand the Report Header node.

The screen now looks like Figure 11-8.

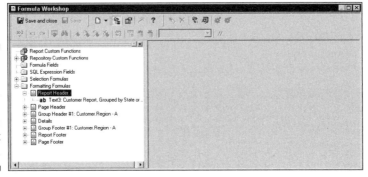

Figure 11-8:
Formula
Workshop,
showing a
formula in
the Report
Header.

4. Right-click the report title entry (Customer Report, and so on) and choose New Formatting Formula.

The New Formatting Formula dialog box appears.

5. Select Background Color, and then click the Use Editor button.

6. In the Functions pane of Format Formula Editor, expand the Color Constants node and double-click Aqua.

This puts the Aqua function (crAqua) in the formula pane at the bottom of Format Formula Editor.

7. Click the Check icon to check the syntax.

8. Click the Save and Close button to save the new formula and close Formula Workshop.

When Formula Workshop disappears, you see that the report now has an aqua-colored report heading.

You can add or change the formatting of any aspect of a report in the same way. Do a little looking around in the Report Fields, Functions, and Operators panes of Format Formula Editor to get an idea of what's available.

Changing and Deleting Formulas

In earlier sections of this chapter, you use Formula Workshop to create a formula. It's just as easy to modify an existing formula. Display it in the Formula Workshop formula pane and make whatever modifications you want, then check it and save it. Deleting a formula is even easier. Select it in the Workshop tree, and then click the Delete icon on the Workshop's toolbar.

Data Types

Formulas deal with data, and databases may hold several different types of data. You can manipulate this data with formulas, but you must be careful to do it properly. For example, you can use the common addition, subtraction, multiplication, and division mathematical operators on number type data, but you can't multiply a number by a string. Specific operations apply to specific data types.

Simple data types

Some data types are more complex than others. The simplest data types are number, currency, string, date, time, datetime, and Boolean. Range types and array types are more complex. Let's look at the simple types first.

Number

The number type includes positive and negative integers and real numbers. When you enter number data, however, don't separate each group of three digits with commas. The only non-numeric characters allowed in a number are the decimal point and the negation sign. Following are examples of number-type data:

```
42
-273
3.1415927
93000000.
```

You can perform addition, subtraction, multiplication, and division operations on number data. Just make sure that you don't divide by 0. Doing so will cause an error (not to mention gray hair on your poor old math teacher).

Currency

Currency data is similar to number data, except it starts with a dollar sign ($) and numbers to the right of the decimal point are rounded differently. Following are a few examples of currency type data:

```
$19.95
-$4000000000.
$64000
```

String

Character strings use different operators than those you use with numbers and currency. You can't add two strings, but you can concatenate them. You can convert a string to all uppercase or all lowercase, which is something you can't do with a number.

Strings must be enclosed in either single or double quotes. Here are a few strings:

```
"I Left My Heart in San Francisco"
"$19.95"
'You can put "quoted text" within a string.'
'You can even include an apostrophe in a string''s text'
```

As you can see, sometimes you must use quotes in an unusual way to keep from confusing the string parser. (The *string parser* is the part of Crystal Reports that analyzes and interprets strings, one character at a time.)

Anything within quotes is a string, even if it looks like a number or a currency value.

Date, time, and datetime

As you might surmise, the date data type holds dates, the time data type holds times, and datetime data type holds a combination of the date and time. Date and time data types are somewhat redundant because the datetime data type can hold dates without times and times without dates. You might want to use the date or the time data type anyway, though, because data in those two types takes up less storage space in memory and on the hard disk than the same quantity stored as a datetime data type.

Datetime values are not strings or numbers. They are literals, which are handled differently from the way either strings or numbers are handled. Datetime literals are enclosed in pound (#) signs. This differentiates them from strings (which are quoted) and numbers (which are not enclosed in anything). Following are some examples of values that can be stored in the datetime data type:

```
#July 20, 1969#
#20 Jul 1969 4:18 pm#
#7/20/1969 16:18:00#
#7/20/1969#
#4:18 pm#
```

Boolean

Boolean data is named after the British mathematician George Boole, who invented Boolean algebra, which gave logic a mathematical foundation. Boolean data has only two values, True and False. Crystal Reports accepts Yes and No as synonyms for True and False. Boolean logic has been critical to the development of the digital computer, which uses ones and zeros to represent True and False.

Range data types

Crystal Reports enables you to restrict the values of data elements to a specified range for all data types except Boolean. For example:

A range of `70 To 100` includes values between 70 and 100. Both 70 and 100 are included in the range.

`70_To_100` includes values between 70 and 100. Both 70 and 100 are excluded.

`70_To 100` includes values between 70 and 100. 70 is excluded but 100 is included.

`UpTo 100` includes all numbers up to and including 100, but none beyond.

`"A" To_ "Z"` includes all character strings starting with an uppercase letter, except for strings starting with `"Z"`.

`UpFrom #1/1/2000#` includes all dates after the once-dreaded Y2K day.

Array data types

Arrays are ordered lists of values that are all the same type. In Crystal Reports, an array can be a simple type or a range type. Array elements are enclosed in square brackets, as in this example:

```
[2, 3, 5, 7, 11, 13]
```

This array contains the first six prime numbers. Or try planets:

```
["Mercury", "Venus", "Earth", "Mars"]
```

is an array containing the string values of the names of the terrestrial planets in our solar system.

You can subscript an array by specifying the index in square brackets after the array. (A *subscript* specifies a particular element of an array.) For example, the following use of brackets

```
[2, 3, 5, 7, 11, 13] [3]
```

specifies 5, the third element in the array.

You can also specify a range of elements, as follows:

```
["Mercury", "Venus", "Earth", "Mars"] [3 To 4]
```

This creates a new array, ["Earth", "Mars"].

Variables in Formulas

In the discussion of Formula Workshop, I use the x and y variables to act as placeholders for specific values in the ConcatWith1Space custom function. Whenever the formula parser encounters a variable in a formula, it looks for the value represented by that variable, and then plugs the value into the formula. Because the value of a variable can be changed by the user or assigned in the formula, variables give Crystal Reports considerable flexibility.

Declaring a variable

Before you can use a variable, you must declare it, to make Crystal Reports aware of it. When you declare a variable, you must specify three things: its name, its scope, and its data type. The name could be something simple, such as *x* or *y.* It could also be something more descriptive, such as *topic.*

When you declare a variable's data type, stick Var on the end of the type, as in StringVar or NumberVar. Scope may be local, global, or shared. If a variable is *declared locally,* it is valid only in the formula in which it is declared. If a variable is *declared globally,* it's available to all the formulas in a report that declare it (except for subreports). A *shared variable* is available to all formulas in a report that declare it, including subreports. Subreports are covered in Chapter 12.

Assigning a value to a variable

After you declare a variable, you can assign it a value. Here's an example:

```
//Declare topic1 to be a global variable of String type that
//specifies a book topic.
Global StringVar topic1;
topic1 := "Crystal Reports";
```

You can also declare a variable and assign it a value in a single statement, as follows:

```
Global StringVar topic2 := "SQL";
```

You can now use the variable in a formula.

Control Structures

Control structures enable you to alter the flow of execution from a strict sequential order to something else. For example, you can branch one way or another with an If-Then-Else control structure. You can branch multiple ways with a Select Case structure. You can loop through an expression or a set of expressions multiple times with a For or While Do structure. You can implement business logic (or illogic) to a fare-thee-well with these structures.

If-Then-Else

The If-Then-Else control structure is useful when you want to do one thing if a condition is true and another thing if the condition is false. Suppose you want to give a 5 percent discount to customers who order more than $10,000 worth of products in a single order. Before printing their invoice, you could have Crystal Reports make the calculation for you as follows:

```
//Give 5% discount for orders > $10,000
If {Orders.Order Amount} > 10000.
Then
    {Orders.Order Amount} = {Orders.Order Amount} * 0.95
Else
    {Orders.Order Amount} = {Orders.Order Amount};
```

If the condition is satisfied, Order Amount is multiplied by 0.95, giving a 5 percent discount. Otherwise, Order Amount is unchanged. The change to Order Amount applies only to this report. The data in the database is not affected.

The Else clause is required, even though it doesn't change anything. The data type of the result returned from the Else clause must match the data type of the result returned by the Then clause. If you leave out the Else clause and the condition is not satisfied, the formula returns the default value for the data type.

Select Case

Use the `Select Case` control structure when there are more than two alternatives to choose from and you want to do a different thing in each case. Suppose the 5 percent discount you offered your customers last month resulted in a huge increase in sales, so you decide to expand the offer this month. A `Select Case` statement will do the job:

```
//Give volume-based discounts
Select {Orders.Order Amount}
    Case 15000. To 1000000.:
        {Orders.Order Amount} = {Orders.Order Amount} * 0.93
    Case 12000. To 14999.99:
        {Orders.Order Amount} = {Orders.Order Amount} * 0.94
    Case 10000. To 11999.99:
        {Orders.Order Amount} = {Orders.Order Amount} * 0.95
    Default:
        {Orders.Order Amount} = {Orders.Order Amount};
```

If an order is between $15,000 and $1,000,000, a 7 percent discount is applied. Lesser discounts are applied for smaller orders. Below $10,000, no discount l is applied. If an order comes through for more than $1,000,000, there must be a mistake, so no discount is applied. The `Default` clause is optional. If you omit it, the value of the selection condition is not changed. (It isn't changed in the preceding example either, but you avoid confusion by making it explicit.)

For loop

Like the `If-Then-Else` structure and the `Select Case` structure, the `For` loop alters the flow of execution, but it alters it in a different way. Whereas the `If-Then-Else` and the `Select Case` constructs cause execution to take one path of execution rather than another, the `For` loop causes execution to pass through a single piece of code multiple times.

The `For` loop is the best tool to use when you want to execute a section of code a predetermined number of times. Suppose you have a character field named `Size` in a table named `Product`, and you want to know how many instances of the letter *x* it contains. You can find out with a formula containing a `For` loop:

```
Local NumberVar Index;
Local NumberVar Xcount := 0;
Local NumberVar StringLength := Length ({Product.Size});

//loop through the characters in Size and count x's
For Index := 1 to StringLength Step 1 Do
(If ({Product.Size} [Index] = "x") Then
     (Xcount := Xcount + 1;)
  Else (Xcount := Xcount;)
);
Xcount
```

In the preceding example, Product.Size is treated as a string array, and Index is the subscript that points to each character in the array in turn. Execution steps through the Size field, one character at a time, counting the occurrences of *x* as it goes. If *x* occurs three times in the Size field, Xcount holds a 3. The last line in the formula returns the value of Xcount.

While Do loop

Whereas the For loop is designed for situations in which you know (or can compute) how many iterations of the loop you want to execute, the While Do loop is ideal when you don't know the number of iterations. The While Do loop depends on the Boolean truth value of a condition. As long as the condition remains true, execution continues to loop. When the condition turns false, the current iteration of the loop is completed and looping terminates. If the condition is initially false, the loop is not executed at all.

Suppose that in the preceding example, you wanted to know the character position of the first *x* rather than the total number of instances of *x* in the string. Because you don't know how far into the string the first *x* occurs (if at all), a While Do loop is appropriate:

```
Local NumberVar Index := 1;
Local NumberVar Xpos := 0;
Local NumberVar StringLength := Length ({Product.Size});

//Find location of first x in Product.Size
While Index <= StringLength And Xpos = 0 Do
(If ({Product.Size} [Index] = "x") Then
     (Xpos := Index;)
  Else (Xpos := Xpos;)
);
Xpos
```

Note that if `Index` were initially greater than `StringLength`, the loop would be skipped.

Do While loop

The `Do While` loop is similar to the `While Do` loop, but whereas the `While Do` loop doesn't execute if the condition is not initially satisfied, the `Do While` loop is always guaranteed to execute at least once, regardless of whether or not the condition is satisfied. Sometimes you want the behavior of `While Do`, and other times you want the behavior of `Do While`. Crystal Reports gives you both.

With a `Do While` loop, you can accomplish the same character location task that was illustrated in the `While Do` loop. The code is just a little bit different:

```
Local NumberVar Index := 1;
Local NumberVar Xpos := 0;
Local NumberVar StringLength := Length ({Product.Size});

//Find location of first x in Product.Size
Do
(If ({Product.Size} [Index] = "x") Then
    (Xpos := Index;)
 Else (Xpos := Xpos;)
While Index <= StringLength And Xpos = 0
);
Xpos
```

In this case, the loop is executed once, and the first character of `Product.Size` is checked to see whether it's an "x". This occurs even if the condition is not satisfied because execution doesn't reach the condition until after the loop has been executed once. Thus, if (by some mischance) the value of `Index` was greater than `StringLength`, an "x" located beyond the end of the `Product.Size` string would cause `Xpos` to take on a nonzero value. This could be misleading and cascade into a significant error. It's important to choose your loop type according to whether you want the loop to execute at least once, regardless of whether the condition is satisfied.

Chapter 12

Creating Reports within a Report

- -

In This Chapter

▶ Combining unrelated reports using subreports

▶ Linking a subreport to the data in a primary report

▶ Using subreports with unlinkable data

▶ Creating an on-demand subreport

▶ Passing data between reports and subreports

▶ Troubleshooting problems with subreports

- -

*I*n other chapters, you see how to build reports based on the data contained in several related tables in a database. This is wonderful, but sometimes you want to build a report that displays data from two or more sources that are unrelated or related only indirectly. Crystal Reports meets that need by enabling you to embed one report in another. The embedded report is called a subreport. Subreports allow you to take data from diverse sources and present it on one or a small number of pages, for ease of comprehension.

Combining Unrelated Reports

A standard report created by Crystal Reports can't display data from two tables that are not linked, but a subreport can. You use subreports when you have data tables that are unrelated or have an indirect relationship.

The easiest kind of primary report/subreport combination to produce is one in which the two reports are unrelated but nonetheless of interest to the reader. Because the primary report and the subreport are not directly related to each other, you don't need to worry about linking them. Aside from the details of building the primary report and the subreport, your main concern is the placement of the subreport within the primary report.

You can embed a subreport within another report in two ways. One way is to open the primary report and create a subreport within it from scratch. The other way is to embed an existing report into another report as a subreport. In this section, I show you an example of embedding an existing report into a primary report.

Suppose the management at Xtreme Mountain Bikes wants to see the results of two reports — the Top Seventeen USA Customers report (Top17USA.rpt) from Chapter 9 and the Big Orders report (highest-value orders from customers worldwide) created in Chapter 5 — in a single report. Crystal Reports makes it easy to do: Just add the Big Orders report to the Top Seventeen USA Customers report. Big Orders becomes a *subreport.* From this report, it will be easy to tell not only which customers have a large cumulative total of purchases but also which of them tend to buy in large lots.

To start, follow these steps:

1. **Open the report that you want to use as the main report.**

   To follow along with the example, open the Top Seventeen USA Customers report. (The report file, Top17USA.rpt, is shown in Figure 12-1.) This summary report fits on a single page. The Big Orders report also fits on a single page, so putting it into the report footer of the Top Seventeen USA Customers report gives you a handy two-page report.

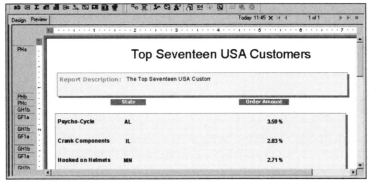

Figure 12-1:
The Top
Seventeen
USA
Customers
report.

2. **Switch to the Design tab.**

   The report sections are displayed, as shown in Figure 12-2. The report footer appears gray, indicating that it's suppressed. To display anything in this section, you must first reverse the suppression.

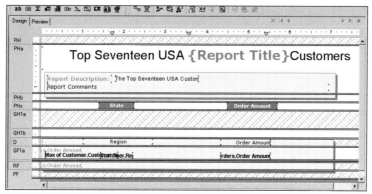

3. **Right-click the area to the left of the report footer section and choose Don't Suppress.**

   Now whatever you put in the report footer will be displayed.

4. **On the Insert Tools toolbar, click the Insert Subreport icon.**

   The Insert Subreport dialog box appears.

5. **Select the Choose a Report option.**

6. **Click Browse.**

   A standard Open dialog box appears.

7. **Use the controls in the Open dialog box to find and select the report that you want to use as the subreport. Then click the Open button to enter it in the Report File Name text box.**

   To follow along with the example, find and open the Big Orders report.

8. **Click OK.**

9. **Drag the placement frame that appears at the cursor location into the Report Footer and expand it to the full width of the page.**

   This gives you the layout shown in Figure 12-3.

   The template for this particular report was not designed for the extra width needed to include all the columns, so it's best used as an illustration, not as a realistic application of a subreport. The idea here is to show you how to include a subreport in a main report; make sure the template for your report can accommodate this operation.

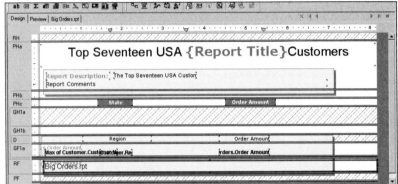

Figure 12-3:
Design
view of the
report and
subreport.

10. Switch to Preview mode.

11. If your report has a parameter field, a dialog box appears. Enter a value and then click OK.

To follow along with the example, enter 9000 for the lower-limit value. Page 1 of the report is unchanged, but now page 2 shows the Big Orders report, which includes all orders of $9,000 or more, as shown in Figure 12-4.

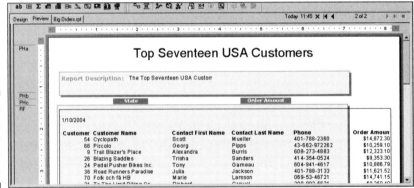

Figure 12-4:
Page 2
of the
report and
subreport.

With a subreport, information that doesn't need to be directly related to information in the primary report can be presented in a compact and convenient form.

Underlay formatting for side-by-side location of subreport

In the preceding example, you inserted a subreport at the bottom of the primary report. For some applications, the subreport works best alongside the primary report for comparison. For this type of formatting (and several others), you use the *underlaying* feature of Crystal Reports, which enables you to lay a subreport under other material in the primary report.

When you underlay the material in any section, it goes "under" the material in the next section. In effect, the next section is overlaid on top — which may seem strange to do. After all, wouldn't underlaying just make the material in both sections unreadable? Yes, if you left it that way — but here comes the trick that makes underlaying worthwhile . . .

Offset the overlaid material *to the right of the underlaid material.* One such use would be to place a chart immediately to the right of the data it's developed from. Another use is to place a subreport immediately to the right of related material found in the primary report.

Both the Big Orders report and the Top Seventeen USA Customers report are too wide to fit comfortably side by side on a standard 8½-by-11-inch sheet of paper in Portrait mode. However, if you know ahead of time that you want to combine two reports as a primary report/subreport combination, you can format them so they work together to effectively convey the information you want to deliver. Here's how:

1. **Place your subreport in the Report Header or a Group Header section.**

2. **Click the Section Expert icon.**

   The Section Expert dialog box appears.

3. **Select the section into which you have placed the subreport.**

4. **Select the Underlay Following Sections option, and then click OK.**

   This operation lays the subreport under the sections that follow it (in effect, putting them on top).

Make sure you've formatted the subreport so it's offset far enough to the right that it doesn't interfere with any content in the primary report.

Drilling down in a subreport

As I explain in Chapter 6, *drill-down* enables you to keep the focus on your summary while also keeping details available offstage. The capability hides detailed information when you want to produce a summary report — while still keeping that information available if a user wants it. If hidden detailed information is available in a summary report, the user's cursor changes to a magnifying glass when it passes over the summary field. Double-clicking while the cursor is a magnifying glass makes the detailed information appear. When you have placed a subreport in a primary report, however, drill-down works a little differently.

Subreport drill-down versus report drill-down

When you pass the cursor over a subreport, the cursor changes to a magnifying glass, regardless of whether the subreport supports drill-down. If you double-click, a preview tab for the subreport appears to the right of the preview tab of the primary report. No additional detail appears in the report (yet), and the cursor changes back to the normal pointer.

After you open the subreport, however, drilling down works just as it does in a normal primary report. When you move the cursor over a summary field that supports drill-down, the cursor changes into a magnifying glass. Double-click to make the detailed information that supports the summary appear. A drill-down tab for that information also appears to the right of the subreport's preview tab.

Handling tab overflow

When you implement drill-down, the tab bar starts to fill up. With the tabs for the primary report (including possible drill-down tabs) and the tabs for the subreport (including multiple possible subreports), the tab bar may run out of space. If it can't display all the tabs at once, click the left and right arrows on the tab bar to move left and right (respectively) through the tabs. In addition, click the red *x* when you want to close the current tab and open the tab immediately to its left. This is a helpful tool for getting rid of tabs that you no longer need.

Figure 12-5 shows the tab bar — including drill-down tabs, left and right movement arrows, and the *x* button that closes the current tab.

Figure 12-5:
Click the
arrows
to move
through the
tab bar.

Linking a Subreport to a Primary Report

One of the most valuable uses of a subreport is to have it supplement related information displayed in the primary report. To set up this useful relationship, you link the subreport to the primary, using a field that's shared by the tables forming the basis of the primary report *and* the subreport. (Alternatively, you can form the link by using formula fields.)

Suppose you have a primary report that holds name and address information for Xtreme's customers in Michigan. Another report — soon to become the subreport — holds order data for Michigan customers.

The primary report, MIcust, is a simple report, containing the CustomerID, Customer Name, Address1 and Address2 fields as well as City, Region, and Postal Code. The fields from the Customer table have been dropped into text fields to allow formatting of lines that contain more than one database field. This is the technique I use in Chapter 7 when creating mailing labels. A filter has been applied so only the customers whose Region is MI appear in the report. The subreport, MIorders, contains Order Date, Order Amount, and Ship Date for all orders made by Michigan customers. It also includes the Customer table, although no fields from that table are displayed. The table is present only to provide a link to MIcust.

To create the full report, follow these steps:

1. **Open the primary report, MIcust.**

   Figure 12-6 shows what the report looks like in Design view.

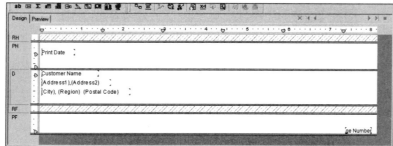

Figure 12-6: Design view of the MIcust report.

2. **Choose Insert⇨Subreport.**

   The Insert Subreport dialog box appears.

3. **Find** `MIorders` **and specify it in the Report File Name box of the Insert Subreport dialog box.**

   You can specify an existing report to use as a subreport or call upon Report Wizard to create a new report to be used as a subreport. For the example, assume that `MIorders` has already been created. Figure 12-7 shows the Design view of `MIorders`.

   To follow along, create a report that looks like Figure 12-7 and that filters out all orders except those where the value of `Region` is `'MI'`.

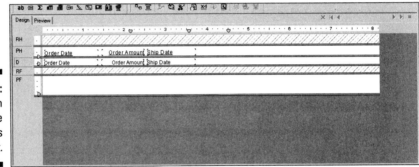

Figure 12-7:
Design view of the MIorders report.

4. **Click OK to dismiss the Insert Subreport dialog box and return to the Design view of** `MIcust`.

   A placement frame appears at the pointer.

5. **Drag the frame into the Details section, to the right of the** `Customer Name` **field.**

   `MIcust` now looks like Figure 12-8 in Design mode and like Figure 12-9 in Preview mode.

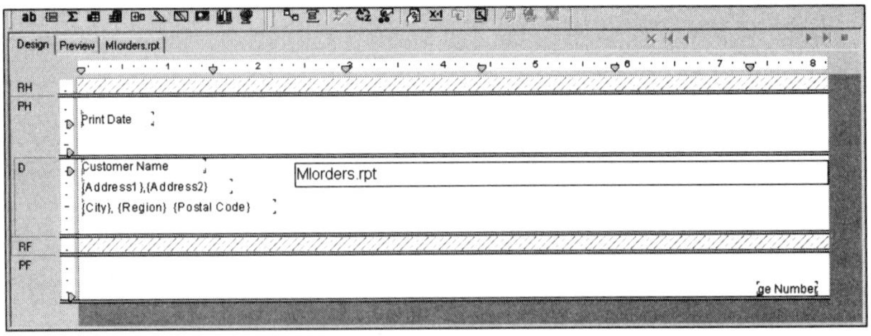

Figure 12-8:
Design view of the report, with the subreport.

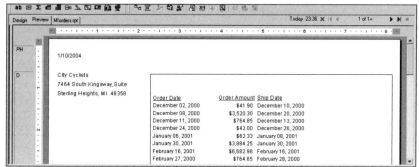

Figure 12-9:
Preview of
the report,
with the
subreport.

To establish the link between the primary report and the subreport, do the
following:

1. **With the primary report open, right-click the subreport.**

   The menu shown in Figure 12-10 appears.

Figure 12-10:
Subreport
menu.

2. **Select Change Subreport Links.**

   The Subreport Links dialog box appears, as shown in Figure 12-11.

3. **Select one or more fields in the Available Fields pane.**

   These fields should be present in one of the tables used in the primary
   report.

   To follow along with the example, choose `CustomerID` as the linking
   field. This makes the Subreport Links dialog box look like Figure 12-12.

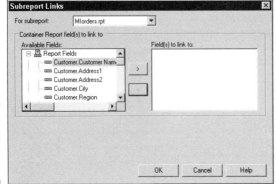

Figure 12-11:
Subreport
Links dialog
box.

4. **Click OK.**

Now the records appearing in the subreport correspond to the primary report records in the same data section.

I used Record Sort Expert to sort the subreport by order date, and then used Format Editor to remove the default border line around the subreport. (To invoke Format Editor, right-click the `MIorders` rectangle in the `MIcust` Design view of the report and chose Format Subreport.)

Subreports need not be linkable

The example in the "Linking a Subreport to a Primary Report" section shows how to link a subreport to a primary report when the linking field is shared by both reports. However, sometimes you'll want to combine two reports that don't have a column in common. Such reports can't be linked in the usual way, but you may be able to link them by using a formula field.

Suppose one of your reports is based on a table that has a `First Name` field and a `Last Name` field. The other report you want to use is based on a table that has a `Full Name` field; no other fields in the two tables are even close to being the same. A solution to the problem would be to create a formula in the first report that concatenates the `First Name` and `Last Name` fields with a single blank space in between. The resulting full name could then be used as a linking field with the `Full Name` field in the second table. Problem solved. (Chapter 11 covers formulas in detail.)

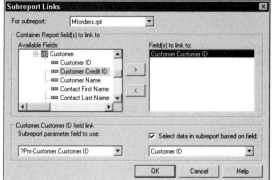

Figure 12-12:
Subreport
Links dialog
box, with
linking field.

On-Demand Subreports Boost Efficiency

On-demand subreports can be valuable when you have a report that contains multiple subreports. The primary report doesn't actually contain the subreports. Rather, it contains hyperlinks to the subreports. The subreports are not read from the database until the user clicks the hyperlink. This way, only subreports that are viewed travel from the database server to the user's client, reducing the load on the network from what it would be if the user downloaded the full report, including all subreports.

To make MIcust an on-demand subreport, follow these steps:

1. **Place MIorders into your primary report, select it, and then choose Format⟿Format Subreport on the Main menu.**

   The Format Editor dialog box appears.

2. **Click the Subreport tab, which is shown in Figure 12-13.**

3. **Select the On-demand Subreport option.**

4. **Click OK.**

   Instead of including each customer's orders in the report, there's now a hyperlink to each order. The report size has shrunk to a single page.

On-demand subreports are purely electronic; they don't work with printed reports. (Ever try to click a printed hyperlink? But you knew that.) On-demand subreports require a database connection.

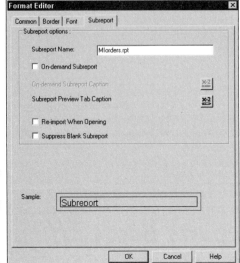

Figure 12-13:
The Format
Editor dialog
box Sub-
report tab.

Passing Data Between Reports

Crystal Reports allows you to pass data from a primary report to a subreport
or from a subreport to its primary report. You can do so by using formulas
containing *shared variables* that are common to a report and all its subreports.
You must declare shared variables in a formula in the main report, and then
declare the same shared variables in any subreports that need to exchange
data with the main report. You may want to pass a shared variable from a
primary report to a subreport for display in the subreport or as a selection
criterion in the subreport.

Before a value can be passed between the main report and the subreport,
these conditions have to apply:

- ✔ A shared variable must be declared *and assigned a value* in a formula in
  the main report.
- ✔ The same shared variable must be declared in a formula in the
  subreport.
- ✔ To pass a value from the subreport to the main report, you must make
  both declarations but assign the value in the subreport.

Troubleshooting Subreport Problems

Sometimes you get odd results from reports containing subreports because of the order in which reports are processed. Formulas in the main report are processed before those in subreports. Thus, if you set the value of a shared variable in a subreport and then pass the variable to a group footer in the main report, you may find that the main report is using the value of the shared variable from the *previous* group rather than from the *current* group. To avoid this problem, create an additional group footer in the main report, such as Group Footer 1b. Place the subreport in Group Footer 1a and retrieve the value of the shared variable in Group Footer 1b. This associates the shared variable with the proper subreport.

As you may expect, reports that contain subreports process more slowly than reports that don't. However, you can do a few things to lessen the problem:

- ✔ If your report contains multiple subreports, consider changing the subreports to on-demand subreports. This way, only the subreports that the user is interested in are downloaded from the server. This tweak could have a major effect on system response time.

- ✔ For linked subreports, make sure that the linking field is indexed. Doing so can bring a tremendous boost to performance.

- ✔ If you're linking a report to a subreport using a formula field, make sure that the formula field is on the main report — and that it corresponds to a database field in the subreport. Requiring a formula calculation in the subreport makes the processing migrate from the server to the client, using network bandwidth and performing calculations on a slower machine.

Chapter 13

Combining Report Elements with OLE

*T*he primary purpose for a report is to present database data to users in a form that's easy to understand. Crystal Reports gives you all the tools you need to do that. Sometimes, however, you want a report that does more than just present database data. You might want to include text from a word processing file, or data that resides in a spreadsheet, or a graphical image stored as a bitmapped image file. To allow the sharing of various kinds of information in different kinds of files, Microsoft developed the OLE (Object Linking and Embedding) architecture.

Overview of OLE

Reports that you create with Crystal Reports can serve as OLE container applications. That is, they can contain OLE objects that were created by other applications called OLE server applications. Microsoft Word and Microsoft Excel are examples of OLE server applications. You can take text from a Microsoft Word file as an OLE object — or take an Excel spreadsheet as an OLE object — and place it in a Crystal report.

Crystal Reports can also function as an OLE server application. You can define a report as an OLE object and place it into a Word text file, an Excel spreadsheet, or any other OLE-compatible container application.

OLE offers an unusual advantage: When you bring an OLE object into Crystal Reports and place it in a report, the object maintains a relationship with the application that created it. The nature of that relationship depends on whether the OLE object is static, embedded, or linked.

Static OLE objects

A *static OLE object* is a snapshot of an object that has been copied from the original application to the container application. You can place a static OLE object in a Crystal report, but after you put it there, you can't edit it or change it in any way (except to delete it). A static OLE object doesn't maintain any connection to the application that created it.

Embedded objects and linked objects

As with a static OLE object, an *embedded OLE object* is downloaded entirely to the container application, with an important difference: An embedded object is no snapshot. It has an "awareness" of which server application it comes from, and you can edit it within the container application. When you double-click an embedded OLE object, it becomes editable. The server application takes over the menus and toolbars to allow editing. For example, if you embed an Excel spreadsheet into a report, you can edit the spreadsheet from within Crystal Reports — using Excel menus and toolbars.

Any modifications you make to an embedded OLE object don't show up in the original file in the OLE server application. If you want to change the original, you have to do that separately.

Linked objects are like visitors; they don't actually move to the container application. What the container application contains is a *pointer* to the linked object (which remains in the server application). This link means that whenever the original object in the server application is updated, the linked object in the container application is updated too. Suppose, for example, that your server application is Excel, and you update the data in the linked spreadsheet. The next time you run your report in Crystal Reports, it pulls the latest data from the Excel file to display in the report.

Linking is best if your report must always reflect the latest data — and if you want the data in multiple applications to remain synchronized. The pointer also takes up less space than embedding a large spreadsheet or Word document, which makes the report faster to load. Reports containing linked objects are, however, less portable than reports containing embedded objects. For the link to work, the original server application must be present on the machine that's running Crystal Reports. By contrast, an embedded object is completely self-contained, needing no link to its source file or application.

Embedding or Linking a File as an OLE Object

Just as there are several types of OLE objects, there are several ways to insert an OLE object into a Crystal report. You can embed an entire file or part of a file into a report as an OLE object. You can also link to a file (or part of a file) defined as an OLE object. In this section, I cover embedding and linking entire files; the next section deals with embedding and linking part of a file.

The file to be embedded can already exist, or you can create one on the spot. In this section, you see how to embed a file in either way. First, in the following steps, you create an OLE object based on a new file.

1. **Display your target report in Design mode.**

2. **Choose Insert⇨OLE Object.**

   The Insert Object dialog box (illustrated in Figure 13-1) appears, listing the types of files you can insert as OLE objects.

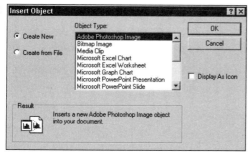

Figure 13-1:
The Insert
Object
dialog box,
showing
some
available
object types.

3. Select the Create New option.

You can either create a new OLE object file or create an OLE object based on an existing file (as described in the next set of steps).

4. In the list box, select an object type.

5. Click OK.

An object-placement frame appears at the cursor position.

6. Drag the placement frame to the appropriate section of the report.

The tool for creating the type of object you have chosen appears. For example, if you chose Bitmap Image, the Paint drawing tools appear.

7. Create the object.

This procedure creates an embedded OLE object. It is editable, and you can add it to the repository if you want (I talk about the repository in Chapter 18). Right-click the object to display a menu that lists all the things you can do with it.

If you want to create an OLE object based not on a new file but rather on an existing file, the procedure is a little different.

In this case, you can do it in seven steps:

1. Display your target report in Design mode.

2. Choose Insert⇨OLE Object.

The Insert Object dialog box appears.

3. Select the Create from File option.

This specifies that you want to create an OLE object based on an existing file.

4. Specify the file that you want to link or embed.

Either type the file's full name (including its path) or browse for it and select it. Figure 13-2 shows an example of what you see.

5. If you want to link to the existing file rather than embed it, select the Link option.

6. Click OK.

An object placement frame appears at the cursor's position.

7. Drag the placement frame to the appropriate spot in the appropriate section of the report.

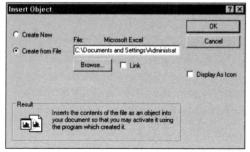

Figure 13-2:
Insert Object
dialog box,
when insert-
ing an object
based on an
existing file.

Embedding or Linking an Object Taken from a File

To embed or link an object taken from an OLE server application (rather than an entire file) into a report, follow these steps:

1. **Copy the object to the Windows clipboard.**

2. **On the Crystal Reports menu, choose Edit⇨Paste Special.**

   The Paste Special dialog box appears.

3. **Select Paste or Paste Link.**

   If you select Paste, the clipboard object is embedded in your report. If you select Paste Link, the object is linked.

When a linked object is updated in the OLE server application, it's likewise updated in your report. If the object is embedded, such an update in the server application doesn't affect it.

Editing OLE Objects

Static OLE objects can't be edited, but you can edit embedded and linked OLE objects easily. To edit an OLE object from Crystal Reports, just double-click it. The appropriate editing tools for that kind of object appear, and you're all set to edit.

If the object is embedded, the changes you make don't affect the original object (lounging back there in its OLE server application). If the object is linked, however the original object will be changed when you edit it from within Crystal Reports.

Chapter 14

Creating and Updating OLAP Reports

Computer geeks have a maddening tendency to refer to things by inscrutable acronyms, sometimes even pseudo-acronyms, such as SQL — which, believe it or not, does *not* stand for Structured Query Language (the sidebar explains why). The letters in BASIC, FORTRAN, and COBOL once stood for something, as did the letters in the late, lamented SNOBOL. OLAP is a new entry in the list of obscure computer acronyms — but at least it's real: OLAP stands for On-Line Analytical Processing. In this case, the name does bear some resemblance to what the technology is actually about.

What's OLAP, and Why Might I Need It?

OLAP is called On-Line because it happens in real time, with the user sitting in front of the screen while there's a direct connection to a database. The results of user actions are immediate (more or less). The operation itself is called Analytical Processing because its main function is to quickly analyze huge quantities of data and deliver meaningful information to the user. The information arrives in a form that the user can readily comprehend and act on.

Who uses OLAP?

Huge amounts of data are stored in relational databases belonging to organizations of all sizes and types. You can retrieve information from these databases using queries written in SQL, or by using a graphical approach such as Query By Example (QBE), which gets translated into SQL and then executed. Either way is great — if you're an SQL guru or someone equally skilled in QBE usage. OLAP is for people who don't even know what a nested `SELECT` is, let alone a `LEFT OUTER JOIN`. OLAP is a tool designed for managers who must make decisions based on a needle of information buried in a haystack of data. OLAP gives people who are not database specialists the capability to find that needle quickly.

Creating multidimensional views

A spreadsheet gives you a two-dimensional view of the data you're displaying. So do most reports you create with Crystal Reports. It's the classic row-and-column approach — a company's line items for income and expense arranged in rows, while months or quarters go in columns. Another example is an instructor's course records — student names in rows, assignment grades and exam scores in columns. Many common situations can be represented very well with these two dimensions. Others, however, require three (or even more) dimensions to convey what the data means.

OLAP is designed to work with these more challenging data sets. A multidimensional OLAP representation of complex data is called an *OLAP cube*. Even though the word *cube* implies three dimensions, an OLAP cube can have more than three dimensions. (Magic? Maybe — but practical.)

What do the letters SQL stand for?

SQL is an industry-standard data sublanguage that descended from a language that IBM developed in the 1970s for its internal use only. The rough prototype language went by the acronym SEQUEL (pronounced the same as the English word), which stood for Structured English QUEry Language. Hey, it made sense at the time; statements in SEQUEL looked a lot like statements in English — but they were more structured. When IBM released its first relational database product (SQL/DS) in 1981, the Big Blue team wanted to deliver a commercial-quality data sublanguage along with it. They performed a major overhaul on SEQUEL, creating (essentially) a new language. To keep the new commercial language from being confused with its ancestor (the prototype SEQUEL), they dropped the vowels and called it

SQL (pronounced *ess-que-ell*). But many people persisted in pronouncing SQL as *sequel* — and that was mistake number one. Mistake number two was the assumption that SQL stood for Structured Query Language — when SQL is *not* a structured language (it breaks the cardinal rule of structured languages by allowing branches to remote locations). Its statements *look* like a structured form of English, but it isn't a structured language, whether for use in a query or otherwise. So where does that leave us? Simple: SQL doesn't actually *stand for* anything. As with C, C++, or C#, it's simply the name of a language — which most people mispronounce and misunderstand — but at least you and I know what they're *really* talking about.

What kinds of reporting tasks might require more than two dimensions? Suppose the company displaying income and expense data by month wants to expand the report to show the data for the last ten years. Income and expense could be one dimension; January through December could be a second dimension, and the years could be a third dimension.

Suppose the instructor is teaching a distance-learning course with clusters of students meeting in 15 different cities. An OLAP cube could have student names in one dimension, assignment grades and examination scores in a second dimension, and student location in a third dimension. Any application that lends importance to more than two aspects of the data is a candidate for storage in an OLAP cube and presentation in an OLAP report.

OLAP Reporting with Crystal Reports

Crystal Reports does not create OLAP cubes — the DBMS that Crystal Reports is working with does that. Crystal Reports currently creates OLAP reports based on four types of data source:

- ✔ Hyperion Essbase (Local Client)
- ✔ IBM DB2 OLAP Server (Local Client)
- ✔ Microsoft OLE DB Provider for OLAP Services 8.0
- ✔ Holos HDC Cube (Local Client)

The most common type of Crystal Reports OLAP report is an *OLAP grid* — a two-dimensional slice through a three-dimensional cube. Multiple slices give the report a third dimension.

Depending on how you want to look at the data, you might slice a cube in differ-ent directions. This process, called (believe it or not) *slicing and dicing,* allows you to play with the data until you display it in the most informative way.

Creating a three-dimensional report

To demonstrate how to create an OLAP report, here's a chance to slice and dice some data from a cube based on the Xtreme database and see what it can tell you. Among the files that come with Crystal Reports 10 is a Crystal Analysis Server cube named `Xtreme.hdc`. It's located on your hard disk, probably at a location similar to the following:

```
D:\Program Files\Crystal Decisions\Crystal Reports 10\Samples\En\Databases\Olap
            Data
```

Here's a step-by-step procedure for creating an OLAP report based on the
Xtreme.hdc cube:

1. **Choose File➪New.**

   Crystal Reports Gallery appears.

2. **Select the OLAP option, and then click OK.**

   The OLAP Report Creation Wizard appears.

3. **Click the Select Cube button.**

   The Crystal OLAP Connection Browser appears, as shown in Figure 14-1.

Figure 14-1:
Crystal
OLAP
Connection
Browser,
showing
OLAP
servers that
are currently
connected.

4. **If the source of your cube is listed on the OLAP Cube tree, select it
   and then click Open (if not, click the Add Server button).**

   The New Server dialog box appears.

5. **In the New Server dialog box, specify the location of your cube
   (whether on a remote server, as a local .CUB file, or as a HTTP cube
   on the World Wide Web) and then click OK.**

   To follow along with the example, for Server Type, select Holos HDC Cube
   (Local Client). Under Server Options, click the button with the three dots
   to the right of the HDC File text box. In the Open dialog box that appears,
   find the Xtreme.hdc file. On my machine it was located here:

```
D:\Program Files\Crystal Decisions\Crystal Reports
        10\Samples\En\Databases\Olap Data
```

Select Xtreme.hdc and click the Open button. This closes the Open
dialog box and returns the focus to the New Server dialog box. Type
something meaningful into the Caption text box, as shown in Figure 14-2,
then click OK.

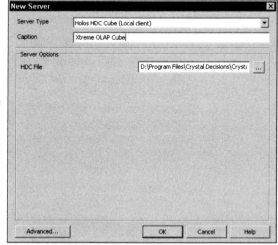

Figure 14-2:
Specify the
server that
holds your
OLAP cube
in the New
Server
dialog box.

6. **The Crystal OLAP Connection Browser now displays your cube as
shown in Figure 14-3. Select it and then click the Open button.**

Figure 14-3:
Crystal
OLAP
Connection
Browser,
showing
the Xtreme
cube.

7. **Verify that the wizard has correctly identified the cube's name and location, as shown in Figure 14-4.**

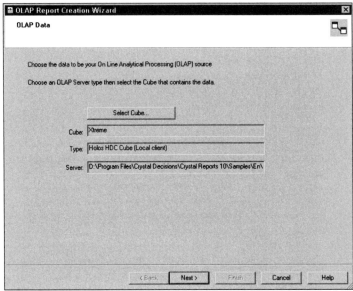

Figure 14-4:
OLAP
Wizard with
a cube
selected.

8. **Click Next.**

   The Wizard's Rows/Column page appears, as shown in Figure 14-5.

9. **Structure the OLAP grid the way you want it.**

   This cube has three dimensions: Monthly, Customer, and Product. The wizard suggests that Customer entries be shown in rows and Product entries in columns. The third dimension, Monthly, can be the basis for slices through the cube. You don't have to accept the wizard's suggestions. You could, for instance, drag Customer entries to the Columns pane and Product entries to the Rows pane, or either of those to the Dimensions pane.

   For this example, I chose to leave the dimensions where they are.

10. **Select the member in the Columns pane.**

    In this example, it is Product.

11. **Click the Select Column Members button below the Columns pane.**

    The Member Selector (shown in Figure 14-6) appears.

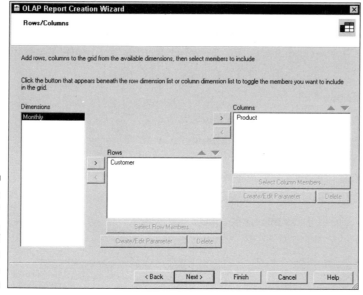

Figure 14-5:
OLAP
Wizard,
Rows/
Columns
page.

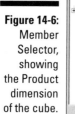

Figure 14-6:
Member
Selector,
showing
the Product
dimension
of the cube.

12. **Expand the tree node displayed.**

    In my case, it is All Products. This lists all of Xtreme Mountain Bike's products. Next just display the bicycles of interest.

13. **Select the specific members you want to show on the report, and then click OK.**

    I chose Descent, Endorphin, Mozzie, Nicros, and Rapel.

14. **Select the member in the Rows pane.**

    In this example, it is `Customer`.

15. **Click on the Select Row Members button below the Rows pane.**

    This displays the Member Selector for rows.

16. **Expand the tree node displayed.**

    In my case, it's the USA node.

17. **Select the specific members you want to show on the report, and then click OK.**

    In my case, I just selected CA for California.

18. **Click Next in the OLAP Report Creation Wizard.**

    The Wizard's Slice/Page page appears, as shown in Figure 14-7.

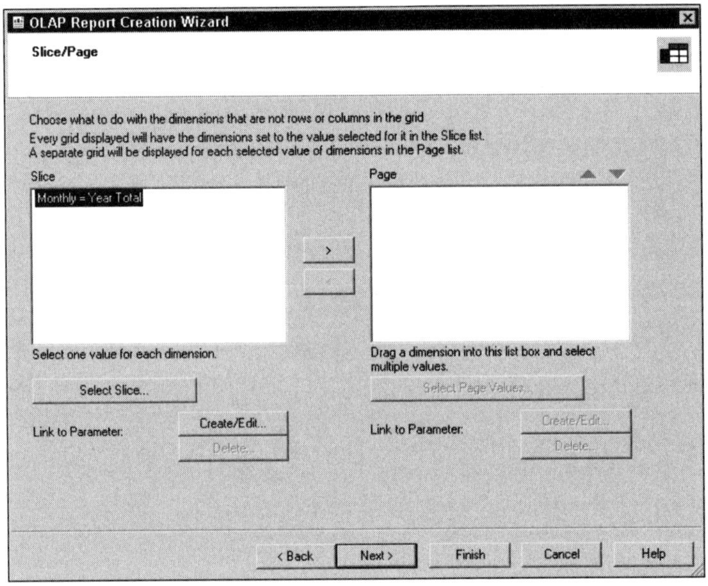

Figure 14-7:
OLAP
Wizard,
Slice/Page
page.

The Wizard suggests that you deal with the Monthly dimension by making a slice based on the year totals for the customers and products in the cube.

19. **For this example, keep it simple and accept the wizard's suggestion.**

20. **Click Next.**

21. **Select a style from the Wizard's Style page, and then click Next.**

    I chose the simple and classic Original style.

22. **If you want to include a chart in your report, select a chart type from the Wizard's Chart page. Fill in appropriate entries for Chart Type, On Change of, and Subdivided by.**

    I chose not to include a chart for this example.

23. **Click the Finish button.**

    A completed report with no associated chart appears in Figure 14-8. Some tweaking is in order, because for the USA slice, some of the order numbers are too large to fit in the boxes provided. These are easy to expand, however, by switching to Design mode and dragging the right-side handles of the Value fields horizontally to the right.

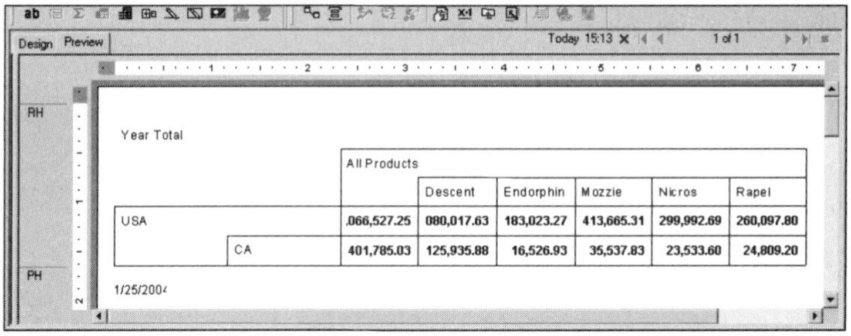

Figure 14-8: The OLAP report based on Xtreme cube.

		All Products					
Year Total			Descent	Endorphin	Mozzie	Nicros	Rapel
USA		,066,527.25	080,017.63	183,023.27	413,665.31	299,992.69	260,097.80
	CA	401,785.03	125,935.88	16,526.93	35,537.83	23,533.60	24,809.20

1/25/2004

Updating an OLAP report

Because an OLAP report is based on an OLAP cube created by a database management system, any change in the underlying cube could cause errors in the production of the report. The report might even come out blank if, for example, the location of the OLAP cube has changed and Crystal Reports can no longer find it. Other problems occur if, for example, a dimension has been removed from the cube or a field used by the report is removed.

To reconnect a report to a cube whose location has changed, perform the following steps:

1. **In the report, select the grid by clicking the border.**

2. **Choose Database↪Set OLAP Cube Location.**

    A dialog box appears, saying, "Warning: It is not possible to undo this command. Would you like to perform the command anyway?"

3. **If you're sure that your OLAP cube location has changed and that your report is no longer valid, click the Yes button.**

   The Set OLAP Cube Location dialog box appears, displaying what Crystal Reports currently thinks the cube location is.

4. **Specify the new OLAP Server location by clicking Select and then use the Crystal OLAP Connection Browser that appears — and possibly the New Server dialog box — to locate the cube.**

5. **After you specify the new server location, in the Crystal OLAP Connection Browser, select the new cube location and click Open. In the Set OLAP Cube Location dialog box, click OK.**

Your OLAP cube is now reconnected to its source database at its new location.

Chapter 15

Enhancing Reports with Charts

. . . .

In This Chapter

▶ Adding visual impact to a report with charts

▶ Finding out about the different chart layouts

▶ Placing charts in the right spot

▶ Creating charts

▶ Troubleshooting problems with chart format and placement

. . . .

*T*he essential purpose of a report is to communicate meaning to its readers. Lines of text and columns of numbers undeniably communicate meaning, but sometimes they don't do so as forcefully as a visual image. The right picture can sometimes be worth much more than a thousand words.

Choosing the Best Chart Type for Your Data

The charting capabilities of Crystal Reports give numbers and statistics an added dimension of communication. Numerical data represented visually in a chart can much more readily reveal trends or show relative sizes. Different types of data are best displayed with different types of charts, and Crystal Reports offers a wide variety to accommodate just about any data set you may have. This section provides a brief summary of each chart type.

Side-by-side bar chart

The *side-by-side bar chart* represents data as a series of bars, lined up side-by-side and extending vertically from the bottom or horizontally from the left edge of the chart. This type of chart is an excellent choice for displaying comparative values, such as the annual sales volume for a company's major divisions for a period of several years. Not only sales totals but also any trends in sales would be evident.

Figure 15-1 is an example of a two dimensional, side-by-side bar chart of the percentages of a person's carbohydrate, fat, and protein intake for a one-week period. If this person is trying to keep to a low-carb diet, he is not doing very well. He is definitely outside the Zone.

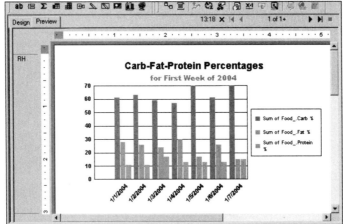

Figure 15-1:
2-D side-
by-side
bar chart.

Another option is the 3-D side-by-side chart, which is shown in Figure 15-2.

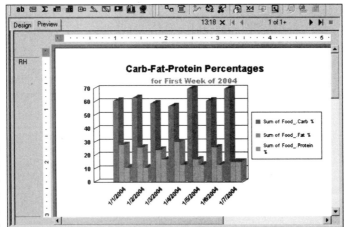

Figure 15-2:
3-D side-
by-side
bar chart.

Stacked bar chart

The *stacked bar chart* also represents multiple series of data as vertical or horizontal bars, but a single bar represents each value for all series. The value of the second series is stacked on top of the value of the first series, the value of the third series stacked on top of the second series' value, and so on. As with the side-by-side bar chart, the stacked bar chart is good for showing the total value of multiple series of data, while also showing how the relative contribution of each series changes over time. Figure 15-3 shows a 2-D stacked bar chart. 3-D stacked bar charts are also available.

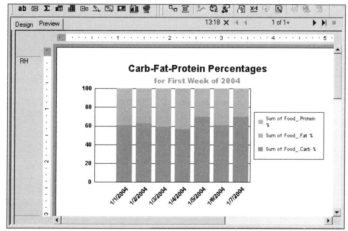

Figure 15-3: 2-D stacked bar chart.

Line chart

A *line chart* displays one or more lines that each connect a series of points. This type of chart is excellent for showing the value of a single variable as it changes over time or the values of several variables with comparable scales. Figure 15-4 shows a line chart of calories consumed daily for the week starting January 1, 2004. This person is not very consistent in his eating patterns. Calorie consumption ranges from about 1900, down to near-starvation level at 1200.

Area chart

In an *area chart,* areas that are filled in with colors or patterns represent the values of variables. This type of chart is good for showing the percentage contribution of a small number of variables to a total. Figure 15-5 shows an area chart displaying the same information that the previously displayed bar charts presented.

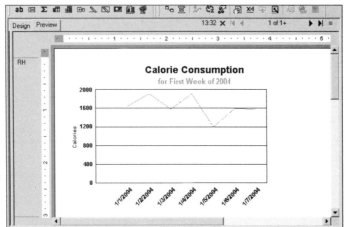

Figure 15-4:
Line chart.

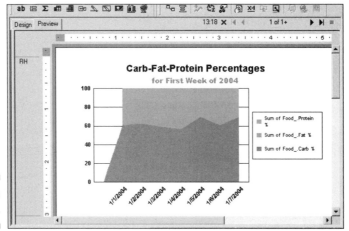

Figure 15-5:
Area chart.

This chart makes it abundantly clear that the bulk of this person's diet was carbohydrates in the time period plotted, with a relatively small amount of protein consumption.

Pie chart

Pie charts are two-dimensional circular charts that display one series of data values, where each value determines how large a sector of the pie that element of the series receives. You might use a pie chart to show the relative contribution each operating division makes to a corporation's sales. Or you might use it to look at food consumption. Figure 15-6 is a pie chart that looks at only the fat data for the first week of 2004. It shows that fat consumption varied quite a bit. Fat consumption on the fourth was more than twice as much as it was on the seventh. It was probably that big piece of pecan pie on the fourth that did it.

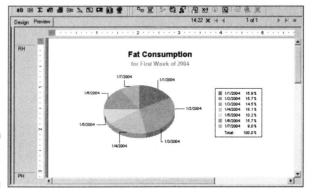

Figure 15-6:
Pie chart.

Doughnut chart

A *doughnut chart* is similar to a pie chart, but the center of the pie is cut out, leaving a 3-D ring that encircles a number that may or may not bear any relationship to what you're trying to emphasize with your chart. It is supposed to show the number of records being represented, but, depending on your data, may not relate to anything pertinent. Figure 15-7 is the doughnut chart for the same data illustrated by the pie chart in Figure 15-6. The doughnut's bites are equivalent to the pieces of the pie. In this case, the number in the center of the doughnut is unrelated to the percentage of fat in a person's meals.

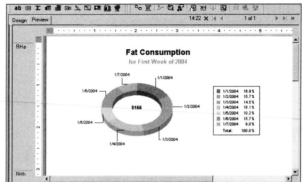

Figure 15-7:
Doughnut
chart.

3-D riser chart

The *3-D riser chart* is a cool way to represent several series of data points. If the number of series and the number of data points are both under about ten, a 3-D riser chart can convey a lot of meaning — and look great too. Values are represented by three-dimensional objects rising out of a three-dimensional plane. Various shapes of objects are available.

Figure 15-8 shows a 3-D riser chart for New Year's week carbohydrate, fat, and protein data. It uses octagon-shaped risers, which I think are the best looking of the several available riser shapes. For some data sets, however, one of the other shapes may be better. Try them all out and see which one communicates your data best.

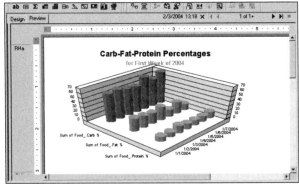

Figure 15-8:
3-D riser
chart.

3-D surface chart

The *3-D surface chart* represents several series of data points with a multicolor surface that sits over a three-dimensional plane. As with the 3-D riser chart, the 3-D surface chart is most meaningful if there are fewer than about ten series and ten data points within each series.

Figure 15-9 is an example of a 3-D surface chart. It gives the data a different look from that obtained with the 3-D riser chart.

XY scatter chart

XY scatter charts are effective when you have a large number of data points and you want to see (for example) whether any clusters show up in the data — and, if so, how compact the clusters are. These graphs are also good at showing whether two variables are correlated. If they are, you'll be able to draw a line with a characteristic slope through the average location of the points. The slope indicates the nature of the relationship. The closeness of the points to the line indicates the strength of the relationship.

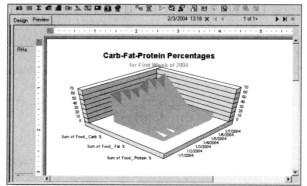

Figure 15-9:
3-D surface
chart.

This chart in Figure 15-10 plots carbohydrate consumption on the horizontal axis against fat consumption on the vertical axis. The two are definitely correlated, because they fall close to a straight line. The variation from a perfect linear relationship is caused by varying protein consumption (not shown) from day to day. The legend to the right of the chart is not legible. The XY scatter chart was apparently not designed for this many data points.

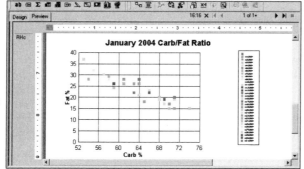

Figure 15-10:
XY scatter
chart.

Radar chart

A *radar chart* is a polar graph that looks somewhat like a radar screen or a plot of an antenna's radiation characteristics. Arrayed around the perimeter are the changing values that generate the chart. The magnitudes of the one or more series of data depicted by the chart are shown by how far they extend from the center toward the perimeter. This type of chart is good for showing how several quantities vary with respect to each other as time or some other variable changes.

The chart in Figure 15-11 shows the same data as the XY scatter chart, but in a very different form. In this chart, the outer jagged line shows the amount of carbohydrate consumed on a daily basis and the inner jagged line shows the amount of fat. Clearly this person is following a high-carb diet.

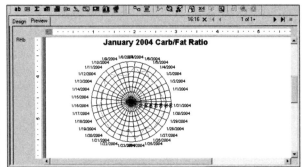

Figure 15-11:
Radar chart.

Bubble chart

A *bubble chart* is similar to an XY scatter chart, except the markers that indicate data points are circles that vary in size. The larger the value of that data point, the bigger the circle. The value of one variable is plotted against the X-axis; the value of a second variable is plotted against the Y-axis, and the value of a third variable is indicated by the size of the bubble. Use this type of chart when you have three series of data that vary with time or with some other fourth variable.

The bubble chart in Figure 15-12, like the XY scatter chart, shows a definite linear relationship between carbohydrate and fat. In addition, the bubble chart explicitly shows the magnitude of the protein variable. It shows that protein consumption ranges from quite low to rather high and the variance seems unrelated to amount of carbohydrate consumed. Once again, the legend to the right of the chart is unreadable. Bubble charts have many of the characteristics of XY scatter charts.

Stock chart

A *stock chart* is familiar to anyone who reads the financial section of a newspaper. It's used to show the daily price ranges of stocks and of indexes such as the Dow Jones Industrial Average. For a given date, a line indicates the range of the variable, extending from the variable's lowest to highest values for that day. Crystal Reports gives you a similar chart; you can create it with or without the little tick marks that identify the opening and closing prices. To include the opening and closing tick marks, you need to have four columns of data: Open, High, Low, and Close.

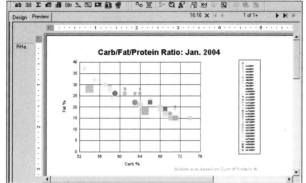

Figure 15-12:
Bubble
chart.

This type of chart is good for showing the differences between two variables. In Figure 15-13, it is immediately obvious that there is a relatively large difference between carbohydrate consumption and fat consumption on January 24, and a relatively small difference on January 8.

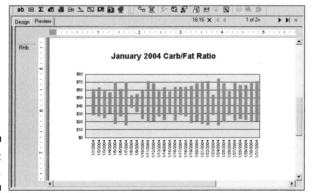

Figure 15-13:
Stock chart.

Numeric axis chart

Numeric axis charts come in six types, as shown in Figure 15-14. They are the numeric axis bar, line, and area charts, and the date axis bar, line, and area charts.

These charts are similar to the ordinary bar, line, and area charts, except their x-axis must be a numeric or date type. The ordinary, bar, line, and area charts are more flexible, but the numeric axis charts may be somewhat simpler to create, assuming that you want the horizontal axis to represent either numbers or dates.

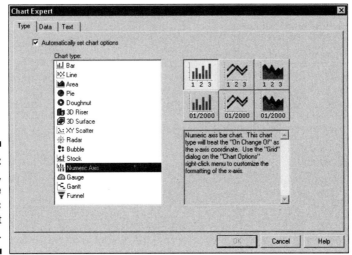

Figure 15-14:
Chart expert,
showing the
six numeric
axis chart
types.

Figure 15-15 is a numerical axis chart showing one month of data on the composition of a person's food intake. As you can see, the person consistently consumes more carbohydrates than anything else, followed by fats, and then proteins. In fact, it looks like carbohydrate consumption is increasing as the month goes on.

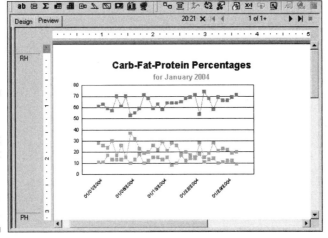

Figure 15-15:
Numerical
axis chart
showing diet
composition
for a one-
month
period.

Gauge chart

A *gauge chart* displays a graphic that looks like an automobile speedometer gauge, with a rotating hand indicating the value of the reported quantity. This type of chart is appropriate only when you have a small number of values to display If you have too many, the gauges get stacked one atop the other in a jumbled mess.

Figure 15-16 shows a gauge chart of a person's food intake for January 19, 2004. It's clear that both fat and protein consumption for that day were below 20 percent and carbohydrate consumption was over 65 percent. This person is apparently eating a high proportion of fruits and vegetables, and very few hamburgers and potato chips.

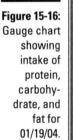

Figure 15-16:
Gauge chart showing intake of protein, carbohy-drate, and fat for 01/19/04.

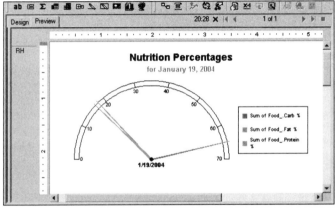

Gantt chart

Project managers often use *Gantt charts* to track progress. Figure 15-17, for example, shows five weeks of data on how quickly Xtreme Mountain Bikes, Inc. ships its products. Each bar represents the interval of time between the entry of an order and when that order was shipped. As you can see, some orders are shipped promptly while others are not. Management can examine which orders were shipped after an excessive delay, and possibly make changes to enable the faster shipment of such orders.

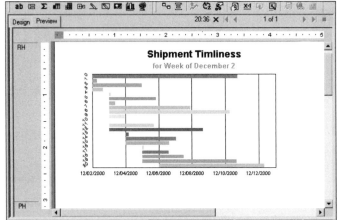

Figure 15-17:
Gantt chart
showing
order
turnaround
for a five-
week period.

Funnel chart

The funnel chart, usually used in customer relationship management (CRM) applications, shows how one series of data points varies over a period of time. Figure 15-18 shows a week of carbohydrate consumption. The chart shows that the subject consumed about the same amount of carbohydrate every day of the week, with perhaps a little more than average on January 5. This type of chart is not particularly applicable to nutrition data, but this example does show what a funnel chart looks like.

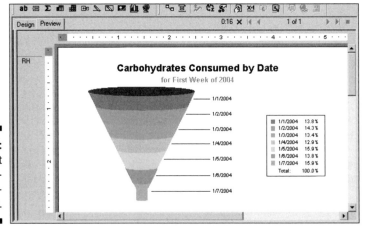

Figure 15-18:
Funnel chart
of carbohy-
drate con-
sumption.

Different Chart Layouts for Different Data Types

Crystal Reports deals with data sets of four different types. The most basic is data retrieved from the database and sent more or less directly to the Details section of the report. No grouping or summarizing is involved. The Advanced chart layout deals with this kind of data; using it, you can filter the data with one or two conditions. You can also group values in several different orders, plot a value for each data record, plot a grand total for all records, and base charts on formulas or running-total fields.

The Group layout provides a higher-level overview than an Advanced layout can. It displays summary information when the value of a specified field changes. Logically enough, you can use the Group layout with only those reports that have at least one group — and at least one summary field for that group.

Figure 15-19 shows the upper-left corner of a cross-tab report of sales for Xtreme Mountain Bikes, Inc. Figure 15-20 shows the right side of the report, displaying the totals and the chart derived from those totals. The Cross-Tab layout is specifically for charting a cross-tab grid, such as the one in Figure 15-19.

The OLAP layout is the structure of a chart based on an OLAP cube. Figure 15-21 shows an example of a chart derived from an OLAP cube. It shows how the various product lines of Xtreme Mountain Bikes are selling in California. Clearly, Bike Shop from Mars is selling a LOT of Xtreme Adult Helmets.

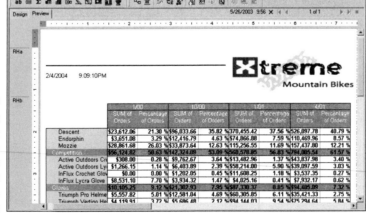

Figure 15-19: Upper-left corner of an Xtreme cross-tab report.

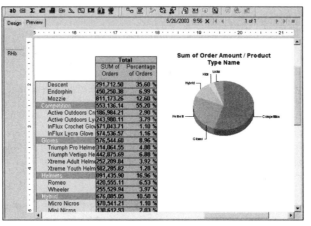

Figure 15-20:
Cross-Tab
chart
showing the
share of
sales due
to each
product line.

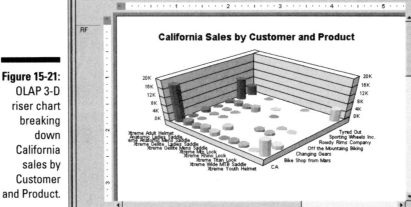

Figure 15-21:
OLAP 3-D
riser chart
breaking
down
California
sales by
Customer
and Product.

A Chart's Placement Affects the Data It Can Represent

A report has multiple sections: a Report Header section, a Page Header section, zero or more Group Header sections, Details sections, as well as Report, Page, and Group Footer sections. Charts can appear in the Report Header and Footer or in Group Headers and Footers.

A chart in the Report Header or Report Footer section draws its data from the entire report. A Chart in a Group Header section draws its data from only that group.

With a chart in the Report Header or Report Footer, you can graphically convey the main point of the report. With charts in either a Group Header or Group Footer, you can show a chart that displays the important information specific to each group.

Figure 15-22 shows a Report Header chart located above data for one of Xtreme Mountain Bikes, Inc.'s customers in California. It shows the values of the sales that Xtreme's various salespeople have made to this customer.

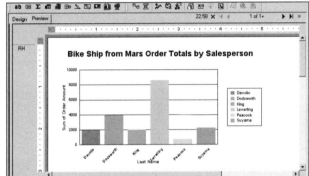

Figure 15-22:
A chart in the Group Header section.

Using Chart Expert

The tool you use to create all the charts shown in this chapter is Chart Expert. You can open Chart Expert by clicking the Chart Expert icon on the Standard toolbar or by choosing Insert⇨Chart on the main menu. The Chart Expert dialog box appears.

Whirlwind tour of the Chart Expert dialog box

The default tab that you see when you first open Chart Expert is the Type tab.

Type tab

The Type tab is shown in Figure 15-23. On this tab, you can select the type of chart you want to include in your report. As you can see, six different bar charts (three 2-D charts and three 3-D charts) are available. The other types of charts have multiple variants as well.

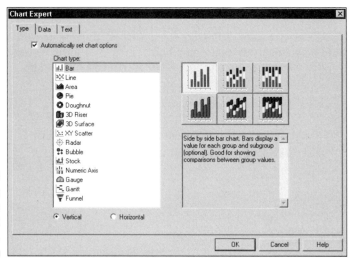

Figure 15-23:
Type tab
of Chart
Expert.

If you leave the Automatically Set Chart Options check box checked, you don't have to worry about the other tabs. The Chart Expert makes default assumptions and displays your chart immediately. In many cases, the result will not be exactly what you want, so you usually have to uncheck this box.

When you select the Vertical option, the bars rise vertically from the bottom of the chart. When Horizontal is selected, the bars move horizontally from left to right. These options don't appear when you have selected a chart that doesn't distinguish between vertical and horizontal (such as a pie chart).

Data tab

The Data tab, which is shown in Figure 15-24, has three areas: Placement, Layout, and Data. In the Placement area, you specify where the chart will go in the report. It can go in a group header or footer or in the report header or footer. The Layout options are described in an earlier section ("Different Chart Layouts for Different Data Types"). In the Data area, you specify what data to show in the chart and what event will trigger the chart display. The triggering event is the change in the value of some field.

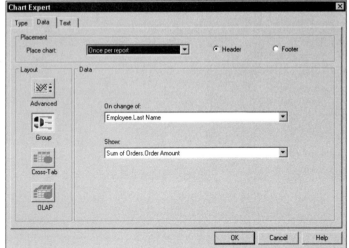

Figure 15-24:
Data tab
of Chart
Expert.

Text tab

The Text tab in the Chart Expert, which is shown in Figure 15-25, is where you add some text to the chart. The two areas are Titles and Format. In the titles area, the Auto-Text boxes are checked by default. This means that Chart Expert selects a title for you, based on the fields the chart uses. (Usually the default choice is not the best, though it's somewhat descriptive.) The Format area at the bottom of the dialog box displays the default fonts chosen for the different types of text objects on the chart. You can select a different font for each of the Title, Subtitle, Footnote, and Legend title categories by clicking the Font button. Doing so displays a Font dialog box where you can specify the font you want.

Options tab

If you unchecked the _Automatically set chart options_ check box on the Type tab, one or two additional tabs appear — the Options tab (always present in such a case) and the Axes tab (present for only some types of charts). The Options tab is shown in Figure 15-26. The areas on this tab are Chart color, Data points, Customize settings, and Legend. You can specify a chart color of either Color or Black and White. Black and White, for use with black and white printers, uses different patterns to show the different areas.

Even if you have a black and white printer, it may be better to specify color anyway. The different colors will show up as different shades of gray on a black and white printer and may be easier to interpret.

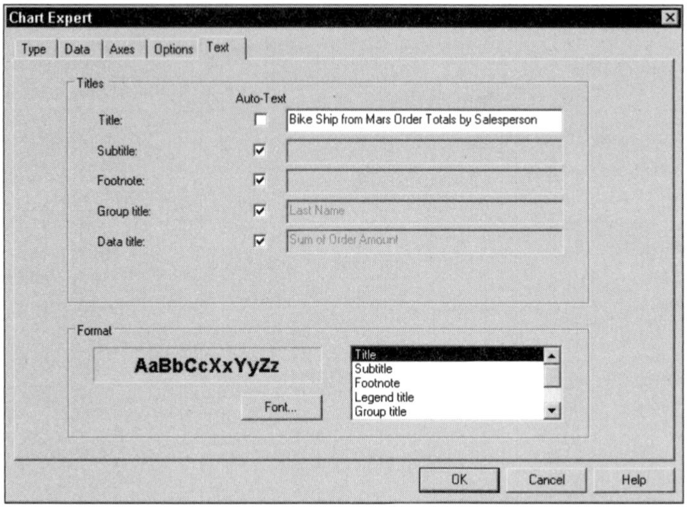

Figure 15-25:
Text tab
of Chart
Expert.

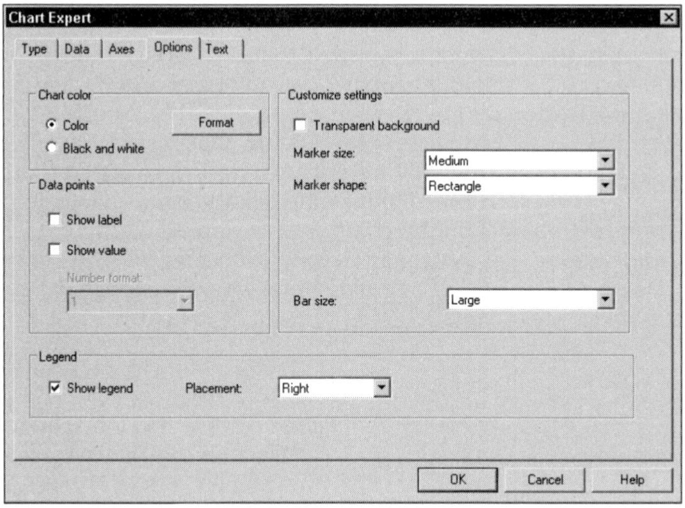

Figure 15-26:
Options tab
of Chart
Expert.

The Data points area allows you to put labels and values in the vicinity of points on the graph. Sometimes these are helpful, but often they just clutter up the chart, without adding much additional information. In many cases leaving both options unchecked is a good idea.

The Customize settings area has a Transparent background check box. You would use this if you were going to underlay content beneath the chart and make the underlaid content visible. You can select from several marker sizes, marker shapes, and bar sizes (for a bar chart). The defaults are good choices to start with.

On charts, a *legend* is not a tale of heroic deeds handed down from long ago. It's an explanation of what the various elements of the chart represent.

Creating a chart

In this section, you run through the steps of using Chart Expert to create a chart. It's not difficult after you do it a few times, but in the beginning there are behaviors that might have you scratching your head. Before you can create a chart, you must have a report and the report must have data upon which to base the chart:

1. **Open a report and switch to Design mode.**

   For the example, use the Customer Orders, by State or District (Mexico) report from Chapter 8 as the basis for the chart. The chart shows the relative contributions of the various states or districts. Figure 15-27 shows what you should see.

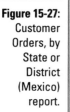

Figure 15-27: Customer Orders, by State or District (Mexico) report.

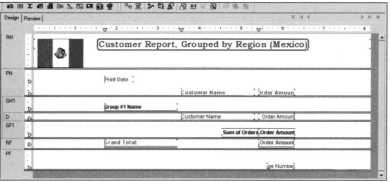

2. **Click the Chart Expert icon or choose Insert⇨Chart.**

   The first decision you need to make is chart type.

3. **Switch to the Type tab, if necessary, and make your selections.**

   To follow along with the example, make the following choices:

   a. **Click to remove the check mark from the Automatically Set Chart Options check box.**

      This means you can have full control over how the chart will look.

   b. **In the Chart type selection pane, select Pie (probably the best way to show the fraction of sales orders coming from each state).**

      The Vertical and Horizontal options at the bottom disappear because they don't apply to pie charts.

4. Switch to the Data tab and make your selections.

To follow along with the example, make the following choices:

a. Place the chart in the report footer by selecting the Footer option in the Placement area. *Once per report* is the only option in the pull-down menu because (for this example) I specified summary data for each state or district, not for individual customers within each state or district.

b. Keep the default layout of Group.

The Group layout is okay because this will be a summary report, pulling one number from each group.

c. In the Data area, keep the default choices of On change of: Customer.Region **and** Show: Sum of Orders.Order Amount.

Again, Crystal Reports has guessed correctly. You want the pie chart to start a new segment when Customer.Region changes. Customer.Region is the field that contains the state or district names. Also, the quantity you want to depict with the chart is the Sum of Orders.Order Amount field. The Chart Expert didn't have to be too smart to select this field because it's the only numeric field in the report.

5. Click the Options tab and make your selections.

To follow along with the example, make the following choices:

a. In the Chart color area, select the Color option.

b. In the Data points area, select the Show Label option.

c. In the Customize settings area, select Detach Pie Slice and then Largest Slice.

d. In the Legend area, select the Show Legend option, keep Right Placement, and leave Layout as Percentage.

6. Click the Text tab and make your selections.

To follow along with the example, make the following choices:

a. Uncheck the Title Auto-Text box and replace the default title with Orders by State or District.

b. Uncheck the Subtitle Auto-Text box and type for Mexico.

c. In the Format area, accept the defaults or change them to fonts you like better.

7. When you're finished, click OK to add the chart to your report.

The bottom of the report page now looks like Figure 15-28. The pie chart is displayed, the largest slice is pulled out, and the legend appears on the right.

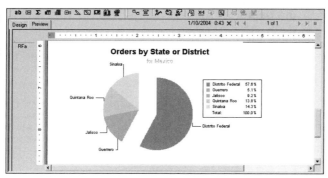

Figure 15-28:
Pie chart
for the
Customer
Orders by
State or
District
(Mexico)
report.

Drilling down from a chart

The steps in the previous section created a chart based on a report in which the details were hidden. Because the details were *hidden* and not *suppressed,* you can drill down to see them if you hover the cursor over the subtotal fields in each group footer. When the cursor changes from the arrow shape to the magnifying-glass shape, a double click drills down to the detail of the group.

You can do the same thing with the chart. When you hover over one of the pie slices in the chart, the cursor changes to the magnifying glass drill-down cursor and you can double-click. You see the same detail that you'd see if you drilled down from the associated group footer. At the same time, a new tab appears to the right of the Preview tab, corresponding to the group you drilled into. From now on, when you want to view the detailed information for that group, you need only click its tab.

Figure 15-29 shows the chart with the drill-down cursor hovering over the Sinaloa pie segment. Double-clicking shows the detail for that state.

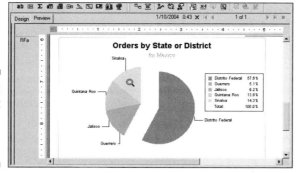

Figure 15-29:
Report
chart, with
drill-down
cursor.

Changing a chart

After you've created a chart on a report and viewed it, you may want to change it. Perhaps the audience for the report has changed and a new chart type would be more appropriate. Perhaps some changes would improve the chart. Here is how you do it:

1. **Right-click somewhere in the chart and choose Chart Expert.**

   Chart Expert appears, with all the options and other selections that you have made.

2. **If you want to change the type of chart, do so on the Type tab.**

3. **If you want to change the layout, do so on the Data tab.**

   You can change any of the parameters that you originally set when you created the chart.

4. **When you've made all your changes, click the Chart Expert's OK button.**

   The changes are instantly incorporated into the chart.

Troubleshooting Chart Problems

Sometimes the chart you're creating for a report just doesn't turn out the way you expect it to. This is less likely to happen as you gain experience with Crystal Reports, but in the beginning, it may occur frequently. Some problems result from a beginner's unfamiliarity with the powerful Crystal Reports features. It's also possible to envision a report simply *isn't* possible, regardless of the power of your report writer. Other problems occur if you try to squeeze too much information into too small a space.

Selecting data to make a chart readable and meaningful

Earlier, this chapter shows how to create a chart that displays cumulative sales orders for all the states and districts in Mexico where Xtreme Mountain Bikes, Inc. has customers. Suppose you want to create a similar chart for the United States. The report would be essentially the same, but with a different selection condition (`Customer.Country` is equal to `USA` instead of `Mexico`). However, if you build the same report in the same way, but this time for the U.S.A. rather than Mexico, you might get something like Figure 15-30.

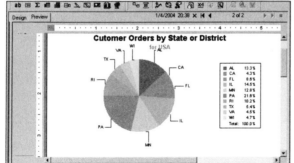

Figure 15-30:
The chart
is getting
busier.

If you had sales in all 50 states plus the District of Columbia, you'd have too many states to make a good pie chart. The result would not communicate very well (tiny slices, hard to see, that sort of thing). But if you display only the states with the ten largest sales volumes, you get a reasonable chart.

The placement of chart elements matters

When you created the chart for Mexico, you kept the default legend placement on the right side of the page. If you select a bottom placement, however, your chart will look quite different, as shown in Figure 15-31.

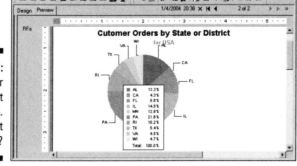

Figure 15-31:
Customer
Order chart
for USA.
What
happened?

The legend at the bottom is so tall that it covers up a big chunk of the chart. If you ever encounter bizarre behavior such as this, check to see whether one element of the chart is hogging the area that rightfully belongs to another element. If it is, you can usually find a way to rearrange things so that everything is displayed.

Chapter 16

Adding Geographic Detail with Maps

In This Chapter

▶ Discovering different map layouts and map types

▶ Creating group, cross-tab, and OLAP layout maps

▶ Troubleshooting maps problems

*M*any reports contain geographic information — and that's easier to comprehend when you add maps that show how the information relates to relevant geographic locations. For example, the Xtreme database contains information on customers located in various cities, regions, and countries around the world. A sales manager may want to know which localities have a concentration of customers or a lack of customers, high sales volume or low sales volume.

All the reasons that make charts a valuable addition to a report apply to maps as well. For data that has a geographical connection, maps are even more valuable. If you can identify a fact (such as a sales total) with a particular city, state, or country, you lock that fact into the reader's mind much more securely than you would if you displayed only a table of numbers.

Crystal Reports has a built-in feature for adding maps to reports, with several different layouts and map types. The various choices enable you to create a map that does the best job of communicating important parts of your report.

Crystal Reports Maps

Before you can create a map with Crystal Reports, you must have a data source with one or more geographical fields (such as City, Region, or Country). Depending on the specific data you have (and on how you want to display it geographically), you can choose the kind of map likeliest to have the most impact on readers. You can choose both the map layout and the type of map.

Map layouts

Four map layouts are available: Advanced, Group, Cross-Tab, and OLAP. Each layout is designed for a specific kind of report, as follows:

- ✔ The Group layout is usually best when your report has groups and you want to associate a map with each group.
- ✔ The Cross-Tab layout is designed to be a part of a cross-tab report.
- ✔ The OLAP layout is designed for use with a report containing an OLAP grid.
- ✔ The Advanced layout is for any map that doesn't fall into the other three categories. It works well for reports that don't have groups or summaries, as well as reports that do.

Map types

In addition to the four map layouts, you can choose one of five map types. If the data you're reporting has a geographic component, one of these map types is probably the best way to show the geographical relationships of the data. The major value of Crystal Reports maps is that they associate some numerical quantity (such as a sales total) with a geographic location in a memorable visual impression that is likelier to be retained.

Ranged type

For numerical quantities that can take on an almost infinite variety of values (such as sales totals), it's helpful to aggregate records with similar values into *bins* — digital storage areas for related records. Each one holds the records for a range of values — a subset of the total range of values. By assigning each bin a different color, shade of gray, or other indicator of magnitude, you can associate geographical regions on a ranged map with specific quantities, making comparisons easy. You can establish bin size in four ways:

- ✔ **Equal count:** With an equal count ranged map, the same number of regions (or as close to the same number as possible) appears in each bin. For example, if the regions are the fifty states of the United States and ten different bins show ranges of sales volume, each of ten different shades of gray can be applied to five states. The five states with the highest level of sales would perhaps be shown as white, and the five states with the lowest level of sales would be shown as black, with progressively darker shades of gray in between, moving from high sales volume to low.

  This map type is best when values are unevenly distributed among the regions. It prevents a situation in which most regions are the same color, with only one or a few that fall into different bins and thus have different colors.

✔ **Equal range:** This map type has bins of equal size (or as close to equal as possible), regardless of how many records fall into each bin. Equal range maps are most useful when the distribution of values being displayed is fairly uniform, with approximately equal numbers of records in each bin.

✔ **Natural break:** This map type applies only to reports that contain summary values. It assigns separate clusters in the data into separate bins.

✔ **Standard deviation:** This map type is used to show statistical analysis. It is best used with three bins, no more, no fewer. The middle bin shows regions associated with values within *one standard deviation of the mean* of the entire data set. The bins above and below hold the regions that are more than one standard deviation removed from the mean.

Dot density type

The *dot density* type of map is good for giving the reader a general idea of where concentrations of records are located and the overall distribution of records. One dot is placed on the map for each record. A company might use this type of map to show the locations of their dealerships. The map would make obvious which regions are adequately covered and which are not — but wouldn't be good at conveying quantitative information.

Graduated type

The *graduated* type of map is similar to the ranged type, putting a symbol in the middle of each region (instead of giving an entire region a specific color or shade of gray) to represent the numerical value associated with that region. The size of the symbol corresponds to the magnitude of the associated value. The default symbol is a circle, but you can use a different symbol if you want.

Pie chart type

The *pie chart* type of map associates a pie chart with each geographic area being displayed. It's useful only when you're comparing the values of several related items in a geographic region. For example, if you want to know the relative sales levels of Xtreme's five major product categories in each region, a pie chart associated with each region on the map would give you a visual picture of that comparison.

Pie charts make sense only if the values of all segments of the pie add up to 100 percent of the total.

Bar chart type

As with pie charts, *bar charts* associated with maps are useful only when you're comparing the values of several related items in a geographical region. Unlike pie charts, bar charts don't require that the total of all values represented by the bars add up to 100 percent. You can use bar charts to show, for instance, the relative sales of bicycles and helmets for the regions of interest, ignoring the other products that Xtreme sells.

Map placement

Where you place a map on a report depends on the information you want it to display. If the map uses data taken from the entire report, you will want to place it in the Report Header or Report Footer section so it can access the needed data. If you want to associate a map with a specific group in the report, place the map in the Group Header or Group Footer for that group. You can also place a map in a subreport of your main report. (See Chapter 12 for information on subreports.)

Creating a Map Step by Step

To create a map, start with a report that has the kind of data best illustrated by a map. This means the report should have at least one geographical field, such as city, state, or country. It also should have at least one numerical field, the value of which varies from one geographical location to another. Certain kinds of maps, such as the pie chart and bar chart types, have additional constraints, as noted previously.

Creating an advanced layout map

This section uses the Advanced layout to add a map to a report:

1. **Load the Customer Orders, by State or District (Mexico) report.**

   This report was created in Chapter 8 and enhanced with a chart in Chapter 15.

2. **On the Insert Tools toolbar, click the Insert Map icon.**

   The Data tab of Map Expert appears.

3. **In the Placement area, select Once Per Report for the Place Map option, and then select the Footer option.**

   This places the map in the report footer.

4. **In the Layout area, click the Advanced icon.**

   The display of the Data area changes, as shown in Figure 16-1.

5. **Drag** `Customer.Region` **from the Available fields pane to the Geographic field box.**

   The `Customer.Region` field automatically appears in the On Change of box also.

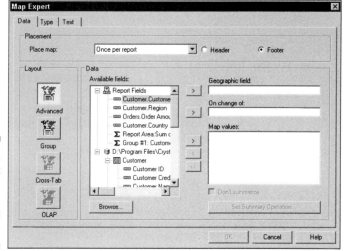

Figure 16-1:
Map Expert
with
Advanced
layout
selected.

6. **Drag** `Report Area:Sum of Orders.Order Amount` **from the Available fields pane to the Map values pane.**

7. **Click the Type tab.**

    The default type shows as Ranged, which is what you want, so keep it. The other defaults are good too, so leave Number of Intervals at 5, Distribution Method at Equal count, Color of Highest Interval at White, and Color of Lowest Interval at Black.

8. **Verify that the Allow Empty Intervals option is checked.**

9. **Click the Text tab.**

10. **Type a Map title and legend titles, if appropriate, and then click OK.**

    Map Expert generates your map, as shown in Figure 16-2.

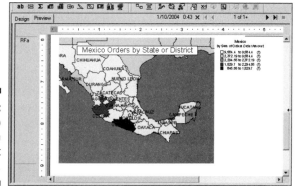

Figure 16-2:
The map
appears in
the report
footer.

The five states or districts appear in five shades of gray as you specified. The top-producing Distrito Federal is white — and a little difficult to see because it encompasses only Mexico City. The state of Guerrero is black because it has the lowest order total. The three other states that have Xtreme customers have three different shades of gray.

Now you know how to add a map to a report. You can make various alternate choices — different types, different fields, different options — but the procedure for any of the Advanced layout reports is essentially the same. The procedure for the other layouts is a little different.

Creating a Group layout map

To create a map with a Group layout, your report must have at least one group and at least one summary field for that group. To illustrate this, you can use the Customer Orders, Grouped by State or District (USA) report created for the United States in Chapter 6 (refer to Figure 6-13). The Mexico report doesn't have enough states to show grouping.

To create a Group layout map, do the following:

1. **Click the Insert Map icon.**

2. **Make sure that the Data tab of Map Expert is displayed.**

3. **In the Placement area, specify a placement of once per report in the footer.**

4. **Confirm that in the Layout area, Group is selected.**

5. **In the Data area, retain the** On Change of: Customer.Region **option and the** Show: Percentage of Sum of Orders.Order Amount **option.**

6. **Switch to the Type tab and verify that Ranged is selected, the Number of Intervals is 5, and the Distribution Method is Equal count.**

   Leave Color of Highest Interval as White, and Color of Lowest Interval as Black. Leave Allow Empty Intervals checked.

7. **Click OK.**

   The map shown in Figure 16-3 appears. It's clear that Pennsylvania does substantial business, but (surprisingly) California and Virginia do relatively little. Considering California's weather, Xtreme should be selling a lot more bikes there. This bears looking into.

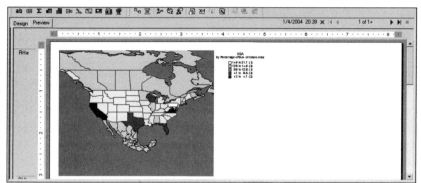

Figure 16-3:
Map
showing
distribution
of orders
from the U.S.

Creating a Cross-Tab layout map

To create a cross-tab layout, your report must have a cross-tab summary field and the rows or the columns must contain a geographical field. In Chapter 10, you built such a report that shows Xtreme's sales from several provinces of Canada (Sales by Province). You can use that report as the base for a Cross-Tab layout map.

To create a map showing the relative sales figures for Canadian provinces that contain Xtreme customers, do the following:

1. **Click the Insert Map icon, or choose Insert⇨Map.**

   The Data tab of Map Expert appears.

2. **In the Placement area, select Footer.**

3. **Click the Cross-Tab icon to change the Data area to the Cross-Tab function.**

4. **In the Data area, for Geographic field, select** `Customer.Region`.

5. **Leave Subdivided By with a value of** `None`.

6. **Verify that Map on contains** `Sum of Orders.Order Amount`.

7. **Click the Type tab, and then select the Ranged type.**

8. **Adjust the options the way you want them, and then click OK.**

   Crystal Reports draws your map, which should look something like Figure 16-4. It's easy to see that British Columbia has the largest order volume and Manitoba has the smallest.

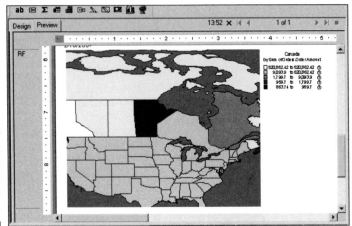

Creating an OLAP layout map

The procedure for creating a map with an OLAP layout is similar to the procedure with a cross-tab layout. The main difference is that the report must contain an OLAP grid rather than a cross-tab object. One of the dimensions of the grid must be a geographical field. Chapter 14 describes creating a report with an OLAP grid — but it doesn't have a geographical dimension, so a map with an OLAP layout would make no sense in that report.

To add a map to a report that *does* have a geographical dimension, follow these steps:

1. **With any report that has a geographical dimension open in the workspace, click the Insert Map icon (on the Insert Tools toolbar).**

   Map Expert appears.

2. **In the Placement area, select either Header or Footer.**

3. **In the Layout area, click the OLAP icon if it's not already selected.**

4. **In the Data area, select a geographical field in the On Change Of pulldown list.**

5. **If you're adding a pie chart or bar chart to the map, select a field in the Subdivided By pull-down list. For a ranged map, leave this option at None.**

6. **For a simple map (such as the one in this example), leave the Other Dimensions option alone.**

7. **Click OK.**

   Crystal Reports draws the map you've specified, basing it on the information in the OLAP grid.

Including maps in subreports

You can include maps in subreports. The procedure for including a map in a subreport is the same as that for a report, except the subreport Design tab must be active. (That makes so much sense, I almost hate to mention it. Oops. Too late. There it is, in indelible print.)

Changing maps

Speaking of indelible print, after you add a map to a report, it's not cast in concrete. You can change it easily. Just right-click the map and choose Map Expert. Now you have the same control over the map as you had when you first created it.

Troubleshooting Map Problems

If you create a map and it doesn't look the way you expect it to, check to make sure that the Preview tab is active. If the Design tab is active, Crystal Reports displays a generic placeholder map in the location where the actual map is located.

If you create a map and all you see is a blank rectangle, check to make sure you based the map on a geographical field. If you based it on a non-geographical field, Crystal Reports displays a non-geographical map — of, in effect, nothing.

If you create a map of the Ranged type and you don't get the spectrum of colors or shades of gray that you expected, check to make sure that the distribution method you chose is appropriate for the data you're illustrating.

Part IV
Crystal Reports in the Enterprise

The 5th Wave   By Rich Tennant

"Well, I got in touch with Enterprise like you said, and all of a sudden there's some Kirk guy in my living room asking me to keep an eye on this for him."

In this part . . .

Besides being a great standalone report writer, Crystal Reports is an integral part of an enterprise-spanning data retrieval, analysis, documentation, and publishing system. In this part, I show you how Crystal Reports fits into the bigger picture of effective communication in a large organization.

Chapter 17

Crystal Enterprise Components

C rystal Enterprise is an enterprise-level companion product of Crystal Reports, designed for online viewing of reports by users across an entire enterprise. Hundreds or even thousands of users can view the same Crystal Reports report simultaneously. With Crystal Enterprise, you can expose reports to users who don't have Crystal Reports and who may not even have access to the database behind a given report. All such users need is a browser running on a workstation in your organizational intranet, on an extranet, or on the World Wide Web. Unlike static HTML pages, reports viewed with Crystal Enterprise show the effects of updates to the underlying database without the need for re-exporting. Drill-down also works in the same way it would if the report were viewed with Crystal Reports.

Understanding Business Views

In earlier chapters, you see how to create a report based on a single data source, such as an Access database or an Excel spreadsheet. An enterprise with multiple disparate databases, however, needs reports that draw data from multiple sources — and Crystal Enterprise provides that capability in its Business Views feature. A *Business View* is a collection of *Business Elements* (abstract objects that transform the tables in the Data Foundation into visual components that give a clearer picture of the data from a business perspective); it provides the highest level of abstraction for report developers and end users.

Setting up a Business View is not the responsibility of the report developer, but rather of the system administrator. Even so, report developers in an enterprise should understand what business views are and how they are created.

The Three Muska-Tiers

All right. Crystal Enterprise does not really employ Athos, Porthos, and Aramis — but it does have a three-tiered structure. The three tiers are:

- **Data tier:** The data tier consists of the multiple databases that contain the data used by the views and objects in the reports that developers build. That's about all there is to say about the data tier.

- **Business tier:** The business tier is where the "heavy lifting" gets done, and so it gets its own section, following.

- **Client tier:** The client tier includes Crystal applications, such as reports created with Crystal Reports. The designers and users of these applications see only the (virtual) tables and fields that are available in the specific Business View that was created for them. Different people with different data needs will have access levels. Two people running the same report may see different things depending on the Business View the report is based on.

The Business Tier

The business tier is the domain of system administrators, who use the Business View Manager to create and modify Business View objects. These objects are used to create the views and other objects that reports are based on.

With the Business View Manager, the administrator can specify Data Connections, set security levels, and selectively control access to the different data sources in the data tier. End users who are executing Crystal Reports have access to only the data specified by the Business View Manager.

A business view can contain five different kinds of objects: Data Connections, Dynamic Data Connections, Data Foundations, Business Elements, and Business Views. The rest of this section explains each of these objects in turn.

Data Connection

If you have connected to a data source in Crystal Reports (and it's a pretty good bet that you have, if you've read this far), then you know how to make a

Data Connection with the Business View Manager. The procedure is practically identical, with a little bit of extra security thrown in. To illustrate how similar making a Business View Data Connection is to connecting to a database when you are developing a Crystal report, let's connect to our old friend `xtreme. mdb`. Here's a step-by-step procedure:

1. **Select Business View Manager from the Crystal Enterprise 10 start menu.**

   The Business View window appears, holding the Log On dialog box shown in Figure 17-1.

Figure 17-1:
Crystal
Enterprise
Log On
dialog box.

2. **Enter your password and authentication, and then click OK.**

   The Welcome to Business View Manager window, shown in Figure 17-2, appears.

3. **Double-click the Data Connection icon.**

   The Choose a Data Source dialog box appears, as shown in Figure 17-3.

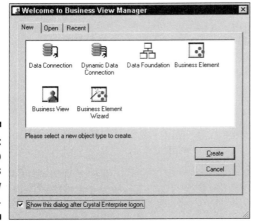

Figure 17-2:
Welcome to
Business
View
Manager.

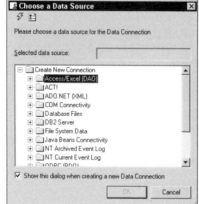

Figure 17-3:
Select a
data source
from the
list of data
source
types.

4. Double-click the Access/Excel (DAO) type.

This produces the Access/Excel (DAO) connection dialog box. Click the
ellipsis button to the right of the Database Name field, find `xtreme.mdb`
and select it. This will give you something that looks like Figure 17-4.

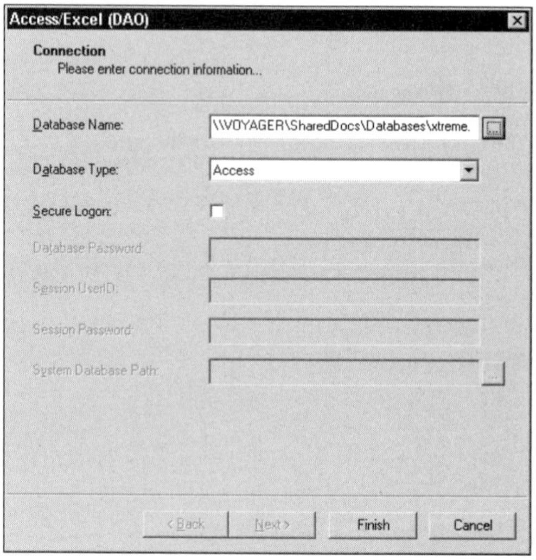

Figure 17-4:
Dialog box
showing
connection
to xtreme.
mdb.

5. Click the Finish button to establish the connection, and then click OK in the Choose a Data Source dialog box.

6. In the Set Data Connection Password dialog box that appears next (see Figure 17-5), enter your user name, password, and runtime prompt mode choice. Choose Never Prompt for Runtime Prompt Mode.

Figure 17-5:
Setting the
connection
password.

If you store data-source logon credentials in the Repository (see Chapter 18), you should set the Runtime Prompt Mode to Never Prompt so users who are already authenticated don't have to enter user name and password again to use this data connection. In addition, you should specify Never Prompt if this connection is one of several that are part of a Dynamic Data Connection. If, on the other hand, you prefer to have users log on to data sources individually, then don't store logon information in the Repository — and be sure to set the Runtime Prompt Mode to Always Prompt.

7. On the Business View Manager's File menu, click Save.

The Save As dialog box appears.

8. Replace the default Object Name with a descriptive name.

To follow along with this example, name the object Xtreme Development. If you were building a real production system, you might go through development, testing, and production stages. This is the first leg on that journey.

9. Click the Save button.

You have now established and named a connection to a database.

An administrator can create multiple data connections to multiple data sources. By using Dynamic Data connections, she can make these multiple data sources available to a developer's report.

Dynamic Data Connection

To illustrate a Dynamic Data Connection, let's add a couple more data connections. Create them in the same way you created Xtreme Development, but name them Xtreme Test and Xtreme Production. Once those connections are created, you can build a Dynamic Data Connection.

1. **From the File menu, select New⇨Dynamic Data Connection.**

   This displays the Choose a Data Connection dialog box, shown in Figure 17-6.

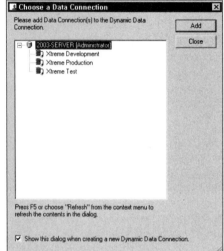

2. **Select the Xtreme Development Data Connection and then click the Add button.**

3. **Select the Xtreme Production Data Connection and then click the Add button.**

4. **Click the Close button.**

   After you close a new Dynamic Data Connection, you can replace the default name with a meaningful name in the next step.

5. **In the Property Browser, select the default name and replace it.**

   For this example, rename the connection `Dynamic Xtreme`. After a Dynamic Data Connection is created, you can modify it by adding new connections or deleting existing ones (as in the next step).

6. **Add a connection by clicking the Add button in the lower-left corner of the window.**

   Doing so brings up the Choose a Data Connection dialog box.

7. **Double-click the Xtreme Test Data connection to add it to the Dynamic Xtreme Dynamic Data Connection, and then click Close.**

8. **Click File⇨Save to save the Dynamic Xtreme Dynamic Data connection.**

The Save As dialog box appears, giving you the opportunity to change the Object Name.

9. **Because Dynamic Xtreme already has a descriptive name, click the Save button to save it as it is.**

Data Foundation

After you've created a Dynamic Data Connection, the next step is to select data items from each Data Connection to make available to report developers. The Data Foundation is the tool designed for that task — an abstraction layer you can use to insert or join different kinds of data objects from different Data Connections. Such objects include tables, views, stored procedures, SQL command objects, formulas, SQL expressions, parameters, filters, and custom functions. This section creates a Data Foundation in a step-by-step process.

Adding tables

To add a table, follow these steps:

1. **On the File menu, select New⇨Data Foundation.**

   The Choose a Data Connection dialog box will appear.

2. **Select Dynamic Xtreme and Click OK.**

   The Set parameter values dialog box pops up.

3. **In the Value drop-down menu, select Xtreme Development and click OK.**

   The Insert Data Tables dialog box appears, as in Figure 17-7.

4. **Expand the Tables node to display a list of tables.**

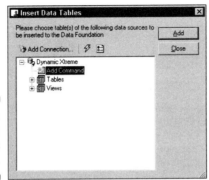

Figure 17-7:
Insert Data
Tables
dialog box.

5. **Select the following tables by holding down the Ctrl key while clicking each one:**

   ```
   Customer
   Employee
   Orders
   Orders_Detail
   Product
   Product_Type
   Supplier
   ```

6. **Click Add, followed by Close.**

Linking tables

You will need to link the tables you have just added to Xtreme Foundation, so that records in one table match related records in another table. For example, you want the orders made by customer Smith to be linked to customer Smith. This linking is done with columns fields that are common to both tables being linked. In a Data Foundation, you can link a table from one data source to a table that comes from a different data source.

Business View Manager has a feature called Smart Linking. It will automatically link the tables in a Data Foundation. It is a good idea to check the result, to make sure Business View Manager has put in all the links you want and has not inserted any extraneous links. Smart Linking relies on matching names of fields or matching keys in different tables. You can add and delete links manually if you want to use fields with differing names to link two tables (or if you want to change the linking done by the Smart Linking feature).

Let's link. Here's the procedure:

1. **Right-click in the main Data Foundation window.**

   This displays the shortcut menu.

2. **Select Smart Linking By Name.**

   This links the tables by field name, as shown in Figure 17-8.

   The `Customer` table is linked to the `Supplier` table by `Postal Code`, a field that both tables have. For the purpose of this application, however, the fact that a customer and a supplier might have the same `Postal Code` is of no significance. This not-so-Smart Link should be deleted.

3. **Right-click the link between the `Customer` table and the `Supplier` table.**

   A shortcut menu pops up.

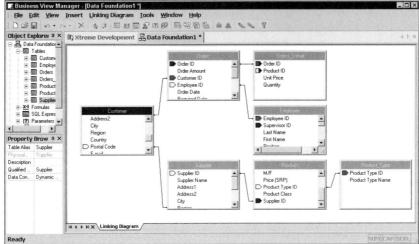

Figure 17-8:
The tables
are linked
by field
name.

4. **Click Delete Link on the shortcut menu, and the link disappears.**

   Linking `Customer` to `Supplier` is one thing that Smart Linking did that it should not have done. It also failed to do something that it should have done: It did not link the `Orders_Detail` table to the `Product` table. You can do that manually. (Looks like people are still smarter than computers in some ways.)

5. **Click the `Product ID` field in the `Orders_Detail` table, and drag down to the `Product ID` field in the `Products` table.**

   A link appears, as shown in Figure 17-9.

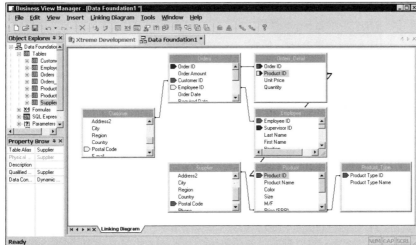

Figure 17-9:
The Orders_
Detail table
has been
manually
linked to
the Product
table.

Inserting formulas

In Chapter 11, I discuss formulas in Crystal Reports. You can also create formulas with Crystal Enterprise's Business View Manager, in much the same way as in Crystal Reports. The difference is that Business View Manager is a tool that system administrators use to provide a friendly environment for report developers. All the tables are there, regardless of what database they reside in. They appear as virtual tables to the report developer. They are already linked. Any needed formulas are provided, as are other database objects that the report developer might need. Crystal Enterprises migrates the harder tasks to its system administrator so people with a lower skill level can create reports in Crystal Reports, based on the Business Views created with the Business View Manager.

To create a formula with Business View Manager, suppose your report developers want to report on how long an employee has been employed by the firm. This is important for the awarding of sabbaticals and the scheduling of anniversary parties. Take the following steps:

1. **On the Insert menu, select Insert Formula.**

   The Business View Formula Editor, looking strikingly like the Crystal Reports Formula Editor, appears (as in Figure 17-10).

2. **Make sure Crystal Syntax is selected in the Formula Editor toolbar above the window area.**

3. **In the Functions window, expand** Functions, Date and Time, **and** DateDiff, **and then double-click** DateDiff(intervalType, StartDateTime, endDateTime) **to select it.**

   DateDiff (, ,) appears in the formula's text window, with the cursor blinking just to the right of the opening parenthesis.

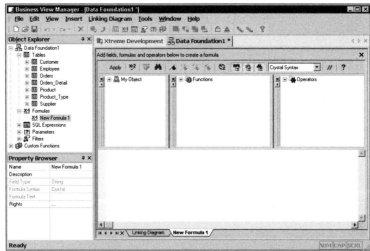

Figure 17-10:
The Formula Editor in Business View Manager looks like the Formula Editor in Crystal Reports.

4. **Fill in the missing values as follows:**

```
DateDiff ("yyyy", {Employee.Hire Date}, CurrentDate)
```

5. **Click the X+2 check icon in the Formula Editor toolbar to check for syntax errors in your formula.**

   With any luck, a message box pops up and says, No errors found. If it says something else, look back at your formula and correct the error.

6. **Click Apply in the Formula Editor toolbar to save the formula.**

   Your new formula should now appear in the Object Explorer on the left side of the window, with the name New Formula 1.

7. **Click New Formula 1 in the Object Explorer to select it.**

8. **In the Property Browser, change the name of the formula to** Years of Service.

   You do this by selecting the old name (New Formula 1) in the Property Browser and replacing it with Years of Service.

9. **Save the formula by clicking the floppy-disk icon in the Business View Manager toolbar.**

10. **Save the Data Foundation as** Xtreme Foundation.

Additional objects

In addition to tables and formula, you can also create SQL expressions, filters, parameters, and custom functions in a Data Foundation. The purpose of all this object creation is to relieve the report developers who will be using Crystal Reports in conjunction with Crystal Enterprise from the task of creating them. An additional benefit of creating these objects here is that it imposes standardization upon the organization. Report developers have access to exactly the information the system administrator has decided they need in order to do their jobs. Sensitive information is withheld from people who have no need to see it. Information that people *do* need is available in the most easily understood form. That easily understood form is a Business View, which is made up of Business Elements.

Creating a Business element

A Business Element is an abstract object that transforms the tables in the Data Foundation into visual components that make clearer business sense than raw numbers or undigested tables. You can create new Business Elements that correspond to tables but contain only the fields you want your report developers to use. Here's an example:

1. **On the File menu, click New⇨Business Element Wizard.**

   The Business Element Wizard shown in Figure 17-11 appears.

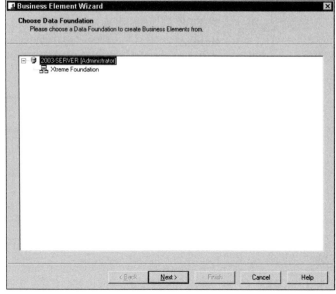

Figure 17-11:
The
Business
Element
Wizard
shows the
Xtreme
Foundation
Data
Foundation.

2. **Select Xtreme Foundation and then click Next.**

   The Create Business Elements dialog box appears.

3. **From the pane on the left, expand the Tables node and select Customer.**

4. **Click the > arrow to move the Customer table over to the Business Elements pane.**

5. **In the Business Elements pane, expand the Customer node to display its fields.**

6. **Select Customer Credit ID and then click the < arrow to remove that field from the Business Element.**

7. **Click Next.**

   The Save to Repository dialog box appears.

8. **Click Next.**

   The *What to do next* dialog box is displayed.

9. **Select Create more Business Elements and then click Finish.**

   The Choose Data Foundation dialog box reappears.

Now you can add another Business Element.

1. **Select Xtreme Foundation again and then click Next.**

2. **In the Create Business Elements dialog box, move the** Employee **table over to the Business Elements pane.**

3. **Remove the following fields that contain sensitive information:**

   Home Phone

   Extension

   Photo

   Notes

   Emergency Contact First Name

   Emergency Contact Last Name

   Emergency Contact Relationship

   Emergency Contact Phone

4. **Add the** Years of Service **formula to the Business Element and click Next.**

5. **On the Save to Repository page, click Next.**

6. **On the What to Do Next page, select Exit and then click Finish.**

Creating a Business View

With the Business Elements created, you can at last create a Business View and offer the highest level of abstraction to your report developers and end users. To the report developer, the Business View appears as an abstract database connection; Business Elements appear as virtual tables that contain Business Fields.

The Business Elements created in the previous section provide a basis for building a Business View in the following steps:

1. **From the File menu, select New⇨Business View.**

   The Insert Business Elements dialog box pops up, as shown in Figure 17-12.

2. **Select Customer and click Add, and then select Employee and click Add again.**

3. **Click the Close button to dismiss the Insert Business Elements dialog box.**

   The Business View now contains the Customer and the Employee Business Elements.

4. **Click File⇨Save.**

   The Save As dialog box appears.

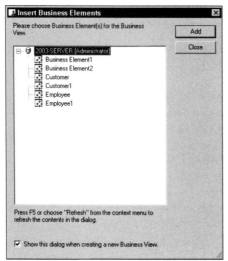

Figure 17-12:
The Insert
Business
Elements
dialog
box lists
Business
Elements
available
for this
Business
View.

5. **In its Object Name field, replace the default name with** Xtreme Business View, **and then click Save.**

   With the Business View you have just created, report developers using Crystal Reports can now build reports based on the Business View, rather than basing their reports on actual tables. This provides centralized control of exactly which information is available for inclusion in reports — and exactly which information is not available.

Crystal Enterprise Admin Launchpad

The Crystal Enterprise Admin Launchpad is the system administrator's point of entry into managing a Crystal Enterprise system. It is browser-based, as shown in Figure 17-13.

There are links to documentation, administrative tools, and the User Launchpad. There are also Web links to the latest versions of Crystal Enterprise documentation and to other resources. The most frequently used link is the link to the Crystal Management console. When you click it, a Crystal Management Console Logon screen appears, asking for your User Name, Password, and Authentication Type. Figure 17-14 shows this screen.

Figure 17-13:
The Admin Launchpad screen.

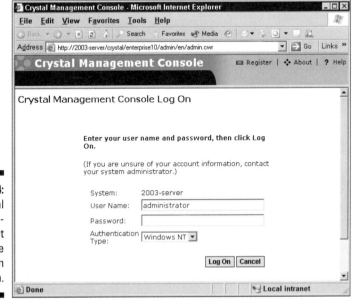

Figure 17-14:
Crystal Management Console Logon screen.

Crystal Management Console

Figure 17-15 shows the Crystal Management Console — which (in general) Crystal Reports application developers never get to see. It's designed to be used only by system administrators, giving them one point from which to control

- ✔ What objects are included in the system
- ✔ How the specified objects are organized
- ✔ Who can use the system
- ✔ What privileges the specified users have
- ✔ What the Web Desktop looks like

The Web Desktop is the screen that developers and users interact with to create, modify, or run reports. With the Crystal Management Console, administrators can also maintain calendars and schedule events.

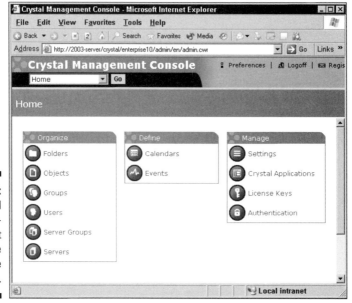

Figure 17-15: Crystal Management Console Home screen.

Crystal Enterprise User Launchpad

The Crystal Enterprise User Launchpad, similar to the Admin Launchpad, is aimed at users rather than system administrators. (In this context, the people who develop applications with Crystal Reports and the people who run those reports are all considered users.) Figure 17-16 shows the User Launchpad.

In addition, the Crystal Enterprise Web Desktop offers links to user documentation, sample reports, the Admin Launchpad, and other resources.

Figure 17-16: Crystal Enterprise User Launchpad main screen.

Crystal Enterprise Web Desktop

The Crystal Enterprise Web Desktop, shown in Figure 17-17, is a model of simplicity.

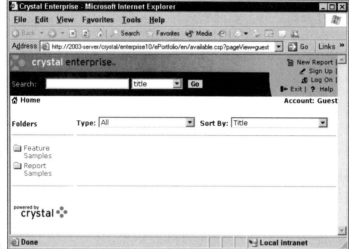

Figure 17-17:
Crystal
Enterprise
Web
Desktop.

Reports and other objects accessible through Crystal Enterprise are organized into folders. Users can interact with those objects through the browser interface. They can run reports, drill down into them, and interact with them in any and all ways possible for users of a full implementation of Crystal Reports.

Crystal Configuration Manager

The Crystal Configuration Manager (CCM) is the system administrator's tool for managing the major components of Crystal Enterprise. Figure 17-18 shows the components of Crystal Enterprise that operate under the surface, allowing users to interact with reports across their network.

Happily, as long as the system administrator is doing his or her job, report designers never have to worry about the CCM.

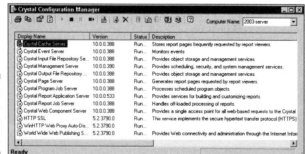

Figure 17-18:
Crystal Con-
figuration
Manager.

Crystal Import Wizard

The Crystal Import Wizard is a tool for importing the environment from a previous installation of Crystal Enterprise or Crystal Info into a Crystal Enterprise 10 system. Acceptable source installations are

- ✔ Info 7.5
- ✔ Crystal Enterprise 8
- ✔ Crystal Enterprise 8.5
- ✔ Crystal Enterprise 9
- ✔ Crystal Enterprise 10

The Crystal Import Wizard facilitates the upgrade of an earlier system to the current version, or migration from one Crystal Enterprise 10 system to another. System administrators can migrate users and groups, folders, report objects, rights, events, and server groups.

Developers and users of Crystal Reports would typically never use the Crystal Import Wizard to create or use a report. System administrators use it to smooth the transition from one system to another. When used correctly, it enables developers and users to start operating in a new Crystal Enterprise 10 environment with a minimum of hassle. All their rights, privileges, and report objects are still available to them. The only difference they notice is the enhanced capabilities of the Crystal 10 environment, compared to the earlier environment they migrated from.

Crystal Publishing Wizard

To make a report accessible to users on a network who don't have Crystal Reports, you must *publish* the report. The easiest way to do this is with a part of Crystal Enterprise called Crystal Publishing Wizard. The wizard walks you step-by-step through a procedure that adds a report created in Crystal Reports to the reports already available through the Crystal Enterprise Web Desktop. As with all the other Crystal Enterprise functions, this operation would normally be accomplished by system administrators in an organization's information systems department, not by an individual report designer.

1. **Launch the Crystal Publishing Wizard and log on.**

   The Select a File page (shown in Figure 17-19) asks you to select a report object from the list displayed. If you do not see the object you want in the list, you can click Add Files to find it and add it to the list.

Figure 17-19:
Crystal
Publishing
Wizard's
Select a
File screen.

2. **The list is empty, so click Add Files to add the file you want to select, and then click Next.**

   After you select a file from the list, the Specify Location page shown in Figure 17-20 appears. You get to tell it where to go (to publish the report object, that is).

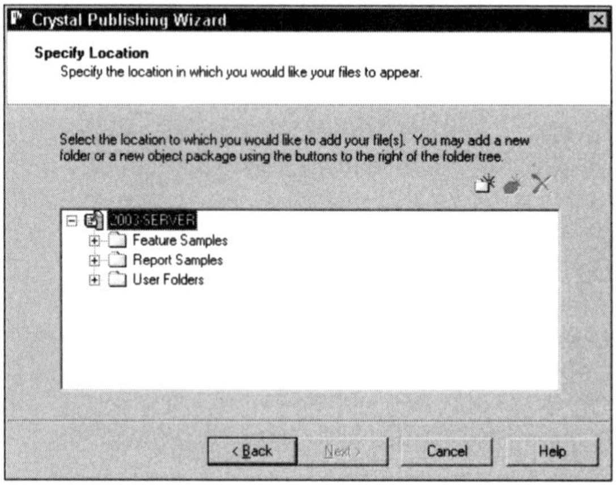

Figure 17-20:
Choose
where
to publish
the report
object on
the Specify
Location
page.

3. **Specify where to publish the report and then click Next.**

   The Location Preview page gives you the opportunity to move the object you have just specified, or other objects to different locations, if you want.

4. **If you are satisfied with where things are, click Next to move on.**

5. **In the Schedule Interval page shown in Figure 17-21, specify when you want the report to run.**

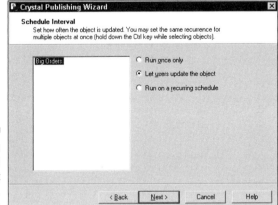

Figure 17-21:
Schedule
report
running.

You can run it once, on a schedule, or let users decide when to run it.

6. **Make your choice for when to run the report, and then click Next.**

   The next screen asks whether you want to refresh your report's repository fields. I talk about repository fields in Chapter 18. If your report does not contain any repository fields, this page has no effect.

7. **Click Next.**

   The last thing the Crystal Publishing Wizard does before publishing your report is to ask whether you want to change any of the report's properties (title, database logon information, parameter values, and so on) before it is published.

8. **Choose either to review and modify the properties or to leave them as they are, and then click Next.**

   The Wizard starts the publishing process. It displays one last dialog box, listing the reports that you have selected for publication.

9. **Click Next one more time and then after the publication operation is complete, click Finish.**

   Users can now view the report when they use the Crystal Enterprise Web Desktop.

Chapter 18

Crystal Repository

- -

- -

*A*s its name implies, Crystal Repository is a central location where you can store report objects. It delivers two benefits to the report developer:

✔ **You can store different types of objects there.** The Repository saves you from reinventing the wheel. After you create an object — a text object, bitmapped image, custom function, or SQL command — you can store it in the Crystal Repository. From there, you can add it to any other reports that you or your colleagues create.

✔ **The Repository remains connected to all the reports that have drawn objects from it.** This means you can take an object from the Repository into a report, update it, and then return it to the Repository. All other reports that contain that object are automatically updated. This saves you from having to keep track of which versions of a particular object are in which reports. You have to manually update the object only once, rather than in all the reports that use it.

The Repository holds the master copy of any object it contains, and that master copy can't be modified while it's in there. To update an object, you must move it into a report, modify it there, and then move it back into the Repository. This eliminates the possibility of object corruption in the Repository due to concurrent access by two users.

The Repository that shipped with Crystal Reports 9 is stored in an Access database. The Crystal 10 Repository is hosted by the Crystal Management Server system database, which is a part of Crystal Enterprise 10. If you already have a Crystal Reports 9 Repository, you can migrate the whole thing to Crystal 10, using the Crystal Repository Migration Wizard.

Storing Your Valuables in Crystal Repository

After you create an object in one report, you can put it into the Repository, where it remains available for reuse in other reports and by other developers. Adding a report object to the Repository is easy, but the methods differ depending on the type of object. The following sections describe these methods.

Adding folders to your Repository

If you keep the objects in the Repository organized, you can find them more easily when you want to add them to your reports. To impose order, you can add folders and subfolders in a tree structure to hold objects in the Repository. You have complete freedom in organizing those folders any way you want. The first step is to launch Repository Explorer, as follows:

1. **In Crystal Reports 10, open a report — any report.**

2. **On the Standard toolbar, click the Repository Explorer icon.**

    A Log On to Crystal Enterprise dialog box appears.

3. **Log on to Crystal Enterprise.**

    The Repository Explorer appears at the right edge of the screen.

4. **Click the Insert a new folder icon.**

    A new folder appears, with the default name New Folder.

5. **Give the new folder a meaningful name, and then press Enter.**

    For this example, name the folder Xtreme. Your screen should look similar to Figure 18-1.

Adding text and bitmapped objects to the Repository

To illustrate how to add a text object or a bitmapped object to the Repository, use the Customer Orders by State or District, Mexico report from Chapter 6. Figure 18-2 shows what it looks like.

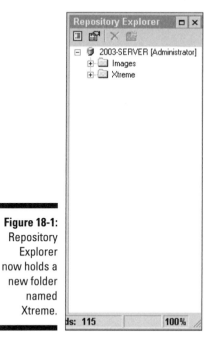

Figure 18-1:
Repository
Explorer
now holds a
new folder
named
Xtreme.

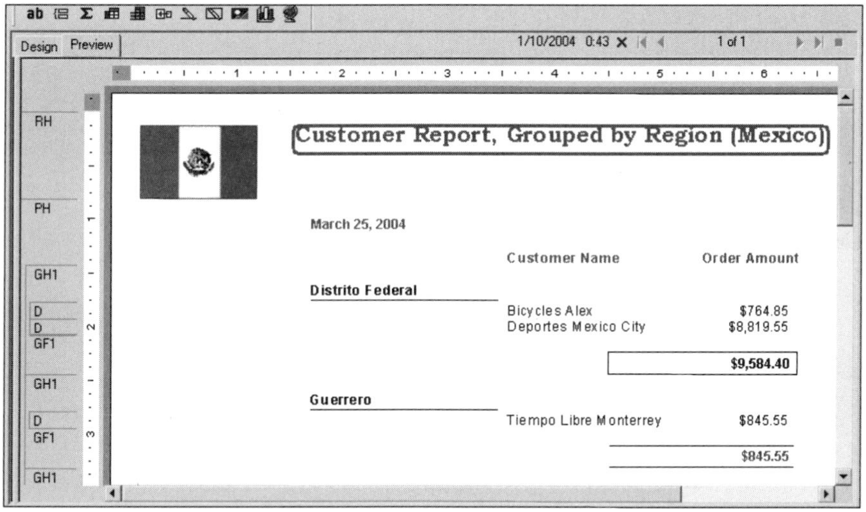

Figure 18-2:
The
Customer
Orders by
State or
District,
Mexico
report.

Suppose you plan to create other reports about sales in Mexico, and want to retain the Mexican flag in the Repository. The flag is an image, but you're likely to be putting other flags in there as well, along with other kinds of images. To keep things straight, first create an Images folder, and then create a Flags sub-folder of the Images folder. Next place the Mexican flag image in the Flags folder, like this:

1. **With your server selected, click on the Insert a new folder icon. When the new folder appears, name it** Images.

2. **With the Images folder selected, click on the Insert a new folder icon. When the new folder appears, name it** Flags.

3. **To add an image to your newly created Repository subfolder, select the image and then drag it to the subfolder in Repository Explorer.**

   For the example, select the image of the Mexican flag and drag it to the Flags folder.

4. **When the Object Information dialog box pops up, enter a name for the object.**

   You may also want to add the author's name and a description, although that information is optional. (I entered the information shown in Figure 18-3.)

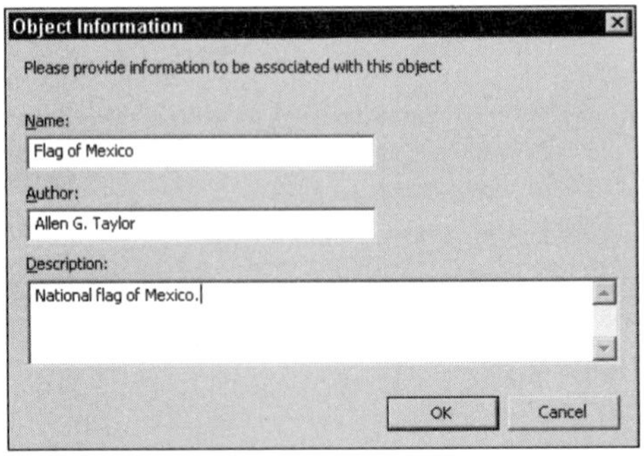

Figure 18-3:
Give the
object a
name.

5. **Click OK.**

   The object is added to the folder in the Repository.

6. **Verify that the object is in the Repository by clicking on the plus sign to the left of the Flags folder.**

   Your new object should now appear in the Repository Explorer tree.

You can add a text object in a similar manner. Just drag it to the appropriate folder in Repository Explorer and name it. From that point on, the object resides in the Repository, still connected to the report you took it from.

Adding custom functions to the Repository

You can create custom functions for use in the formulas you create with Formula Workshop. (Formula Workshop and the creation of custom functions are covered in Chapter 11.)

Putting custom functions in the Repository so they can be reused is a great labor saver. Adding a custom function to the Repository from Formula Workshop is easy; Chapter 11 provides a step-by-step procedure.

Adding SQL commands to the Repository

Relational databases are created and manipulated by commands in SQL. You can add such commands to the Repository in much the same way you would add text objects, image objects, or custom functions. In Chapter 24, I give an overview of SQL commands. For a more complete exposition of SQL, refer to my *SQL For Dummies* (published by Wiley).

For now, here's how to add an existing SQL command to the Repository, where it will be readily available next time you need it:

1. **In the Selected Tables pane of the Database Expert dialog box, find the command you want to add to the Repository.**

2. **Right-click the command and choose Edit Command.**

   The Modify Command dialog box appears.

3. **Select Add to Repository, and then click OK.**

   The Add Item dialog box appears.

4. **Specify a name and Repository location for the command.**

   From now on, the command appears in the Repository node of Database Expert, the Set Datasource Location dialog box, and the Data screen of Report Creation wizards.

Using Repository Objects in a Report

Moving an object from the Repository to a report is essentially the reverse of moving an object from a report to the Repository. There is one method for text and image objects, a second method for custom functions, and a third method for SQL commands.

To add a text object or an image object to a report, follow these steps:

1. **On the Standard toolbar, click the Repository Explorer icon.**
2. **Expand the Text Objects or Images folder, whichever is appropriate.**
3. **Drag the desired object into your report, at the location where you want it.**

   That's all there is to it.

Adding a custom function to a report is only a little more complicated:

1. **On the Expert Tools toolbar, click the Formula Workshop icon.**
2. **In Formula Workshop, expand the Repository Custom Functions node.**
3. **Right-click the desired custom function and choose Add to Report.**

   The function is now added to the report. If the function you added requires other functions for its operation, those functions are automatically added too.

Adding an SQL command is similar to adding a custom function:

1. **On the Expert Tools toolbar, click the Database Expert icon.**
2. **In Database Expert, expand the Repository folder.**
3. **Right-click the command you want to add and choose Add to Report.**

   The SQL command is now part of your report. SQL commands are covered more extensively in Chapter 24.

Modifying a Repository Object

After an object is in the Repository, it's available for inclusion in multiple reports. When these reports are opened, the Repository is checked to see whether the object has been updated since the last time the report was open. If the object has been updated, the new version is downloaded to the report.

You don't have control over when other users might open reports that contain an object you want to modify — so Crystal Reports doesn't allow the modification of Repository objects. To update (or otherwise modify) a Repository object, you must first disconnect the object from the Repository, and then change the object. After the change is complete, you can add the object back to the Repository. The next time anyone opens a report that contains that object, your updated object is the one supplied.

To see how to modify a text object in the Repository, follow these steps:

1. **Open a report in Design view.**

   You might want to open the Mexico Orders, with Running Totals Sorted by Date report from Chapter 6. However, for this example, any report will do.

2. **From the Flags folder of Crystal Repository, drag the Flag of Mexico object to the left edge of the Report Header.**

3. **In Design view in the report, right-click the flag object you just dragged into the report and choose Disconnect from Repository.**

4. **Right-click the flag object again and choose Format Graphic from the menu that pops up.**

   The Format Editor appears.

5. **Click the Border tab and change the Left, Right, Top, and Bottom Line styles to Single, and then click OK.**

6. **Drag the modified graphic object from the report back to the Flag of Mexico icon in Repository Explorer.**

   The Add or Update Object? dialog box appears.

7. **Click the Update button, and then click OK.**

   The Modify Item dialog box appears.

8. **Click OK.**

   The Mexican flag in the Repository now has a single black line border around it.

Updating Reports Automatically Using Connected Repository Objects

You may want to set an organization-wide policy that whenever a Repository object is updated, all the reports that use that object will receive the update the next time they're opened. Doing so guarantees that all reports that use a Repository object are using the same version. On the other hand, people who create reports may not want to surrender control of their report to whoever makes a Repository update. In such a case, they would not want their reports to be automatically updated when opened after a Repository update. Crystal

Reports can be configured to work in either of these two ways. In addition, you can decide — on an individual basis — whether you want a specific report to receive updated Repository objects.

To have all reports that use Repository object receive updated objects when they're opened, configure Crystal Reports in the following manner:

1. **Choose File⇨Options.**

   The Options dialog box appears.

2. **Click the Reporting tab.**

3. **Select the Update Connected Repository Objects on Open option.**

4. **Click OK.**

   From now on, whenever any report is opened, the version numbers of the Repository objects it contains will be compared against the current version numbers of those objects in the Repository. If the Repository contains a newer version, it replaces the older version in the report.

If you don't want the automatic update feature, make sure that Update Connected Repository Objects on Open is *not* checked.

To update the Repository objects in a single report — rather than globally for all reports — note the dialog box that you use to open a report (Figure 18-4 shows an example). At the bottom of that dialog box is an option that reads Update Repository Objects. Repository objects will be updated on the report you open, but not on any others.

Figure 18-4:
Note the
Update
Repository
Objects
option.

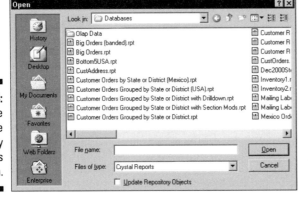

Deleting Objects from the Repository

Sooner or later, Repository objects become obsolete and should be deleted. Of course, you don't want just anyone deleting Repository objects that other people might want to continue using in their reports. Removal of a Repository object is simple. You can do it in three easy steps:

1. **On the Standard toolbar, click the Repository Explorer icon.**

2. **Move to the appropriate folder in the Repository Explorer and select the object you want to remove.**

3. **Press the Delete key, and then click the Yes button to respond to the Confirm Delete dialog box.**

    The object is removed.

Any reports that already include a deleted object will still contain it, but the object can't be included in any other reports from this point on.

Wow. That seems drastic and potentially dangerous. How do you control who has permission to delete Repository objects?

Fortunately, the Repository is stored in a relational database — and relational databases have built-in protections against unauthorized tampering. One of those protections is basic to the database's structure: The database administrator assigns permissions to all users. One of those permissions is the right to delete records from database tables. Only those users who have been granted permission to do so may delete objects from the Repository. (Naturally, the DBA should choose such people with care.)

Chapter 19

Maintaining Security

. . . .

In This Chapter

▶ Examining Crystal Enterprise security features

▶ Freeing users from the worries of security

▶ Granting rights and privileges

. . . .

*S*ecurity and confidentiality of information has always been a concern of organizations that understand that information has value. Today, however, emphasis on security is at an all-time high. Malicious hackers have been much in the news for penetrating even highly secure government installations. Corporate victims of such attacks have suffered leaks — thousands of credit card numbers, highly confidential source code, and other extremely sensitive records have been compromised or stolen.

Realistically, total protection of that important data from every conceivable threat is probably impossible to guarantee. But you can make access to it extremely difficult for unauthorized people to gain.

Crystal Enterprise 10 provides your reports with a sturdy, multilayered security structure that can deter all but the most determined and most sophisticated attempts at penetrating your valuable documents. Although Crystal Enterprise is a distributed system — thus more vulnerable to being compromised than a standalone system that can be physically isolated — its security infrastructure is quite robust. In this chapter, I discuss the security features that administrators can implement, show how administrators can take the burden of security off the end user, and describe the ways that administrators can control access to specific reports.

Restricting Access

The best way to keep people from misusing or tampering with the information contained in your reports is to deny them access to the reports in the first place. Crystal Enterprise uses a multilayer authentication process to ensure that reports are available for viewing or update only to those people authorized to view or update them.

Logon tokens

One mechanism that helps restrict access is the *logon token* — an encoded string that contains a user's session information and also defines its own usage attributes. The usage attributes apply restrictions to the token to reduce the chance that it will be used improperly. Two security features of logon tokens serve to reduce the risk of abuse by malicious users:

- ✓ Each token is valid for only a specified number of minutes before it expires.
- ✓ A logon token can be used only a specified number of times.

Sessions and session tracking

A *session* is a connection between a client and a server over which information can be exchanged. A *session state* is a set of data items that describes the session's attributes, its configuration, or its content. Over a Web connection, each session is restricted to a single page. The Web browser retains the state of only the current page. When you move to a different page, the state of the previous one is discarded. As a result, Web sites and Web applications must store the state.

Crystal Enterprise stores state information in two ways — with cookies and with session variables:

- ✓ A *cookie* is a small text string that resides on the client computer. It stores the session state for later use. For example, a user's logon token is stored in a cookie.
- ✓ A *session variable* is a portion of the server's memory that stores session state. A user's authentication type is stored as a session variable. As long as a session is maintained, the system will not reprompt the user for authentication or authorization information. The system will destroy a user's session variable when the user logs off or when a predetermined interval without user activity has passed. The default is 20 minutes. If a user has not made a request within the last 20 minutes, the session will be terminated.

Primary authentication

When users first attempt to log on to the system to gain access to reports, they are prompted for a user name, password, and authentication type. Crystal Enterprise supports four different types of authentication: Enterprise, Windows NT, LDAP, and Windows AD. Every authorized user must have one of these four authentication types. Enterprise authentication is native to Crystal Enterprise; the other three types are inherited from their respective operating environments.

The logon information is used in several ways. While a user is logged on, one user license is consumed on the system. When the user logs off, the license is released and once again becomes available. At logon, a logon token is generated and placed in a cookie in the user's Web browser. This token serves as the user's valid ticket to the system's resources until it expires. Token expiration protects the system when a user inadvertently leaves his or her computer without logging off.

Secondary authentication and authorization

Primary authentication gets a user into the system, but it does not yet allow them to do anything. People who are authorized to see some reports or perform some actions may not be authorized to view other reports or perform other actions. The secondary authentication and authorization process manages what users can see and what they can do.

When a user attempts to view, run, schedule, or otherwise act upon an object that Crystal Enterprise manages, the system checks to see whether the user has sufficient rights to do what he or she is attempting to do:

1. The system checks whether the user has a valid logon token. If a valid token is not present, primary authentication is repeated.

2. If a valid token is present, the system checks whether the user's session has timed out. If it has, the user is logged back on with the logon token. The user is not prompted for credentials again.

3. When the user attempts to perform an action, such as refreshing the data in a report, the system checks the logon token yet again to make sure the user is authorized to perform that action on that object.

Protecting the environment

In securing a client/server environment that incorporates Crystal Enterprise, there are two cases to consider:

✔ Communication between a Web browser and a Web server

✔ Communication between a Web server and Crystal Enterprise

The Web server must secure communication between the Web browser and the Web server; Crystal Enterprise does not get involved in this process. Normally a firewall separates a Web server from the rest of an organization's intranet (which includes Crystal Enterprise). Crystal Enterprise supports firewalls, as well as a wide variety of configurations.

Web activity auditing

With Crystal Enterprise, you can log Web activity, including time, date, IP address, and port number to monitor not only the amount of traffic on your system, but also where it is coming from. To set up this auditing function, your system administrator must configure the properties of the Web Component Server.

Combating malicious logon attempts

Accounts with Enterprise authentication are protected in several ways that go beyond what is implemented for accounts with Windows NT, LDAP, or Windows AD authentication. In that sense, Enterprise authentication is more secure. With Enterprise authentication, the system administrator can

✔ Enforce mixed-case passwords.

✔ Require a minimum number of characters (N) in the password.

✔ Disable accounts after N failed attempts to log on.

✔ Reset the failed logon count after N minutes.

✔ Re-enable an account after N minutes.

✔ Require users to change their password every N days.

✔ Disallow the use of the N most recent passwords.

✔ Require a wait of N minutes to change a password.

✔ Disable the capability of a user logged on as Guest to create a new user account.

Easing the Security Burden

All the heavy-duty security packed into Crystal Enterprise could potentially be a major burden on users. To relieve that burden (at least to some extent), Crystal Enterprise features Single Sign On and supports the idea of an active trust relationship.

Single Sign-On

Users can sign on anonymously as a Guest with Enterprise authentication. Guests only have access to folders and objects that are open to *all* authorized users. Users who sign on with either Windows NT or Windows AD authentication do not need to explicitly enter their credentials again. They retain whatever rights have been assigned to their group.

Active trust relationship

Crystal Enterprise contains many components, each one a potentially separate security domain. The fact that Crystal Enterprise supports an *active trust relationship* means that authentication secured in one such domain is recognized by all other domains. Thus users can draw information from disparate sources without having to present authentication credentials at each domain boundary. This facility, combined with Single Sign-On, substantially reduces the user's burden of operating in a highly secure environment.

Controlling Access to Specific Reports

Some authenticated users are authorized to view and operate on everything in the system. Such people are usually called *administrators.* Administrators have the authority to control other users' access by creating groups and assigning privileges and rights.

Creating groups to control access

Most users normally have lesser privileges than administrators. For example, Crystal Enterprise enables administrators to create groups and to assign users to these groups — giving each group only the access privileges necessary to do its job. Users of the system need not be concerned about this unless they happen to need access to some object but aren't authorized to view it. In such a case, users must convince the system administrator that they have a legitimate need for the access. The administrator can then upgrade the privileges of the group — or create a new group that *does* have the required privileges, and make it available for those particular users to join.

Granting rights to control access

By setting the access rights for a group, system administrators can maintain control over who sees a report object and who has the power to modify a report object. Administrators have two ways of granting (or denying) rights to users:

- ✔ **The Rights window:** Accessible by system administrators through the Crystal Management Console, the Rights window lists all groups defined on the system — along with each group's current access level. Here administrators can set and change each group's access level.

  Possible levels are Inherited Rights, No Access, View, Full Control, and Advanced. Members of a group inherit the rights of the group. A group with No Access rights to a folder or an object cannot do anything with that folder or object. View rights allow viewing, but nothing else. Full Control grants all available advanced rights. It is the only access level that allows users to delete objects. The Advanced access level does not include a predefined set of rights. It allows you to set the rights of other users or groups.

- ✔ **The Folders screen:** This window is also accessible by system administrators through the Crystal Management Console. The Rights tab of the Folders screen shows the groups that have access to each folder, and identifies their current access levels. Administrators can set and change a group's folder access on this tab.

  Possible folder access levels are Inherited Rights, No Access, View, Schedule, View On Demand, Full Control, and Advanced. A person with Schedule rights can view an object, such as a report, and schedule when the report is to be run. A person with View On Demand rights has Schedule rights plus the ability to refresh the data "on demand" against the data source.

Chapter 20

Navigating with Report Parts

. . . .

In This Chapter

▶ Choosing what part(s) of a report or of several reports to display

▶ Enabling users to move from one report object to another

▶ Employing highly selective drill-down

▶ Hyperlinking between reports

. . . .

*R*eport Parts, a relatively new facility within Crystal Reports, allows developers to extract and display only selected parts of a report (called *report objects*) while the rest of the objects on the source pages are not displayed. With Report Parts, advanced developers can integrate key elements of an existing report — such as summary data, tables, and charts — into workflow applications that users can access through a Web portal, PDA, cell phone, or other wireless device.

In this chapter, I discuss the two ways you can use Report Parts:

✔ **Report Part Drill-down:** This method uses a drill-down capability that is a more restricted method than the standard drill-down available when you perform regular page navigation.

✔ **Another Report Object:** This method involves defining a hyperlink path to other objects in the same report (or in a different report).

Using the Report Parts facility requires the use of a scripting language such as VBScript to create the Report Parts Viewer. After you create the Report Parts Viewer, it must be integrated into the HTML code that produces the Web application that actually presents the Report Parts to their audience.

Understanding Report Parts Navigation

The Report Parts facility is a tool that report developers can use to focus attention on the specific parts of a report that are relevant to a given user community. By crafting different Report Parts for different user communities, developers can address multiple audiences with a single report. The members of each audience see only the information that concerns them; other parts of the report aren't displayed.

You can view reports in several ways:

- ✓ **Through the Crystal Reports development environment:** Keep in mind, however, that not everyone who needs to view the reports will be a report designer. Those who are not designers won't have Crystal Reports installed.

- ✓ **Through Crystal Enterprise via the Crystal Enterprise Web Desktop:** Users employing this method need only a browser and the assigned privileges of a licensed Crystal Enterprise *seat*.

- ✓ **Through one of several viewers:** These are available via the standalone Report Application Server (see the nearby sidebar, "What's a Report Application Server?" for more information). One viewer works offline, and need not be connected to anything. All it needs is the report file.

    Most of the viewers available are *page viewers,* programs that display entire report pages. However, the *Report Parts Viewer* shows only specific report objects, without showing the rest of the page the objects are on. With the Report Parts Viewer, a user can see one part of a report and then hyperlink to another part of the same report (or of a different report) to get specific related information. Thus the report designer can give users exactly the information they need, whichever report it's in.

The Report Parts Viewer is not a preexisting tool in the way that the regular Crystal Reports Viewer is. It is not available from the Crystal Enterprise User Launchpad. To embed the Report Parts Viewer in a Web page, the report developer must first invoke it with an ASP or JSP page (written in VBScript or JavaScript). I don't go into those details here. Writing ASP or JSP pages is more related to building Web sites than to creating Crystal Reports documents. You may want to concentrate on mastering Crystal Reports for the time being, and let a Web guru do the ASP or JSP coding.

What's a Report Application Server?

The Report Application Server (RAS) is a software tool included with Crystal Reports, designed for building, customizing, and delivering reports over a network. In conjunction with its SDK (Software Development Kit), RAS connects to a Web server to provide users with access to Crystal reports. RAS is more of a tool for system administrators — report designers probably would not use it — but in the absence of Crystal Enterprise, its presence on a network is necessary in order for remote users to view a report.

Using Report Parts to Navigate

You can move from one report object to another via hyperlink. For such *navigation* to work, however, the second report must be managed by Crystal Enterprise or by the standalone Report Application Server. This type of navigation is available only in the DHTML viewers, which are zero-client, server-side viewers. You can link directly from an object in one report to an object in another report.

Note: A *zero-client, server-side viewer* requires nothing on the client machine other than a browser. The viewer itself resides on the server.

The Report Parts Viewer and any of the page viewers both support hyperlink navigation, but what the user sees it different in the two cases:

- ✔ **Using Report Parts Viewer:** When users are navigating between Report Parts (using the Report Part Viewer), they link from one report object to another report object. Both report objects are designated as Report Parts — the only things that the users see when they follow a chain of hyperlinks. The rest of the page remains out of view.

- ✔ **Using a page viewer:** When users view a report with a page viewer and the report uses page navigation, they are linked from one object to another, but can see the entire page that these objects are on.

Navigation is set up using the Hyperlink tab on the Format Editor dialog box. I illustrate this action with a couple of examples in the following sections.

Using the Report Parts Drill-down method

Drill-down is a standard capability of regular page navigation (see Chapter 6 for more about drill-down), but Report Parts drill-down is more restricted. The Report Part Viewer emulates the drill-down functionality of Crystal Reports but does not provide full drill-down capability. You can drill down from summary fields, group charts and maps, and fields in a report's group headers and group footers. Report Parts drill-down from or to objects in a report's page header or page footer is not supported. Furthermore, all destination objects (the objects you are linking to) must be in the same report section.

Performing a Report Part drill-down involves three steps:

1. Defining the Initial Report Part settings.
2. Creating a Report Part Drill-down hyperlink.
3. Publishing the report into the Crystal Enterprise environment.

After these steps are completed, the Report Part is ready for viewing.

Defining Initial Report Part settings

Following is a step-by-step example of Report Part Drill-down. The first thing you must do is define the Initial Report Part settings.

1. **Open the report that holds the first Report Part. You will define its default home object as the starting point of the Report Parts Drill-down.**

   For this example open the Customer Orders Grouped by State or District with Drill-down report created in Chapter 6. In Design Mode, it looks similar to Figure 20-1.

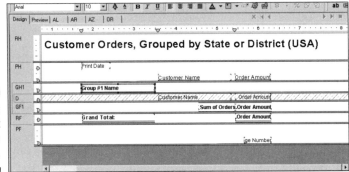

Figure 20-1:
A report
has been
opened.

2. **Right-click the object you want to set as the default home object and select Copy from its shortcut menu.**

   In Design mode, right-click the text object in the Report Header RH and select Copy from its shortcut menu.

3. **On the File menu, click Report Options.**

   A Drill-Down dialog box may appear, offering a cryptic message such as

   ```
   You cannot perform this command and keep your Drill-down,
            Cube View and Alerting tabs. If you continue, the
            Drill-down, Cube View and Alerting tabs will be
            closed. Do you want to continue?
   ```

4. **Click OK.**

   The Report Options dialog box (Figure 20-2) appears.

5. **In the Initial Report Part Settings area, click Paste Link.**

   The Object Name and Data Context fields are filled in automatically with the name and data context of the home object you selected.

6. **Click OK.**

Figure 20-2:
The Report
Options
dialog box
enables you
to specify
Initial
Report Part
Settings.

Creating a Report Part Drill-down hyperlink

Now that your Initial Report Part Setting is in place, you can create a Report Part Drill-down hyperlink.

1. **Open a report and then right-click the object you have selected to be the destination of the hyperlink.**

   For our example, using the Customer Orders Grouped by State or District with Drill-down report, right-click the Group #1 Name field in the GH1 report section. Doing so displays a pop-up menu.

2. **From the pop-up menu, select Format Field to display the Format Editor.**

3. **Select the Hyperlink tab.**

   Figure 20-3 shows the Format Editor.

4. **In the DHTML Viewer Only area, select Report Part Drill-down.**

   The Hyperlink information area appears, showing a Details entry in the Available Fields pane. You can expand this entry to see what fields you may select as destinations for the hyperlink.

5. **Expand the Details entry, as shown in Figure 20-4.**

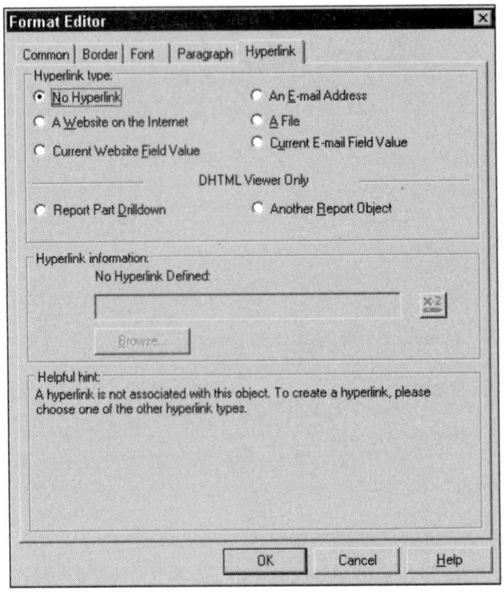

Figure 20-3:
The
Hyperlink
tab of the
Format
Editor.

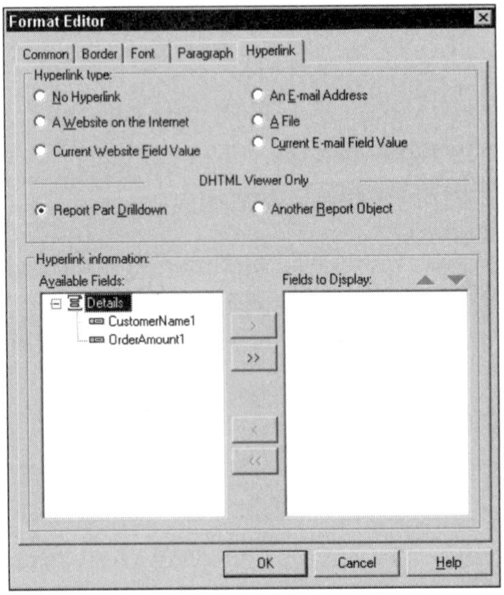

Figure 20-4:
There are
two possi-
bilities for
destination
fields.

6. **Select the field you want to use as the destination of the hyperlink and move it over to the Fields to Display pane.**

To follow along with the example, select `CustomerName1` and then click the arrowhead pointing to the Fields to Display pane. In this case, you only want to display the names of the customers, not the amount they have ordered.

7. **Click OK to establish the hyperlink and dismiss the Format Editor.**

8. **Click File⇨Save.**

You now have a report in which drill-down displays only the data you want to display rather than whole pages.

Publishing a Report Parts Drill-down report

To view this report, you use the Report Parts Viewer, which is embedded in a Web application. Before you can view the report, you must publish it into the Crystal Enterprise environment. Follow these steps to get that done:

1. **Start the Crystal Enterprise Publishing Wizard, and log on.**

2. **On the Publishing Wizard's Select A File pane, click Add Files. The reports in the Databases folder will appear.**

3. **Select the report you want to publish and click Open.**

   To follow along with this example, select `Customer Orders Grouped by State or District with Drill-down.rpt`. The Select a File pane will look similar to Figure 20-5.

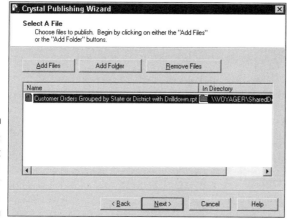

Figure 20-5: A report has been selected for publication.

4. Click Next to display the Specify Location pane. Select the folder you want to publish to, as shown in Figure 20-6, and then click next.

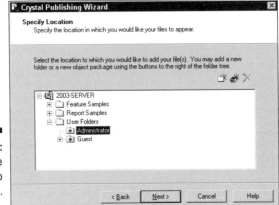

Figure 20-6:
Select the folder to publish to.

5. In the Location Preview pane, verify that the report you specified will be placed into the folder you specified, and then click Next.

6. In the Schedule Interval pane, specify how often you want the report to run.

For our example, select Let Users Update the Object.

7. Click Next.

The Repository Refresh pane appears. With it you can specify whether you want to refresh the report's repository fields. For our example, there are no repository fields, so this pane has no effect.

8. Click Next to show the Change Default Values pane.

For our example, select Publish Without Modifying Properties.

9. Click Next.

The next pane tells you that publishing may take some time, so you don't worry unduly if the system does not respond immediately.

10. Click Next.

The Wizard performs the publishing operation.

11. Click Finish.

If the foregoing seems like a lot to go through to make a report available to its intended users, you're right. But weigh the hassle factor against the importance of careful control over what gets published on your network, and how it gets published. Balancing security and convenience is always tricky. That's why system administrators get paid the big bucks.

Viewing a Report Parts Drill-down report

When the report has been published on your intranet, it's available for viewing. Users can access it by entering the appropriate URL into their browsers and going to the Web page that contains the report. The Report Parts Viewer built into the code of that page displays the Report Parts appropriate to each user, enabling drill-down to deeper levels of relevant detail.

Using the Another Report Object method

Report Part Drill-down is one of the two ways you can use Report Parts. The other way is to select Another Report Object. Using this option, you can define a hyperlink path to objects in the same report (or in a different report). If you are defining a path to a different report, that report must either be managed by Crystal Enterprise or it must be part of a standalone Report Application Server environment. As with Report Part Drill-down, all destination objects must reside in the same report section. Linking to another report is very similar to creating a Report Parts Drill-down report.

To link from one Report object to another Report object in either the same or a different report — and this need not be a drill-down operation — follow these steps:

1. **Open the source and target reports.**

2. **In the source report, right-click the destination object and select Copy from its shortcut menu.**

3. **Select the intended home object in your target report, and then select Format Field under the Format menu.**

4. **In the Format Editor, click the Hyperlink tab and then select Another Report Object in the DHTML Viewer Only area, as shown in Figure 20-7.**

5. **In the Hyperlink Information area, click the Paste Link button.**

   The Report Title, Object Name, and Data Context fields are automatically filled in.

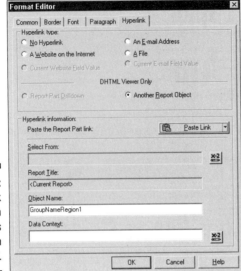

Figure 20-7:
The link
between
objects
has been
selected.

6. **Click OK.**

This establishes a hyperlink between your home object and a destination object. Now you can create a series of hyperlinks in the same manner, allowing users to move from one object to the next, to the next.

Chapter 21

Crystal Analysis 10

Crystal Analysis 10 is a software tool for doing Online Analytic Processing (OLAP). As I discuss in Chapter 14, Crystal Reports itself has a facility for displaying OLAP data. If you want to do really complex analysis, however, you need a more sophisticated tool: Crystal Analysis 10.

Crystal Analysis is not a feature of Crystal Reports per se — it's a part of the Crystal 10 suite — and you can access its capabilities via Crystal Enterprise. The relationship is straightforward: Crystal Enterprise provides the technology that puts Crystal Reports on line, and Crystal Analysis displays OLAP data so you can analyze your reports in an online environment. Crystal Enterprise makes Crystal Analysis documents — specialized analytical reports — available to online users (who access them through a browser).

Because Crystal Analysis is only indirectly related to Crystal Reports, I don't go into great depth about its capabilities. Instead, I describe how to start Crystal Analysis and produce a simple report. From there, you can experiment with more advanced functions. My objective in this chapter is not to make you an expert on Crystal Analysis, but rather to expose you to the full range of capabilities of the Crystal 10 product suite, including Crystal Reports 10, Crystal Enterprise 10, and Crystal Analysis 10.

Digging Deeper into OLAP

OLAP is a way of pulling meaningful information out of multidimensional data sources. Whereas a relational database management system such as Microsoft Access, Oracle, IBM DB2, or Microsoft SQL Server does a great job of structuring data in two-dimensional tables, such products are not as efficient at dealing with data that has three or more dimensions. Crystal Analysis 10 handles that job by using OLAP technology.

Here's an example of such multidimensional data: Imagine you have to display sales figures for a line of products, across all the regions in a country, for a span of five years. You have to work with three dimensions: product, region, and year. The sales organization that wants the figures is probably interested in reports showing product sales by region, product sales by year, and product sales by region by year.

Since product, region, and sales are independent, they can be represented — graphically and conceptually — as three dimensions that are "perpendicular" to each other. Such data sets incorporating more than two dimensions are called *cubes*. (Data sets with four or more dimensions are still called cubes, even if theoretical mathematicians would rather call them hypercubes.) The way a cube looks depends on which dimension is facing you. You can also take "slices" out of a cube — for example, Product by Region would be one slice of a three-dimensional cube; Region by Time would be another. Crystal Analysis gives you the flexibility to display your data in a variety of ways.

Each page on a Crystal Analysis report can display a worksheet and a chart. Both the worksheet and the chart on any given page share the same viewpoint of the cube being analyzed. Other pages can show other viewpoints. You can (for example) create a static application that the user can view (but not manipulate), or you can allow interactivity. If users want to look at the data in ways you didn't anticipate, you're ahead if you can enable them to choose members and reorient dimensions. (In practice, you may want to allow some classes of users to only view a static application.)

Creating a Crystal Analysis Report

When you first start Crystal Analysis, you are greeted by the Welcome screen shown in Figure 21-1. There are two ways to create a Crystal Analysis application, the easy way and the *really* easy way. First I show you the easy way (starting with a blank application) and then provide a step-by-step walkthrough of the really easy way (using an Application Expert).

Using a blank application

To create a new analysis application starting with a blank application, follow these steps:

1. **In the Welcome dialog box's Create a New Analysis Application area (refer to Figure 21-1), select As a Blank Application and then click OK.**

   The Connection Browser appears, listing the available OLAP servers. If the server containing your cube is not listed, add it. (With any luck, a system administrator has already taken care of this for you.)

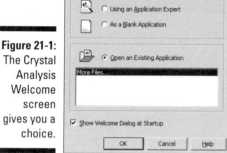

Figure 21-1:
The Crystal Analysis Welcome screen gives you a choice.

2. **If the server that holds your cube *is* listed, click to expand it and to show a list of available catalogs.**

3. **Click the appropriate catalog to display a list of the cubes it contains.**

4. **Select your cube and then click Open.**

   The New Page dialog box appears. You can now choose from a number of standard page layouts. These layouts contain various combinations of Worksheets, Dimension Explorers, and Slice Navigators.

5. **Click a template to select it and then click OK.**

   After selecting a page layout, you can delete any of the components on it that you don't want, or add new components.

The components you can add to your layout are

✓ **Worksheet:** The Worksheet looks much like a spreadsheet, but unlike a spreadsheet, it gives you a dynamic view of your data. You can change your view of the Worksheet's rows and columns, but also your view of any other dimensions the Worksheet might have. You can make these changes with simple drag-and-drop operations. One advantage of this capability is that you can easily spot trends in the data as you view one time slice after another.

✔ **Chart:** As you might expect, charts present a cube's data in a graphical way. If a chart and a Worksheet appear on the same page, the chart shows the same data that the Worksheet shows. If you change the view of the data on the Worksheet, or with a Dimension Explorer or a Slice Navigator, the chart is automatically updated to show the new view. You can change the type of chart displaying the data, or adjust its formatting. In some cases, you can also drill down into a chart to see the data that underlies it.

✔ **Dimension Explorers:** Users can employ these tools to explore the dimensions of a cube, select members for an analytic application, or reorient the cube's dimensions. You can do all these things with a Worksheet too, but Dimension Explorers make the job easier.

✔ **Slice Navigators:** There are multiple ways to slice and dice a cube. The more dimensions it has, the more ways it can be sliced. Slice Navigators are simple controls that you can use to change your application's view from one slice to another. The Worksheet includes a Slice Navigator, but you can also add a separate one to an application page.

✔ **Analysis Buttons:** These buttons provide a handy way to perform common tasks, such as changing the current view of a Worksheet or chart, drilling down on the selected member, opening a Crystal Report, or sending an e-mail containing data from the application.

✔ **Text Boxes:** Text Boxes give you a means of putting text on the screen. For example, it is a good idea to label Analysis Buttons with Text Boxes, so users know what the buttons are for.

Using the Application Experts

The *really* easy way to create a Crystal Analysis application is to use one of the Experts that address some of the most common analytical tasks. The Experts included with Crystal Analysis 10 are the Financial Reporting Expert, the KPI (Key Performance Indicator) Reporting Expert, the Sales Analysis Expert, and the Web Reporting Expert.

In the following steps, I take you through an application development, using one of these Experts. The others work in the same way, but with different assumptions about the type of data you are dealing with.

1. **In the Welcome to Crystal Analysis dialog box shown in Figure 21-1, select Using an Application Expert, and then click OK.**

   The New Application dialog box shown in Figure 21-2 appears.

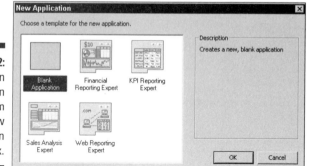

Figure 21-2:
You can
select an
Expert from
the New
Application
dialog box.

2. **Select one of the Experts and then click OK.**

   To follow along with this example, select the Sales Analysis Expert.

   The Select OLAP Data Source dialog box appears.

3. **For this example, click the + sign to the left of Local Server to expand the Local Server node, and then click the + sign to the left of Budget Reports to display the Budget Reports cube.**

   Figure 21-3 shows what the Expert should look like at this point.

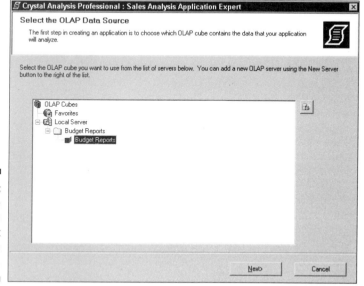

Figure 21-3:
You have
selected the
Budget
Reports
cube.

4. **Click Next to display the Identify the Products dimension page of the Sales Analysis Expert (Figure 21-4).**

   The Sales Analysis Expert requires you to identify a Products dimension.

5. **For this example, select Account Lines for the Products dimension and then click Next.**

   The Identify the Time dimension is next (Figure 21-5). Identify one of the remaining dimensions as the Time dimension and then click Next.

6. **Choose Month for the Time dimension.**

   The next Expert page asks you to Identify the Measures dimension.

7. **Choose Measures for the Measures dimension and then click Next.**

   The next page asks you to identify the Sales dimension member.

8. **For this example, choose Actual and then click Next.**

   The next page asks you to identify the Costs dimension member. (I'm getting the idea that this cube contains *quite* a few dimensions.)

9. **Select Budget and then click Next.**

   The next page asks you to identify the Margin dimension number.

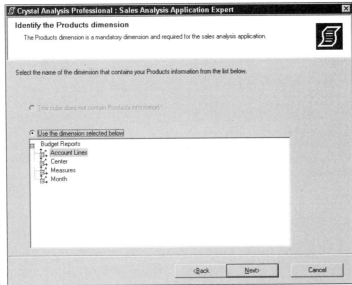

Figure 21-4:
You must select the Products dimension.

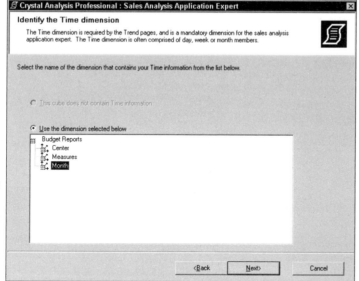

Figure 21-5:
You must
select
the Time
dimension.

10. **Leave the selection at This Cube Does Not Contain Margin Information and then click Next.**

    The next page asks you to identify the Versions dimension.

11. **Leave the selection at This Cube Does Not Contain Versions Information and then click Next.**

    The next page asks you to identify the Organization Hierarchy dimension.

12. **Leave the selection at This Cube Does Not Contain Organization Hierarchy Information and then click Next.**

    The next page asks you to identify the Year dimension.

13. **Leave the selection at This Cube Does Not Contain Year Information and then click Next.**

    The next page asks you to identify the Customers dimension.

14. **Leave the selection at This Cube Does Not Contain Customers Information and then click Next.**

    Now that you've identified all the dimensions that you care about, the page shown in Figure 21-6 asks you to specify the default members used for sectioning unused dimensions.

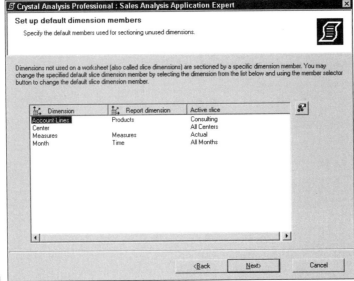

15. **Click Next.**

    The Select Pages dialog box appears, where you select the pages you want to include in the application.

16. **For this example, select Row by column - Products by Measures, and Trend - Measures by Time, as shown in Figure 21-7.**

17. **Click the Finish button.**

    Your application is displayed, as shown in Figure 21-8. It shows a lot of information about several variables — but the best part is that you can change the view and look at the data in a different way, and then you can change it again.

You can try various configurations until you find the one that conveys the information the best. You might find two or three views that convey various aspects of the information. Use as many as you like.

Crystal Analysis 10 is the Veg-O-Matic of the twenty-first century. It may not retail for only $9.95, but it certainly does slice and dice.

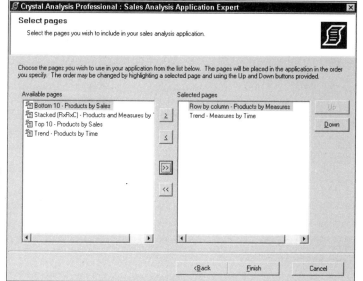

Figure 21-7:
Select the
pages
to include
in your
application.

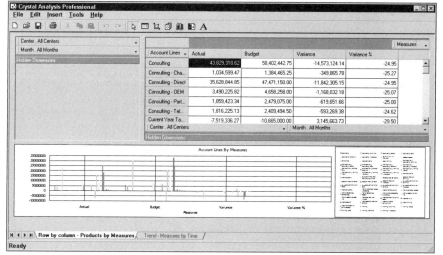

Figure 21-8:
An example
Crystal
Analysis
report.

Part V

Publishing Your Reports

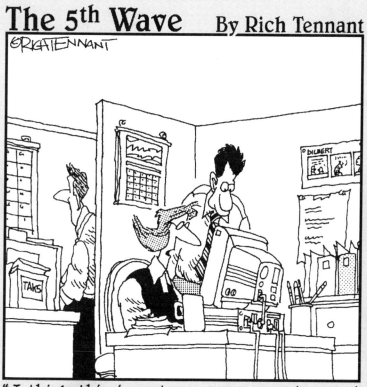

The 5th Wave   By Rich Tennant

"I think this inventory management report would really benefit by having an appropriate video clip attached to it. How about this one of a sink hole swallowing up a trailer park?"

In this part . . .

You will have a fine sense of accomplishment after you complete an excellent report that clearly conveys the information that you intended to deliver. However, your efforts will all be for naught if no one reads the report. Publishing your report to its intended audience is an important final step in the report-creation process. You can publish a report using various methods. You might make the report available on your organization's local area network, or you might print copies on a printer and distribute them. You might fax the report to people at remote sites, or you might put it up on a Web site. Crystal Reports supports all these methods of report distribution. Your handiwork will be visible to all who should see it. And in the case of posting on a Web site, your handiwork will be visible to the world.

Chapter 22

Distributing and Viewing Reports

. . . .

In This Chapter

▶ Printing reports

▶ Faxing reports

▶ Exporting reports to different places

▶ Discovering a few troubleshooting tips

. . . .

*W*hen creating a report in Crystal Reports, the ultimate goal is to get the report into the hands of people who can use the information that the report contains. These people may not have access to a computer running Crystal Reports, so several methods of distributing reports are available that don't depend on Crystal Reports being present. You can print the report on paper, send it directly from your computer via fax, or export it to a variety of destinations.

Printing Your Report

After you have completed report development, your report is ready to print. This is the easiest way to produce a finished report. Choose File➪Print➪ Printer on the main menu or click the printer icon on the Standard toolbar. The Print dialog box, shown in Figure 22-1, appears, telling you the name of the default printer and asking you which pages to print, how many copies to print, and whether to collate copies.

Make the appropriate selections and then click OK. That's all there is to it. Your report is printed as you specified. Distribute the printed copies to the people who should get them. Now your job is truly finished.

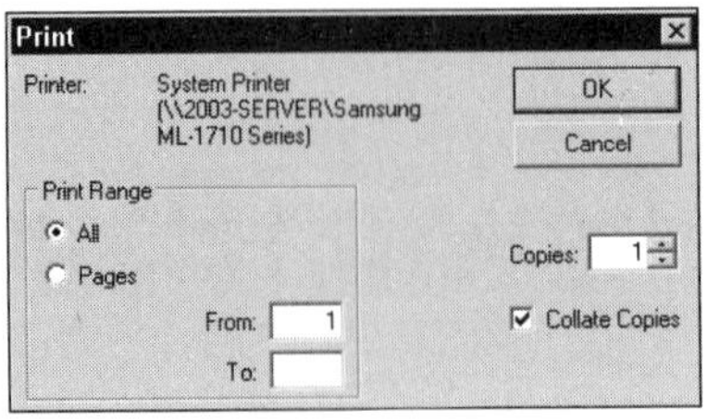

Figure 22-1:
The Print
dialog box,
showing
default
assump-
tions.

Print	☒
Printer: System Printer (\\2003-SERVER\Samsung ML-1710 Series)	OK / Cancel

Print Range
- ⦿ All
- ○ Pages

Copies: 1

☑ Collate Copies

From: 1
To:

Faxing a Report

Maybe the intended recipients of your report aren't close enough for you to hand them a printed report, and FedEx isn't fast enough to get it to them when they need it. In this case, you can fax the report directly from your computer, provided your computer is equipped with fax software and either has a modem connection to the telephone network or is set up to send faxes over the Internet.

To fax a report, you must change your default printer to a fax driver. Do this as follows:

1. **Choose File⇨Printer Setup.**

2. **Select your fax driver in the list of printer drivers installed on your computer.**

   If you don't find a fax driver among the list of installed printer drivers, it probably means that your computer is not set up to send faxes. You have to install fax software before you can fax any reports to recipients at remote sites.

3. **Click OK.**

4. **Click the Printer icon.**

   The Print dialog box appears. This time, your fax driver appears instead of your printer driver.

5. **Make the appropriate selections and then click OK.**

   Your fax software appears.

6. **Follow the software's instructions to send your report to its intended recipients.**

Exporting a Report

Crystal Reports can send reports to a variety of destinations, in a format that is appropriate for those destinations. You can export a report to Microsoft Excel as a spreadsheet in the Excel .xls format or to Microsoft Word as a word processing document in the Word .doc format. That's just scratching the surface, however.

Here's a list of file formats to which you can export a report:

- Adobe Acrobat (.pdf)
- Crystal Reports (.rpt)
- HTML 3.2
- HTML 4.0
- Microsoft Excel 97–2000
- Microsoft Excel 97–2000 (data only)
- Microsoft Word (.doc)
- ODBC
- Record style (columns no spaces)
- Record style (columns with spaces)
- Report Definition
- Rich Text Format (.rtf)
- Separated Values (.csv)
- Tab-separated text
- Text (.txt)
- XML

When you export a report to any format other than Crystal Reports format, you may lose some or all of the report's formatting. Crystal Reports tries to retain as much formatting as possible, but in some cases, not much can be saved.

You may export a report to several destinations:

   ✔ An application

   ✔ A disk file

   ✔ A Microsoft Exchange folder

   ✔ Lotus Domino

   ✔ Lotus Domino Mail

   ✔ MAPI (Microsoft Mail)

If you export to an application such as Microsoft Word or Microsoft Excel, Crystal Reports launches the target application and opens the report file in it. If you export to a disk file, Crystal Reports opens a dialog box that allows you to specify a drive, directory, and filename for the report file. Using Lotus Domino Mail or MAPI, you can send a report directly to a person's electronic mailbox. Using Lotus Domino, you can send a report directly to a person's desktop.

Whether you're distributing your report as a printed document, fax, or computer file, Crystal Reports makes it easy for you to get the report out in a timely fashion and in the form you want.

Troubleshooting Output Problems

Little can go wrong when you're attempting to print a Crystal Reports report to your system's printer. If you can print a document from your word processor or another application, you should be able to print from Crystal Reports. If you can't print from any of your applications, check to confirm that the printer is on and properly connected to your computer. Make sure that your printer is identified as your computer's default printer.

If you can't fax a report, make sure that your fax software is properly installed. Confirm that it works when sending a document from your word processor. If your system won't send a word processor document, the fault is not with Crystal Reports. Make sure that your fax driver is identified as your computer's default printer.

If you have trouble exporting a report, make sure that you have correctly specified the format and the destination. Like printing and faxing reports, exporting is pretty foolproof after you set up your connections properly.

Chapter 23

Displaying Reports Online

As organizations become more interconnected electronically, an emerging trend is to communicate more over the network than by passing paper around. Organizational intranets have become the communications medium of choice in many cases. Beyond the organization's borders, extranets and the Internet have assumed more important roles. Crystal Reports takes advantage of this trend. Report features such as drill down and subreports require the reader to be online. It's not hard to drill down into a sheet of paper, but when you do, you don't see very much, and it tends to ruin the surface of your desk.

Exporting to a Static HTML Page

Web pages, whether they're designed to be viewed by a small group of people on a company intranet or by a worldwide audience on the Web, are implemented by using Hypertext Markup Language (HTML). A report created in Crystal Reports can go online in several ways. Exporting to a static HTML page is the easiest but also the most limited. The only thing that gets exported is what is visible on the screen.

When you export a report to a static HTML page, take note of the word *static*. The data in the report is a snapshot of the data at the time of the export. The exported report won't be updated when the data in the original report changes. To display the changed data, you have to export the report again.

For many applications, you don't need to go beyond static HTML. In those cases, exporting is as easy as 1-2-3. Well, actually, it's as easy as 1-2-3-4:

1. **Open the report that you want to export, and display the screen — the main report or subreport — that you want to present to your online audience.**

2. **Choose File⇨Export.**

   The Export dialog box appears.

3. **In the Format drop-down list, select HTML 4.0. In the Destination drop-down list, select Disk File. Then click OK.**

   The Select Export File dialog box appears, as shown in Figure 23-1.

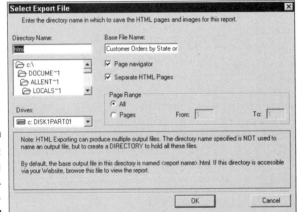

Figure 23-1:
Exporting
static HTML
is simple.

4. **Choose the drive and directory where you want to place the HTML file, make your formatting choices, and then click OK.**

   An HTML version of your report is created and stored in the directory you selected.

When you export a report to another format, such as HTML 4.0, you will likely lose some of the formatting of the original report. Crystal Reports does its best to preserve the original formatting, but the appearance of the exported report probably won't match the original exactly. If you're not happy with how the exported report looks, you may have to make changes to the original to come up with a design that is less affected by the change of file type.

Figure 23-2 shows the top of the Customer Orders, by State or District (Mexico) report as it exists in Crystal Reports. Note that the title is enclosed in a box with rounded corners.

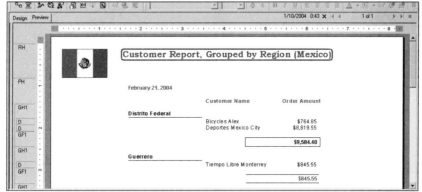

Figure 23-2: The Customer Orders, by State or District (Mexico) report in Crystal Reports.

After exporting the report to HTML 4.0, it looks like Figure 23-3.

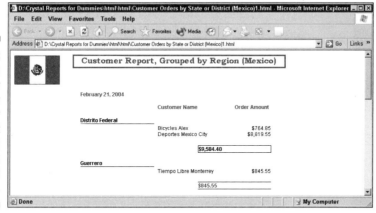

Figure 23-3: The Customer Orders, by State or District (Mexico) report as an HTML 4.0 file.

The two reports look virtually identical, except that the corners of the box enclosing the title are no longer rounded. More complex formatting features, however, may not translate as well in the exported report. Judge each case individually.

After you save your report to a disk file, you can upload the file to your Web server in the same way that you upload any other files that appear on your site.

Adding a Hyperlink to a Report

One of the most valuable features of Web-based content is the capability to quickly move between pages by using hyperlinks. By clicking a hyperlink associated with a word, a phrase, or an image, you can instantly display a new page that provides more detail.

Crystal Reports enables you to add hyperlinks to your reports without your having to become a HTML scripter. Here's how to do it:

1. **In your report, select the object that you want to turn into a hyperlink and then click the Insert Hyperlink icon on the Expert Tools toolbar. (Or right-click the selected object and choose Format Field.)**

   The Hyperlink tab of Format Editor appears, as shown in Figure 23-4. If the Hyperlink icon on the Expert Tools toolbar appears dimmed, you can't use the object you selected as a hyperlink.

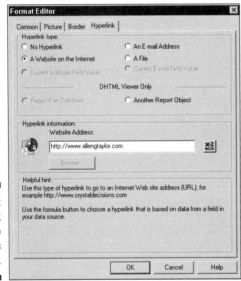

Figure 23-4:
The link shown is to the author's Web site.

2. **Select the type of hyperlink that you want.**

3. **To link to a Web site, type a Web site address in the Hyperlink Information box.**

4. **Click OK.**

As you can see in Figure 23-4, you can link to several places in addition to Web sites. Here's a brief description of the options available:

- ✔ **No Hyperlink:** Removes a hyperlink from the selected object.

- ✔ **A Website on the Internet:** Links to a Web site.

- ✔ **Current Website Field Value:** Select this when you want to link to the URL contained as a value in the selected object. This option appears dimmed if no URL is contained as a value in the selected object.

- ✔ **An E-mail Address:** Enables users to send e-mail messages to a recipient that you specify.

- ✔ **A File:** Links to a file on the user's computer.

- ✔ **Current E-mail Field Value:** Select this when you want to send an e-mail message to the address contained as a value in the selected object. This option appears dimmed if no address is contained as a value in the selected object.

- ✔ **Report Part Drilldown:** Specifies which detail object is displayed when the user drills down on a report part. (Report parts are explained in the next section.) This type of hyperlink works only with DHTML viewers such as Internet Explorer 4.0 and above or Netscape Navigator 4.72 and above.

- ✔ **Another Report Object:** Links directly to the object that the user specifies. The destination object may be in this report or in another report. Details are up next.

To link to a Web site on the Internet, follow these steps:

1. **Open the source report and select the object that you want as the originator of the hyperlink.**

2. **Click the Insert Hyperlink icon.**

   The Hyperlink tab of Format Editor appears.

3. **In the Hyperlink Type area, select A Website on the Internet.**

4. **In the Hyperlink Information area, fill in the URL of the Web site to which you want to link.**

   Figure 23-5 shows what Format Editor looks like at this point.

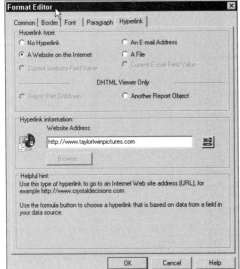

Figure 23-5:
The Hyper-
link tab
of Format
Editor with
the target
Web site
address
entered.

5. **Click OK to establish the link.**

   Now when the cursor hovers over the source object, it turns into the hyperlink hand. Clicking the source object launches your default browser and displays the target Web site.

Chapter 24

SQL Commands

Crystal Reports 10 has a feature called SQL Commands. SQL is an internationally accepted standard language for dealing with relational databases. Report writers such as Crystal Reports retrieve data from such databases. They do so by translating the data retrieval part of the report into an SQL statement that's sent to the database. The database management system executes the SQL statement on the data in the database, and then sends the result set back to the report writer, which formats and displays it.

As you may know, some concepts that you can express in one language are impossible to translate accurately into another language. I ran into this problem while trying to communicate with a taxi driver in Beijing, China, using my community college Mandarin. I ended up on the wrong side of town, late at night. A similar problem can happen with database reports.

If you want to zero in on a particular data set, the specification of which is difficult or impossible to express using the admittedly handy wizards and dialog boxes that Crystal Reports provides, you may be able to get what you want by speaking the database's native language, SQL. SQL is not a particularly easy language to learn, although a book such as my *SQL For Dummies* (published by Wiley) can make it about as easy as possible. If you make the effort to learn SQL, you can extend the power of Crystal Reports. By using the new SQL Commands feature of Crystal Reports, you can add anything you want to your report. And if the information you want is buried somewhere in your database, you can retrieve it with SQL.

Creating an SQL Statement

To create an SQL statement, you must start with a report. Here's a step-by-step procedure for adding an SQL statement to one of the sample reports that comes with Crystal Reports:

1. **With the Xtreme sample database connected, open the sample report called** Formulas.rpt.

   Mine is in D:\Program Files\Crystal Decisions\Crystal Reports 10\Samples\En\Reports\Feature Examples. Yours is probably in a similar place.

2. **On the Expert Tools toolbar, click the Database Expert icon or choose Database⊃Database Expert.**

   The Database Expert dialog box appears, as shown in Figure 24-1. The Xtreme sample database should be displayed in the Selected Tables pane, with the Customer and Orders tables listed under it.

3. **Connect to the Xtreme database. In the Available Data Sources pane, double-click the Add Command node.**

   The Add Command to Report dialog box appears, as shown in Figure 24-2.

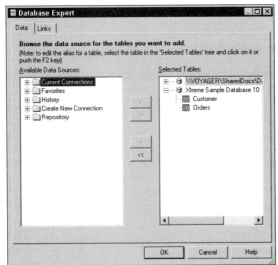

Figure 24-1:
Database
Expert.

Figure 24-2:
This is
where you
add the SQL
statement.

4. **Type the following SQL statement in the left pane:**

```
SELE19CT
     Customer.[Customer ID],
     Customer.[Customer Name],
     Customer.[Last Year's Sales],
     Customer.Region,
     Customer.Country,
     Orders.[Order Amount],
     Orders.[Customer ID],
     Orders.[Order Date]
FROM
     Customer Customer INNER JOIN Orders Orders ON
          Customer.[Customer ID] = Orders.[Customer ID]
WHERE
     (Customer.Country = "USA" OR
     Customer.Country = "Canada") AND
     Customer.[Last Year's Sales] < 10000.
ORDER BY
     Customer.Country ASC,
     Customer.Region ASC
```

Figure 24-3 shows the Add Command to Report dialog box after the SQL command has been entered.

The specific database driver that your system uses may differ from the driver that my system uses. My system accepts square brackets around field names that contain blanks or other punctuation. Yours may accept single or double quotes instead. If your system has Access, look at the syntax of the SQL that it generates, and use the same thing. It's important that Crystal Reports be able to distinguish between field names and quoted strings such as "USA". It also needs to be able to properly handle field names that include punctuation, such as Last Year's Sales.

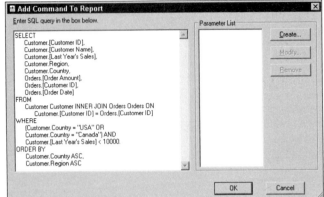

Figure 24-3:
The SQL
command
has been
entered.

5. **Click OK.**

   You are returned to Database Expert.

6. **Click OK.**

   Database Expert displays the Link view.

7. **Click OK.**

   In my case, a Visual Linking dialog box appears, stating

   ```
   Unable to smart link unlinked tables. Foreign key rela-
        tionships may not be present for the tables, or
        the database driver may not support the retrieval
        of this information. Would you like to try smart
        linking using field names instead?"
   ```

   You can safely ignore this announcement.

8. **Click OK.**

   Another Visual Linking dialog box appears and says, "Your current link configuration contains multiple starting points. Please be advised that this is generally not supported." You can ignore this one too.

9. **Click OK.**

   You might see more dialog boxes. Click through them until you get to the Refresh Report Data dialog box.

10. **Click OK.**

    When all the dialog boxes go away, Report Designer displays your report. Field Explorer has a new table named Command. Crystal Reports has saved your query as a database table named Command. You can change the name if you want.

Adding an SQL Statement to a Repository

If you create an SQL statement that can be used in more than one report, you may want to save it in the Repository. Doing so saves you the effort of re-creating the statement from scratch. You can then just drag the statement from the Repository to your new report.

When you're creating an SQL statement that may be used in another report, follow this procedure:

1. **In the Selected Tables area of the Database Expert, select the statement that you want to add to the Repository.**

   For this example, select Command, as shown in Figure 24-4.

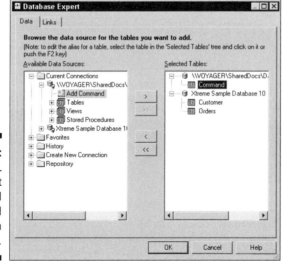

Figure 24-4:
The SQL statement named Command has been selected.

2. **Right-click the statement and select Add to Repository.**

3. **In the Add Item dialog box that appears, fill in an appropriate name and author. The Description and Location fields will already contain the correct information.**

   Figure 24-5 shows the Add Item dialog box for our example.

Figure 24-5:
Information
to identify an
item being
added to the
Repository.

4. **Click OK.**

   The SQL statement is now in the Crystal Repository and is available for
   use by other applications.

Modifying an SQL Statement

Modifying an SQL command is similar to creating one. Here are the steps:

1. **In the Selected Tables pane of the Database Expert dialog box, find
   the statement that you want to edit.**

2. **Right-click the statement and choose Edit Command.**

   The Modify Command dialog box appears, as shown in Figure 24-6. The
   existing statement appears in the left pane, although its appearance may
   vary from one implementation to another.

   If the SQL command that you want to edit is in the Repository, the Edit
   Command menu option appears dimmed. If you have been following along
   with the example, the SQL statement we just created *is* in the Repository.
   As I mention in Chapter 18, you can't edit a Repository object. Instead,
   you must disconnect the statement from the Repository before you can
   edit it. If this is the case, right-click the statement and choose Disconnect
   from Repository, before you right-click the statement again and choose
   Edit Command.

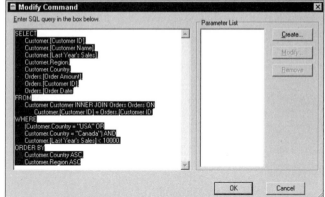

Figure 24-6:
The Modify
Command
dialog box.

3. **Make whatever changes to the statement that you want.**

4. **Click the OK button to execute the change.**

   The revised SQL statement appears in Field Explorer under Database
   Fields. If you select any of the fields under the statement and then click
   Field Explorer's browse button, a browse dialog box appears, displaying
   all the data that the report retrieved from that field. Figure 24-7 shows
   the result of browsing the statement's Customer Name field.

Figure 24-7:
The new
SQL
statement
returns the
data in the
Customer
Name field.

Part VI
The Part of Tens

The 5th Wave   By Rich Tennant

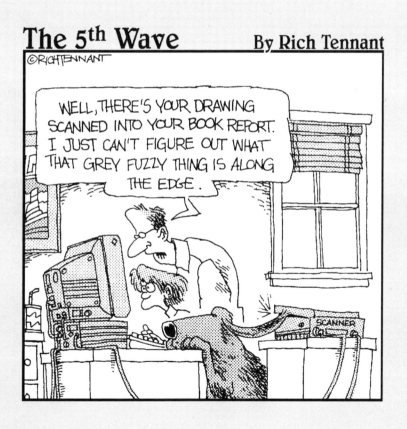

In this part . . .

The Part of Tens distills information found in various places throughout the book into lists of ten pithy pointers to better reports. It's a good idea to reread Chapter 25 before you start each new report generation project and to reread Chapter 26 as you are wrapping up each project. These guidelines may help you to remember something that you could do to improve your report.

Chapter 25

Ten Things to Do Before You Create a Report

*W*ith a great report-writing tool such as Crystal Reports, you might reasonably assume that creating a report is an easy task that doesn't require much thought or effort. That would be a bad assumption. Creating a high-quality report that truly meets users' needs requires considerable thought and effort even before you fire up Crystal Reports for the first time. You should put thought and effort into at least ten things before you apply fingers to keyboard.

Identify the Users

Identifying the users might seem obvious, but it's not as obvious as you might think. Sure, the person who asked you to create the report is probably someone who will use the report. But who else will benefit from using this report? Other people in your client's workgroup? Your client's manager? People in other workgroups or other departments? Perhaps even people in other companies? It's important to identify *all* the probable users.

Interview the Users

After you identify all the people who could benefit from your report, it's important to find out what they need the report to tell them. What information should the report contain? How should the information be presented? The only way to get the complete answer is to interview at least one representative of each class of user. But it's best to interview them all. What's unimportant to one class of users might be vital to another.

Arbitrate Conflicting Demands

It's almost certain that when you have a diverse user community, the needs of one group or individual will conflict with the needs of another. One group may want the information presented in one format, but a second group may insist on receiving the information in a different format. Someone has to find a compromise that's acceptable to all parties. As a neutral outside party, this arbitrator often turns out to be you.

Nail Down the Project's Scope

After everyone agrees on what they want, it's important to get agreement on exactly what will be included in the project. To make sure that the project doesn't keep expanding as you go along, get a signed agreement from the client on the project's scope. This agreement protects both the developer and the client. From the beginning, everyone knows what will be delivered.

Nail Down the Project's Schedule

After you know the project's scope, you can estimate how long it will take you to complete the project. Make sure you plan for adequate time to do a good job. If the schedule is agreed to in advance, you have a solid defense against clients who want you to speed up development so that they can have reports sooner. Quality generally suffers when a reasonable schedule is accelerated.

Verify That the Necessary Data Is in the Database

If you're going to build a report based on data in a database, it helps if the data you need is actually in the database. Sometimes clients ask for a report that their database can't support because the data just isn't there. You need to verify with a database query that the data you need is indeed present.

Determine How the Report Will Be Viewed

You can view a report created in Crystal Reports in several ways. What is the primary way that your user community will view it? Will users view it on a computer that's connected to the database that the report is based on? If so, they can refresh the data to get up-to-the-minute reports. They can also drill down for detail and view the report, including charts and maps, in color.

If users will be looking primarily at printed reports, they can't drill down. The data in the reports is a snapshot of the data when the report was printed, so it may not be up-to-date. Furthermore, if your report is printed on a black-and-white laser printer, color doesn't show up.

Design your report with your users in mind and optimize the report for the best viewing.

Determine the Best Report Type for the Users' Needs

What's the best way to present your client's data? A standard report? A cross-tab report? An OLAP report? Based on the underlying data and how users want it to be presented, choose the most appropriate report type and then build the report based on that type.

Get Agreement on the Report's Appearance

Users may have strong preferences on how they want the information presented. Their ideas of the ideal presentation may differ from what makes the most sense to you. Make sure you develop a report that clearly presents information that's of interest to all the user communities. This may require you to hold meetings for all concerned parties as well as negotiate with various user groups. Make sure everyone will support the report's user interface before you put effort into developing it.

Decide Whether to Include Charts or Maps

Some types of reports can be immeasurably enhanced by the inclusion of appropriate charts or maps. Charts present the data in a way that goes directly to the viewer's brain. Sometimes columns of numbers just don't have the same effect. In those cases, adding charts or maps can be a good idea. In other cases, a chart would not add to an understanding of the data and might actually obscure it. Evaluate each case individually and decide whether charts or maps are appropriate.

Chapter 26

Ten Ways to Give Your Reports More Pizzaz

*Y*ou say you want to make your reports more visually appealing? Crystal Reports can help you do that. In this chapter, I mention ten simple ways to help you lift your reports out of the category of ordinary into the rarified atmosphere of truly extraordinary. You can give your reports maximum impact by tastefully combining several of the techniques in this chapter.

Use the Correct Fonts

Beyond the bare facts presented in a report, you may also want the report to convey a feeling or emotion. Perhaps you want the report to put the reader in a sober, strictly business frame of mind. Or you might want the report to playfully remind readers of things that are fun. You might want to call particular attention to certain parts of the report, while burying other parts in a way that makes them easy to overlook. You can accomplish much of this with a judicious choice of fonts.

A wide variety of font styles are available, and you can use several in the same report, although it's wise to not go overboard with different font styles. Three different styles are usually plenty. You can also vary the size of the font, and whether it is bold, italic, or underlined. By combining all these options, you can have your report project an image that enhances what the bare words and numbers in the report have to say.

Use Color Tastefully

Reports that are meant to be viewed on a computer screen can make use of a full palette of color. So can reports that will be printed on a color printer. Color capability makes it feasible to incorporate charts and maps in your reports, as well as graphical images. You can use color to emphasize text elements or to set off drawing elements such as lines and boxes. You can even give different sections their own unique background colors.

Use your imagination to think of ways to use color to enhance your reports. Remember, however, to not overuse color effects. Make sure that any color effects are appropriate to the material and what you're trying to communicate. Don't use multiple colors just because you can.

Enclose Text in Boxes

One way to make titles and important areas of text stand out is to enclose them in boxes. Crystal Reports makes it easy to enclose text in a box; simply drag the cursor over the text. You can give the box sharp or rounded corners, and you can give it any color available on your palette. Boxes are a good way to call attention to text.

Emphasize Objects with Drop Shadows

You can give a box, such as the one described in the preceding section, even more emphasis by giving it a drop shadow. The drop shadow makes the box appear to come out of the page in a 3-D effect. To get a drop shadow, just right-click the box and choose Format Box. In the Format Editor dialog box that appears, select the Drop Shadow option. When you click OK, the drop shadow appears on your box. The drop shadow feature is available only with rectangular boxes. If you round the corners of your box, the drop shadow feature becomes unavailable.

Produce a Consistent Appearance with Templates

You can determine many of the formatting details of a report with a template. Using a template also helps you to maintain consistency from one report to the next. You can have one template for one type of report and another template for another type. Readers will become accustomed to seeing information presented in a consistent way from one report to the next.

Add an Image

An old bromide says that a picture is worth a thousand words. Sometimes that's true, and sometimes it's not. When a picture can help you get your point across, use it. Crystal Reports makes it easy to insert graphical images into your reports wherever you want them. You can use this capability for corporate logos, photographs, drawings, or images of any kind.

Add a Chart

Numeric data presented in tabular form conveys the facts but often doesn't clearly show trends or relationships among data items. Charts, whether they are line charts, bar charts, pie charts, or some other kind, can show trends and relationships clearly. When trends or relationships in data are important, by all means use a chart to bring out that point and hammer it home.

Add a Map

For some kinds of reports, it's important to show readers where things are. If your data has anything to do with geographical locations, such as sales territories or political boundaries, Crystal Reports' mapping facility can make your report much more valuable. Maps cover the entire globe, showing countries as well as individual states and provinces.

Combine Two Objects with an Underlay

You can give your report a watermark effect by underlaying words or symbols in a light font beneath the main text of your report. You can also use this facility to position a chart or map next to the text that it refers to rather than above or below it. For example, with an underlay, you might line up a chart with the detail section that contains the data from which the chart is drawn.

Separate the Summary from the Details with Drill-Down

The drill-down facility in Crystal Reports makes use of the fact that more and more people view reports on their computer screens rather than read them on paper. Drill-down capability allows viewers to interact with the report, viewing detail when they want to see it and skimming past it when they don't. A person can quickly get the gist of what they want from the report and then move on to make decisions based on what they've learned.

Index

• G •

• **P** •

Notes

Notes

Notes

Notes

FOR DUMMIES®

The easy way to get more done and have more fun

PERSONAL FINANCE

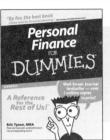
0-7645-5231-7

0-7645-2431-3

0-7645-5331-3

Also available:

Estate Planning For Dummies
(0-7645-5501-4)

401(k)s For Dummies
(0-7645-5468-9)

Frugal Living For Dummies
(0-7645-5403-4)

Microsoft Money "X" For
Dummies
(0-7645-1689-2)

Mutual Funds For Dummies
(0-7645-5329-1)

Personal Bankruptcy For
Dummies
(0-7645-5498-0)

Quicken "X" For Dummies
(0-7645-1666-3)

Stock Investing For Dummies
(0-7645-5411-5)

Taxes For Dummies 2003
(0-7645-5475-1)

BUSINESS & CAREERS

0-7645-5314-3

0-7645-5307-0

0-7645-5471-9

Also available:

Business Plans Kit For
Dummies
(0-7645-5365-8)

Consulting For Dummies
(0-7645-5034-9)

Cool Careers For Dummies
(0-7645-5345-3)

Human Resources Kit For
Dummies
(0-7645-5131-0)

Managing For Dummies
(1-5688-4858-7)

QuickBooks All-in-One Desk
Reference For Dummies
(0-7645-1963-8)

Selling For Dummies
(0-7645-5363-1)

Small Business Kit For
Dummies
(0-7645-5093-4)

Starting an eBay Business For
Dummies
(0-7645-1547-0)

HEALTH, SPORTS & FITNESS

0-7645-5167-1

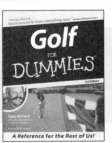
0-7645-5146-9

0-7645-5154-X

Also available:

Controlling Cholesterol For
Dummies
(0-7645-5440-9)

Dieting For Dummies
(0-7645-5126-4)

High Blood Pressure For
Dummies
(0-7645-5424-7)

Martial Arts For Dummies
(0-7645-5358-5)

Menopause For Dummies
(0-7645-5458-1)

Nutrition For Dummies
(0-7645-5180-9)

Power Yoga For Dummies
(0-7645-5342-9)

Thyroid For Dummies
(0-7645-5385-2)

Weight Training For Dummies
(0-7645-5168-X)

Yoga For Dummies
(0-7645-5117-5)

Available wherever books are sold.
Go to www.dummies.com or call 1-877-762-2974 to order direct.

FOR DUMMIES®

A world of resources to help you grow

FOR DUMMIES®

Helping you expand your horizons and realize your potential

INTERNET

0-7645-0894-6

0-7645-1659-0

0-7645-1642-6

Also available:

America Online 7.0 For Dummies
(0-7645-1624-8)

Genealogy Online For Dummies
(0-7645-0807-5)

The Internet All-in-One Desk Reference For Dummies
(0-7645-1659-0)

Internet Explorer 6 For Dummies
(0-7645-1344-3)

The Internet For Dummies Quick Reference
(0-7645-1645-0)

Internet Privacy For Dummies
(0-7645-0846-6)

Researching Online For Dummies
(0-7645-0546-7)

Starting an Online Business For Dummies
(0-7645-1655-8)

DIGITAL MEDIA

0-7645-1664-7

0-7645-1675-2

0-7645-0806-7

Also available:

CD and DVD Recording For Dummies
(0-7645-1627-2)

Digital Photography All-in-One Desk Reference For Dummies
(0-7645-1800-3)

Digital Photography For Dummies Quick Reference
(0-7645-0750-8)

Home Recording for Musicians For Dummies
(0-7645-1634-5)

MP3 For Dummies
(0-7645-0858-X)

Paint Shop Pro "X" For Dummies
(0-7645-2440-2)

Photo Retouching & Restoration For Dummies
(0-7645-1662-0)

Scanners For Dummies
(0-7645-0783-4)

GRAPHICS

0-7645-0817-2

0-7645-1651-5

0-7645-0895-4

Also available:

Adobe Acrobat 5 PDF For Dummies
(0-7645-1652-3)

Fireworks 4 For Dummies
(0-7645-0804-0)

Illustrator 10 For Dummies
(0-7645-3636-2)

QuarkXPress 5 For Dummies
(0-7645-0643-9)

Visio 2000 For Dummies
(0-7645-0635-8)

Available wherever books are sold. Go to www.dummies.com or call 1-877-762-2974 to order direct.

FOR DUMMIES®

The advice and explanations you need to succeed

ELF-HELP, SPIRITUALITY & RELIGION

0-7645-5302-X

0-7645-5418-2

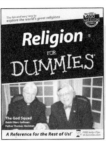

0-7645-5264-3

Also available:

The Bible For Dummies
(0-7645-5296-1)

Buddhism For Dummies
(0-7645-5359-3)

Christian Prayer For Dummies
(0-7645-5500-6)

Dating For Dummies
(0-7645-5072-1)

Judaism For Dummies
(0-7645-5299-6)

Potty Training For Dummies
(0-7645-5417-4)

Pregnancy For Dummies
(0-7645-5074-8)

Rekindling Romance For Dummies
(0-7645-5303-8)

Spirituality For Dummies
(0-7645-5298-8)

Weddings For Dummies
(0-7645-5055-1)

ETS

0-7645-5255-4

0-7645-5286-4

0-7645-5275-9

Also available:

Labrador Retrievers For Dummies
(0-7645-5281-3)

Aquariums For Dummies
(0-7645-5156-6)

Birds For Dummies
(0-7645-5139-6)

Dogs For Dummies
(0-7645-5274-0)

Ferrets For Dummies
(0-7645-5259-7)

German Shepherds For Dummies
(0-7645-5280-5)

Golden Retrievers For Dummies
(0-7645-5267-8)

Horses For Dummies
(0-7645-5138-8)

Jack Russell Terriers For Dummies
(0-7645-5268-6)

Puppies Raising & Training Diary For Dummies
(0-7645-0876-8)

DUCATION & TEST PREPARATION

0-7645-5194-9

0-7645-5325-9

0-7645-5210-4

Also available:

Chemistry For Dummies
(0-7645-5430-1)

English Grammar For Dummies
(0-7645-5322-4)

French For Dummies
(0-7645-5193-0)

The GMAT For Dummies
(0-7645-5251-1)

Inglés Para Dummies
(0-7645-5427-1)

Italian For Dummies
(0-7645-5196-5)

Research Papers For Dummies
(0-7645-5426-3)

The SAT I For Dummies
(0-7645-5472-7)

U.S. History For Dummies
(0-7645-5249-X)

World History For Dummies
(0-7645-5242-2)

Available wherever books are sold. Go to www.dummies.com or call 1-877-762-2974 to order direct.